Bilingual

VISUAL

dictionary

DISCARD

A DORLING KINDERSLEY BOOK

DK

LONDON, NEW YORK, MELBOURNE, MUNICH, DELHI

Senior Editor Angela Wilkes
Managing Art Editor Christine Keilty
Production Editor Lucy Baker
Production Controller Rita Sinha

Designed for Dorling Kindersley by WaltonCreative.com

Hindi Edition
Senior Editor Rohan Sinha
Editor Saloni Talwar
Design Manager Arunesh Talapatra
Senior DTP Designer Harish Aggarwal
DTP Designers Dheeraj Arora, Jagtar Singh
Production Manager Pankaj Sharma
Art Director Shefali Upadhyay
Head of Publishing Aparna Sharma

Hindi Translation by Yatra Books

First published in Great Britain in 2008 by
Dorling Kindersley Limited, 80 Strand, London WC2R 0RL

First published in the USA in 2008 by DK Publishing,
375 Hudson Street, New York, NY 10014

A Penguin Company

08 09 10 9 8 7 6 5 4 3 2 1

CIP catalog records for this book are available from
the British Library and the Library of Congress

UK ISBN: 978-1-4053-3163-0
US ISBN: 978-0-7566-3857-3

Printed by L Rex Printing Co. Ltd, China

Discover more at
www.dk.com

contents
viṣaya sūchī
विषय सूची

42

health
svāsthya
स्वास्थ्य

146

eating out
bāhar khānā
बाहर खाना

252

leisure
manorañjan
मनोरंजन

Bilingual
VISUAL
dictionary

CONTENTS • VIṢAYA SŪCHĪ • विषय सूची

about the dictionary

The use of pictures is proven to aid understanding and the retention of information. Working on this principle, this highly-illustrated English-Hindi bilingual dictionary presents a large range of useful current vocabulary in the two languages.

The dictionary is divided thematically and covers most aspects of the everyday world in detail, from the restaurant to the gym, the home to the workplace, outer space to the animal kingdom. You will also find additional words and phrases for conversational use and for extending your vocabulary.

This is an essential reference tool for anyone interested in languages – practical, stimulating, and easy-to-use.

A few things to note

The Hindi in the dictionary is in the Devnagari script and this is accompanied by a romanization, showing you how to pronounce each word. The entries in the dictionary are always presented in the same order – English, the romanization, then Hindi. Where no suitable Hindi words exist, or are not commonly used, we have retained the English words, but the romanization has been adapted to show how native Hindi speakers pronounce them. You can find out more about this in the Hindi pronunciation guide on page 324-327.

Verbs are indicated by a (v) after the English, for example: **attend (v)**

There is an English index at the back of the book where you can look up a word and find out on which page it appears.

शब्दकोश के बारे में

तस्वीरों के ज़रिए किसी जानकारी को समझना और उसे ग्रहण करना हमेशा सहायक सिद्ध होता है। इसी सिद्धांत के आधार पर तैयार किया गया यह चित्रात्मक द्विभाषी शब्दकोश अंग्रेज़ी और हिन्दी भाषा में बड़ी संख्या में लाभकारी शब्दों को प्रस्तुत करता है।

यह शब्दकोश विषयों के आधार पर विभाजित है और इसमें रोज़मर्रा के जीवन से जुड़े अनेक पक्ष समेटे गए हैं, जिनमें रेस्तरां से जिम, घर से दफ़्तर और अंतरिक्ष से लेकर प्राणी जगत तक के क्षेत्र शामिल हैं। शाब्दिक क्षमता और बातचीत के कौशल को निखारने के लिए इसमें अतिरिक्त शब्द और वाक्यांश भी दिए गए हैं।

भाषाओं में दिलचस्पी रखने वाले व्यक्तियों के लिए व्यावहारिक, उत्साहवर्धक और प्रयोग में आसान यह संदर्भ पुस्तक एक अत्यावश्यक उपकरण सिद्ध होगी।

ध्यान देने योग्य बातें

इस शब्दकोश में हिन्दी मूल देवनागरी लिपि में लिखी गई है। शब्दों के उच्चारण को स्पष्ट करने के लिए उनका रोमन लिप्यंतरण दिया गया है। इस शब्दकोश में शब्दों को इस क्रम में प्रस्तुत किया गया है– अंग्रेज़ी, फिर हिन्दी रूप का रोमन में लिप्यंतरण और फिर देवनागरी में हिन्दी रूप। ऐसी स्थितियों में जहां अंग्रेज़ी शब्दों के समुचित हिन्दी पर्याय नहीं हैं या उनका आम चलन में प्रयोग नहीं होता, वहां हमने मूल अंग्रेज़ी के शब्दों को ही रखा है। हां, उनके रोमन लिप्यंतरण को उनके हिन्दी उच्चारण के अनुसार लिखा गया है। हिन्दी शब्दों के उच्चारण संबंधी विस्तृत जानकारी के लिए पुस्तक के अंत में (पृष्ठ संख्या 324–327) दी गई लिप्यंतरण गाइड देखें।

क्रियाओं को अंग्रेज़ी शब्द के बाद (v) के द्वारा बताया गया है, जैसे: **attend (v)**

इस शब्दकोश के अंत में अंग्रेज़ी तालिका दी गई है जिसमें किसी भी शब्द को देखकर आप उसकी पृष्ठ संख्या जान सकते हैं।

how to use this book

Whether you are learning a new language for business, pleasure, or in preparation for a holiday abroad, or are hoping to extend your vocabulary in an already familiar language, this dictionary is a valuable learning tool which you can use in a number of different ways.

When learning a new language, look out for cognates (words that are alike in different languages) and false friends (words that look alike but carry significantly different meanings). You can also see where the languages have influenced each other. For example, English has imported many terms for food from other languages but, in turn, exported terms used in technology and popular culture.

Practical learning activities
• As you move about your home, workplace, or college, try looking at the pages which cover that setting. You could then close the book, look around you and see how many of the objects and features you can name.
• Challenge yourself to write a story, letter, or dialogue using as many of the terms on a particular page as possible. This will help you retain the vocabulary and remember the spelling. If you want to build up to writing a longer text, start with sentences incorporating 2–3 words.
• If you have a very visual memory, try drawing or tracing items from the book onto a piece of paper, then close the book and fill in the words below the picture.

कोश का प्रयोग कैसे करें

आप भले ही व्यापार के लिए, शौक़ के लिए या विदेश में छुट्टी मनाने जाने के लिए कोई नई भाषा सीख रहे हों या पहले से सीखी हुई किसी भाषा का अपना शब्द ज्ञान बढ़ाना चाहते हों, आपके लिए यह शब्दकोश काफ़ी सहायक होगा और आप कई तरह से इसका प्रयोग कर सकते हैं।

कोई नई भाषा सीखते समय इस भाषा में प्रयोग होने वाले समानार्थी शब्दों (वे शब्द जो दूसरी भाषाओं में भी एक जैसे हों) और भिन्नार्थी शब्दों (वे शब्द जो एक जैसे दिखते हैं, परंतु उनके अर्थ अलग होते हैं) पर ध्यान जरुर दें। आप यह भी देख सकते हैं कि भाषाएं किस तरह एक–दूसरे को प्रभावित करती हैं। उदाहरण के लिए अंग्रेजी भाषा में खाने संबंधी अनेक शब्द यूरोपीय भाषाओं से लिए गए हैं जबकि इसने संस्कृति व तकनीक के क्षेत्र में बहुत से शब्द उन्हें प्रदान किए हैं।

सीखने के लिए व्यावहारिक अभ्यास
• आप अपने घर, दफ़्तर या कॉलेज में घूमते हुए, उन पन्नों को देखने का प्रयास करें, जो इन क्षेत्रों से संबंधित हैं। फिर इस पुस्तक को बंद करके अपने आसपास नज़र दौड़ाएं और यह देखें कि आपको कितनी चीज़ों के नाम याद हैं।
• किसी एक विशेष पन्ने पर दिए गए शब्दों का प्रयोग करके छोटी कहानी, पत्र या संवाद लिखने का प्रयास करें। इससे आपको शब्द और वर्तनी याद रखने में मदद मिलेगी। अगर आप कोई बड़ा आलेख लिखना चाहते हैं, तो दो–तीन शब्दों को मिलाकर छोटे–छोटे वाक्य बनाकर शुरुआत करें।
• यदि चित्रों की सहायता से आपको अधिक याद रहता है तो इस कोश में दिए गए चित्रों को अलग काग़ज़ पर बनाएं और बिना देखे उनसे संबंधित शब्दों को लिखें।

people
log
लोग

body • śarīr • शरीर

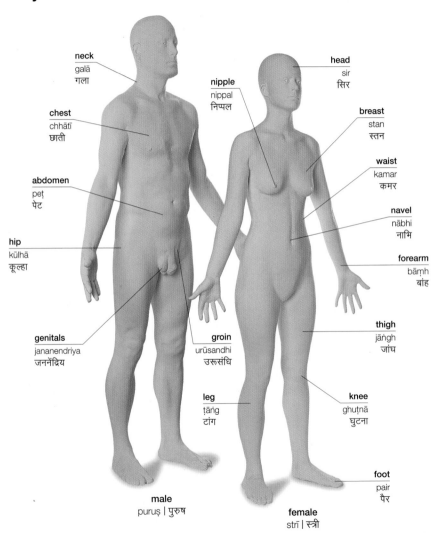

neck
galā
गला

chest
chhātī
छाती

abdomen
peṭ
पेट

hip
kūlhā
कूल्हा

genitals
jananendriya
जननेंद्रिय

nipple
nippal
निप्पल

groin
urūsandhi
उरूसंधि

leg
ṭāṅg
टांग

head
sir
सिर

breast
stan
स्तन

waist
kamar
कमर

navel
nābhi
नाभि

forearm
bāṃh
बांह

thigh
jāṅgh
जांघ

knee
ghuṭnā
घुटना

foot
pair
पैर

male
puruṣ | पुरुष

female
strī | स्त्री

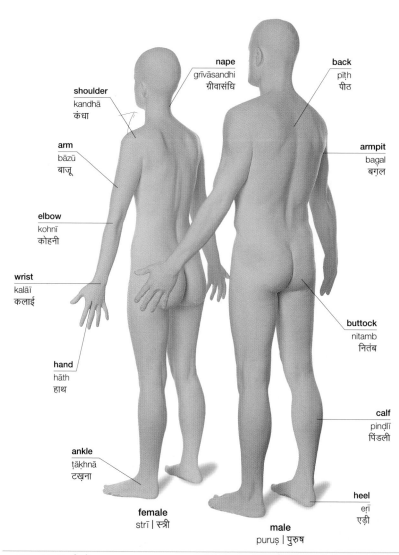

nape
grīvāsandhi
ग्रीवासंधि

back
pīṭh
पीठ

shoulder
kandhā
कंधा

arm
bāzū
बाजू

armpit
bagal
बग़ल

elbow
kohnī
कोहनी

wrist
kalāī
कलाई

buttock
nitamb
नितंब

hand
hāth
हाथ

ankle
ṭākhnā
टख़ना

calf
pinḍlī
पिंडली

heel
eṛī
एड़ी

female
strī | स्त्री

male
puruṣ | पुरुष

face • chehrā • चेहरा

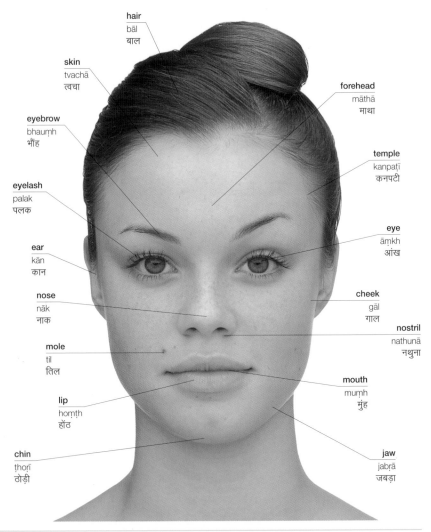

hair
bāl
बाल

skin
tvachā
त्वचा

eyebrow
bhaumh
भौंह

eyelash
palak
पलक

ear
kān
कान

nose
nāk
नाक

mole
til
तिल

lip
homth
होंठ

chin
ṭhoṛī
ठोड़ी

forehead
māthā
माथा

temple
kanpaṭī
कनपटी

eye
āmkh
आंख

cheek
gāl
गाल

nostril
nathunā
नथुना

mouth
mumh
मुंह

jaw
jabṛā
जबड़ा

wrinkle
jhurriyāṃ | झुर्रियां

freckle
jhāīṃ | झाईं

pore
rom chhidr | रोमछिद्र

dimple | gāl kā
gaḍḍhā | गाल का गड्ढा

hand • hāth • हाथ

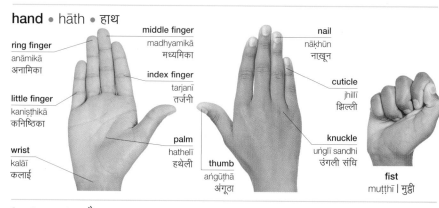

ring finger
anāmikā
अनामिका

middle finger
madhyamikā
मध्यमिका

index finger
tarjanī
तर्जनी

little finger
kaniṣṭhikā
कनिष्ठिका

palm
hathelī
हथेली

wrist
kalāī
कलाई

thumb
aṅgūṭhā
अंगूठा

nail
nākhūn
नाखून

cuticle
jhillī
झिल्ली

knuckle
uṅglī sandhi
उंगली संधि

fist
muṭṭhī | मुट्ठी

foot • pair • पैर

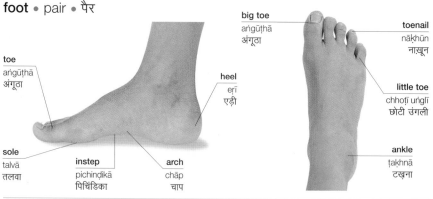

toe
aṅgūṭhā
अंगूठा

big toe
aṅgūṭhā
अंगूठा

heel
erī
एड़ी

toenail
nākhūn
नाखून

little toe
chhoṭī uṅglī
छोटी उंगली

sole
talvā
तलवा

instep
pichiṇḍikā
पिचिंडिका

arch
chāp
चाप

ankle
ṭakhnā
टखना

muscles • māṃspeśiyāṃ • मांसपेशियां

frontal
lalāṭ
ललाट

pectoral
anspeśī
अंसपेशी

deltoid
anscchhad
peśī
अंसच्छद
पेशी

trapezius
pṛṣṭhcchhadā
peśī
पृष्ठच्छदा पेशी

latissimus dorsi
pīṭh kī sabse
chaurī peśī
पीठ की सबसे
चौड़ी पेशी

biceps
dviśir peśī
द्विशिर पेशी

triceps
triśir peśī
त्रिशिर पेशी

abdominals
udarīya
māṃspeśiyāṃ
उदरीय मांसपेशियां

hamstring
jānupṛṣṭh
peśī
जानुपृष्ठ पेशी

buttock
nitamb
नितंब

quadriceps
chatuḥ śirask
चतु: शिरस्क

Achilles tendon
peśībandh
पेशीबंध

calf
piṇḍlī
पिंडली

skeleton • asthipanjar • अस्थिपंजर

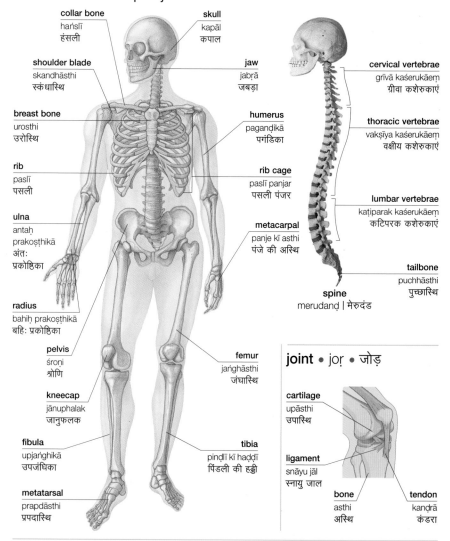

collar bone
haṅslī
हंसली

skull
kapāl
कपाल

shoulder blade
skandhāsthi
स्कंधास्थि

jaw
jabṛā
जबड़ा

cervical vertebrae
grīvā kaśerukāeṃ
ग्रीवा कशेरुकाएं

breast bone
urosthi
उरोस्थि

humerus
pagaṇḍikā
पगंडिका

thoracic vertebrae
vakṣīya kaśerukāeṃ
वक्षीय कशेरुकाएं

rib
paslī
पसली

rib cage
paslī panjar
पसली पंजर

ulna
antaḥ
prakoṣṭhikā
अंत:
प्रकोष्ठिका

metacarpal
panje kī asthi
पंजे की अस्थि

lumbar vertebrae
kaṭiparak kaśerukāeṃ
कटिपरक कशेरुकाएं

radius
bahiḥ prakoṣṭhikā
बहि: प्रकोष्ठिका

tailbone
puchhāsthi
पुच्छास्थि

spine
merudaṇḍ | मेरुदंड

pelvis
śroṇi
श्रोणि

femur
jaṅghāsthi
जंघास्थि

kneecap
jānuphalak
जानुफलक

joint • joṛ • जोड़

cartilage
upāsthi
उपास्थि

fibula
upjaṅghikā
उपजंघिका

tibia
piṇḍlī kī haḍḍī
पिंडली की हड्डी

ligament
snāyu jāl
स्नायु जाल

metatarsal
prapdāsthi
प्रपदास्थि

bone
asthi
अस्थि

tendon
kaṇḍrā
कंडरा

internal organs • āntarik aṅg • आंतरिक अंग

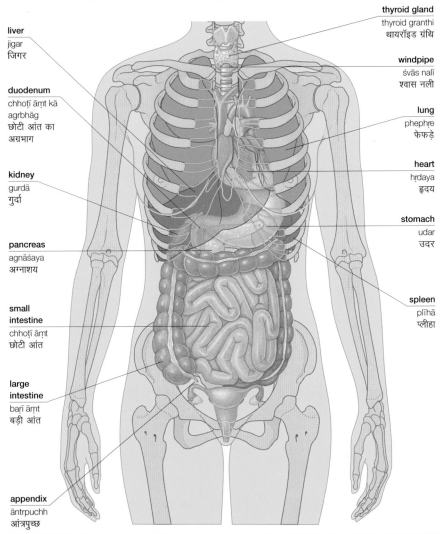

thyroid gland
thyroid granthi
थायरॉइड ग्रंथि

liver
jigar
जिगर

windpipe
śvās naḷī
श्वास नली

duodenum
chhoṭī āṃt kā
agrbhāg
छोटी आंत का
अग्रभाग

lung
phephṛe
फेफड़े

heart
hṛdaya
हृदय

kidney
gurdā
गुर्दा

stomach
udar
उदर

pancreas
agnāśaya
अग्नाशय

spleen
plīhā
प्लीहा

**small
intestine**
chhoṭī āṃt
छोटी आंत

**large
intestine**
baṛī āṃt
बड़ी आंत

appendix
āntrpuchh
आंत्रपुच्छ

head • sir • सिर

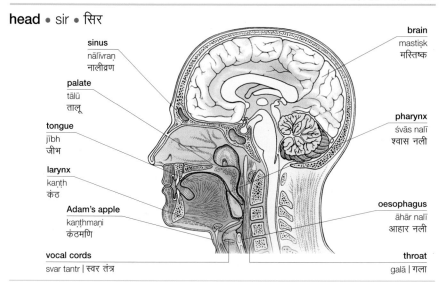

sinus
nālīvraṇ
नालीव्रण

palate
tālū
तालू

tongue
jībh
जीभ

larynx
kaṇth
कंठ

Adam's apple
kaṇthmaṇi
कंठमणि

vocal cords
svar tantr | स्वर तंत्र

brain
mastiṣk
मस्तिष्क

pharynx
śvās nalī
श्वास नली

oesophagus
āhār nalī
आहार नली

throat
galā | गला

body systems • śarīr tantr • शरीर तंत्र

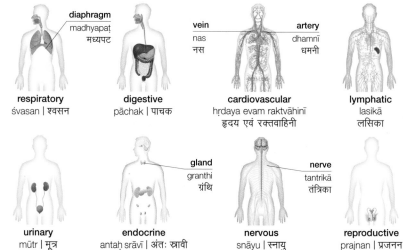

diaphragm
madhyapaṭ
मध्यपट

vein
nas
नस

artery
dhamnī
धमनी

respiratory
śvasan | श्वसन

digestive
pāchak | पाचक

cardiovascular
hṛdaya evam raktvāhinī
हृदय एवं रक्तवाहिनी

lymphatic
lasikā
लसिका

gland
granthi
ग्रंथि

nerve
tantrikā
तंत्रिका

urinary
mūtr | मूत्र

endocrine
antaḥ srāvī | अंतः स्रावी

nervous
snāyu | स्नायु

reproductive
prajnan | प्रजनन

english • hindī • हिन्दी

reproductive organs • prajnanīya aṅg • प्रजननीय अंग

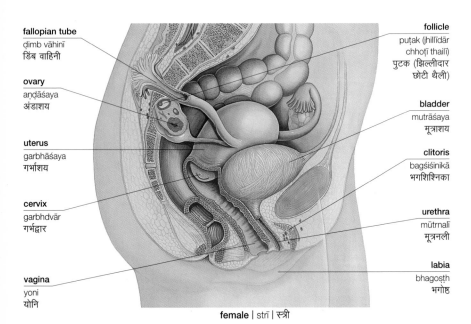

fallopian tube
ḍimb vāhinī
डिंब वाहिनी

ovary
aṇḍāśaya
अंडाशय

uterus
garbhāśaya
गर्भाशय

cervix
garbhdvār
गर्भद्वार

vagina
yoni
योनि

follicle
puṭak (jhillīdār chhoṭī thailī)
पुटक (झिल्लीदार छोटी थैली)

bladder
mutrāśaya
मूत्राशय

clitoris
bagśiśinikā
भगशिशिनका

urethra
mūtrnalī
मूत्रनली

labia
bhagoṣṭh
भगोष्ठ

female | strī | स्त्री

reproduction • prajnan • प्रजनन

sperm
śukrāṇu
शुक्राणु

egg
aṇḍā
अंडा

fertilization | niṣechan | निषेचन

vocabulary • śabdāvalī • शब्दावली

hormone hārmon हारमोन	**impotent** napunsak नपुंसक	**intercourse** sambhog संभोग
ovulation bīj janan बीज जनन	**menstruation** māhvārī माहवारी	**sexually transmitted disease** yaun rog यौन रोग
conceive garbhdhāraṇ karnā गर्भधारण करना	**fertile** urvar उर्वर	

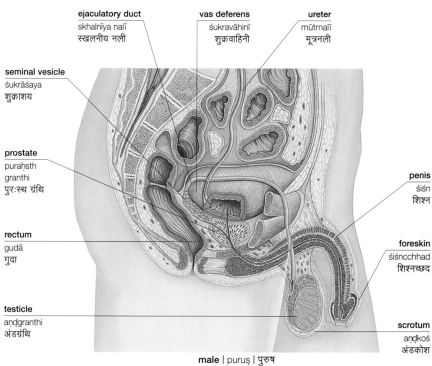

ejaculatory duct
skhalnīya nalī
स्खलनीय नली

vas deferens
śukravāhinī
शुक्रवाहिनी

ureter
mūtrnalī
मूत्रनली

seminal vesicle
śukrāśaya
शुक्राशय

prostate
puraḥsth
granthi
पुर:स्थ ग्रंथि

penis
śiśn
शिश्न

rectum
gudā
गुदा

foreskin
śiśncchhad
शिश्नच्छद

testicle
aṇḍgranthi
अंडग्रंथि

scrotum
aṇḍkoś
अंडकोश

male | puruṣ | पुरुष

contraception • garbhnirodh • गर्भनिरोध

cap
kaip
कैप

diaphragm
ḍāyafrām
डायफ्राम

condom
kaṇḍom
कंडोम

IUD
copper-ṭī
कॉपर–टी

pill
garbh nirodhak
goliyāṃ
गर्भ निरोधक गोलियां

family • parivār • परिवार

grandmother
dādī | दादी

grandfather
dādā | दादा

uncle
phūphā | फूफा

aunt
buā | बुआ

father
pitā | पिता

mother
mātā | माता

cousin
phūpherā bhāī |
फूफेरा भाई

brother
bhāī | भाई

sister
bahan | बहन

wife
patnī | पत्नी

daughter-in-law
bahū | बहू

son
beṭā | बेटा

daughter
beṭī | बेटी

son-in-law
dāmād | दामाद

grandson
potā | पोता

granddaughter
potī | पोती

husband
pati | पति

vocabulary • śabdāvalī • शब्दावली

relatives	parents	grandparents	stepfather	stepson	generation
riśtedār	mātā-pitā	dādā-dādī/nānā-nānī	sautele pitā	sautelā beṭā	pīṛhī
रिश्तेदार	माता–पिता	दादा–दादी/नाना–नानी	सौतेले पिता	सौतेला बेटा	पीढ़ी

partner	children	grandchildren	stepmother	stepdaughter	twins
sāthī	bacche	nātī-nātin/potā-potī	sautelī mātā	sautelī beṭī	jurvāṃ
साथी	बच्चे	नाती–नातिन/पोता–पोती	सौतेली माता	सौतेली बेटी	जुड़वां

mother-in-law
sās | सास

father-in-law
sasur | ससुर

stages • avasthāeṃ • अवस्थाएं

baby
śiśu | शिशु

child
bacchā | बच्चा

brother-in-law
sāṛhū | साढू

sister-in-law
sālī | साली

boy
laṛkā | लड़का

girl
laṛkī | लड़की

niece
bhānjī | भानजी

nephew
bhānjā | भानजा

teenager
kiśorī | किशोरी

adult
vayask | व्यस्क

Mrs
śrīmatī
श्रीमती

titles • sambodhan • संबोधन

Mr
śrīmān
श्रीमान

Miss
kumārī
कुमारी

man
ādmī | आदमी

woman
aurat | औरत

relationships • sambandh • संबंध

manager
prabandhak
प्रबंधक

assistant
sahāyak
सहायक

business partner
sājhedār
साझेदार

employer
mālik
मालिक

employee
karmchārī
कर्मचारी

colleague
sahyogī
सहयोगी

office
karyālaya | कार्यालय

neighbour
paṛosī | पड़ोसी

friend
dost | दोस्त

acquaintance
parichit | परिचित

penfriend
ḵalam mitr | क़लम मित्र

boyfriend
puruṣ mitr
पुरुष मित्र

girlfriend
mahilā mitr
महिला मित्र

fiancé
maṅgetar
मंगेतर

fiancée
maṅgetar
मंगेतर

couple | yugal | युगल

engaged couple | bhāvī var-vadhū | भावी वर–वधू

emotions • bhāvnāeṃ • भावनाएं

smile
muskān
मुस्कान

happy
k̲h̲uśī | ख़ुशी

sad
dukh | दुख

excited
uttejnā | उत्तेजना

bored
ūb | ऊब

surprised
āścharya
आश्चर्य

scared
bhaya | भय

frown
tyoriyāṃ
charhnā
त्योरियां
चढ़ना

angry
g̲ussā | ग़ुस्सा

confused
asmanjas | असमंजस

worried
chintā | चिंता

nervous
ghabrāhaṭ | घबराहट

proud
garv | गर्व

confident
ātmaviśvās | आत्मविश्वास

embarrassed
lajjā | लज्जा

shy
śarmīlā | शर्मीला

vocabulary • śabdāvalī • शब्दावली

sigh (v)	**shout (v)**	**laugh (v)**	**cry (v)**
āh bharnā	chillānā	haṃsnā	ronā
आह भरना	चिल्लाना	हंसना	रोना
shocked	**yawn (v)**	**upset**	
sadmā lagnā	ubāsī lenā	pareśān	
सदमा लगना	उबासी लेना	परेशान	

life events • jīvan kī k̲has ghaṭnāeṃ •
जीवन की ख़ास घटनाएं

be born (v)
paidā honā | पैदा होना

start school (v)
skūl jānā | स्कूल जाना

make friends (v) | dost
banānā | दोस्त बनाना

graduate (v) | snātak
honā | स्नातक होना

get a job (v)
naukrī pānā | नौकरी पाना

fall in love (v)
prem honā | प्रेम होना

get married (v)
śādī karnā | शादी करना

have a baby (v)
santān honā | संतान होना

wedding | vivāh | विवाह

divorce
talāk̲ | तलाक़

funeral
antyeṣṭi | अंत्येष्टि

vocabulary • śabdāvalī • शब्दावली

christening īsaī nāmkaraṇ ईसाई नामकरण	**die (v)** marnā मरना
bar mitzvah yahūdī upnayan यहूदी उपनयन	**make a will (v)** vasīyat banānā वसीयत बनाना
anniversary sālgirah सालगिरह	**birth certificate** janm pramāṇpatr जन्म प्रमाणपत्र
emigrate (v) utpravās karnā उत्प्रवास करना	**wedding reception** vivāh bhoj विवाह भोज
retire (v) kārya nivṛtt honā कार्य निवृत्त होना	**honeymoon** hanīmūn हनीमून

celebrations • utsav • उत्सव

birthday party
janmdin kī parṭī
जन्मदिन की पार्टी

card
kārḍ
कार्ड

birthday
janmdin | जन्मदिन

present
tohfā
तोहफ़ा

Christmas
krismas | क्रिसमस

festivals • tyohār • त्योहार

Passover | yahūdī
parv | यहूदी पर्व

New Year
nav varṣ | नव वर्ष

carnival
kārnivāl | कार्निवाल

procession
śobhāyātrā
शोभायात्रा

Ramadan
ramzān | रमज़ान

ribbon
riban
रिबन

Thanksgiving
thaiṅks giviṅg | थैंक्स गिविंग

Easter
īsṭar | ईस्टर

Halloween
hailovīn | हैलोवीन

Diwali
dīvālī | दीवाली

appearance
veśbhūṣā
वेशभूषा

children's clothing • bāl paridhān • बाल परिधान

baby • śiśu • शिशु

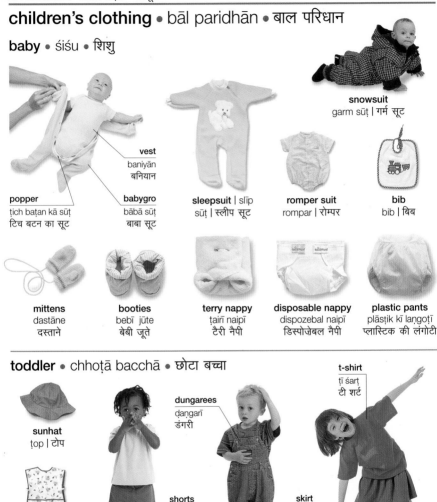

snowsuit
garm sūṭ | गर्म सूट

vest
baniyān
बनियान

popper
ṭich baṭan kā sūṭ
टिच बटन का सूट

babygro
bābā sūṭ
बाबा सूट

sleepsuit | slīp
sūṭ | स्लीप सूट

romper suit
rompar | रोम्पर

bib
bib | बिब

mittens
dastāne
दस्ताने

booties
bebī jūte
बेबी जूते

terry nappy
ṭairī naipī
टैरी नैपी

disposable nappy
dispozebal naipī
डिस्पोज़ेबल नैपी

plastic pants
plāsṭik kī laṅgoṭī
प्लास्टिक की लंगोटी

toddler • chhoṭā bacchā • छोटा बच्चा

t-shirt
ṭī śarṭ
टी शर्ट

sunhat
ṭop | टोप

dungarees
ḍaṅgarī
डंगरी

apron
epren | एप्रेन

shorts
nekar
नेकर

skirt
skarṭ
स्कर्ट

child • bacchā • बच्चा

dress
dres
ड्रेस

hood
ṭopī
टोपी

jeans
jīns
जीन्स

sandals
saiṇḍil
सैंडिल

summer
garmī | गर्मी

raincoat
barsātī | बरसाती

backpack
piṭṭhū baig
पिट्टू बैग

toggle
lambā
baṭan
लंबा बटन

autumn | śarad
ṛtu | शरद ऋतु

duffel coat
garm koṭ
गर्म कोट

scarf
gulūband
गुलूबंद

anorak
barsātī
koṭ
बरसाती कोट

wellington boots
veliṅgṭan
būṭ
वेलिंगटन बूट

winter
sardī
सर्दी

dressing gown
ḍresiṅg gāun
ड्रेसिंग गाउन

logo
logo
लोगो

trainers
ṭrenars
ट्रेनर्स

nightie
nāiṭī
नाइटी

slippers
chappal
चप्पल

nightwear
rātri pośāk | रात्रि पोशाक

football strip
football strip
फुटबॉल स्ट्रिप

tracksuit
ṭraik sūṭ
ट्रैक सूट

leggings
garm pajāmī
गर्म पजामी

vocabulary • śabdāvalī • शब्दावली

natural fibre
prakṛtik reśe
प्राकृतिक रेशे

synthetic
kṛtrim
कृत्रिम

Is it machine washable?
kyā yah maśīn meṃ dhul saktā hai?
क्या यह मशीन में धुल सकता है?

Will this fit a two-year-old?
kyā yah do sāl ke bacche ko ā jāegā?
क्या यह दो साल के बच्चे को आ जाएगा?

men's clothing • puruṣ paridhān • पुरुष परिधान

collar
collar
कॉलर

tie
ṭāī
टाई

belt
peṭī
पेटी

buttonhole
kāj
काज

cuff
kaf
कफ़

pocket
jeb
जेब

jacket
jaikeṭ
जैकेट

button
baṭan
बटन

trousers
painṭ
पैंट

business suit
biznes sūṭ
बिज़नेस सूट

coat
koṭ | कोट

lining
astar
अस्तर

leather shoes
chamṛe ke jūte
चमड़े के जूते

---

vocabulary • śabdāvalī • शब्दावली

shirt	**dressing gown**	**tracksuit**	**long**
ḳamīz	ḍresiṅg gāun	ṭraik sūṭ	lambā
क़मीज़	ड्रेसिंग गाउन	ट्रैक सूट	लंबा
cardigan	**underwear**	**raincoat**	**short**
sveṭar	antaḥ vastr	barsātī	chhoṭā
स्वेटर	अंतः वस्त्र	बरसाती	छोटा

....

Do you have this in a larger/ smaller size?
kyā iskā baṛā/chhoṭā sāiz hai?
क्या इसका बड़ा/छोटा साइज़ है?

May I try this on?
kyā maiṃ ise pahankar dekh saktā hūṃ?
क्या मैं इसे पहनकर देख सकता हूं?

blazer
blezar | ब्लेज़र

sports jacket | sports
jaikeṭ | स्पोर्ट्स जैकेट

waistcoat
vāskaṭ | वास्कट

v-neck
vī galā
वी गला

round neck
gol galā
गोल गला

t-shirt
ṭī śarṭ
टी शर्ट

anorak
ainoraik | ऐनोरैक

sweatshirt
sveṭ śarṭ | स्वेट शर्ट

windcheater
vinḍchīṭar | विंडचीटर

sweatpants
sveṭ painṭ
स्वेट पैंट

sweater
sveṭar | स्वेटर

pyjamas
pajāmā sūṭ | पजामा सूट

vest
baniyān | बनियान

casual wear
rozmarrā ke vastr
रोज़मर्रा के वस्त्र

shorts
nekar | नेकर

briefs
chaḍḍī | चड्डी

boxer shorts | boxer
shorts | बॉक्सर शॉर्ट्स

socks
moze | मोज़े

women's clothing • mahilā paridhān • महिला परिधान

jacket
jaikeṭ
जैकेट

neckline
galā
गला

seam
sīvan
सीवन

sleeveless
āstīn rahit
pośāk
आस्तीन रहित
पोशाक

sleeve
āstīn
आस्तीन

ankle length
lambī pośāk
लंबी पोशाक

evening dress
gāun
गाउन

dress
paridhān | परिधान

skirt
skarṭ
स्कर्ट

blouse
ḳamīz
क़मीज़

hem
kinārī
किनारी

knee-length
ghuṭne tak lambī
घुटने तक लंबी

trousers
painṭ
पैंट

tights
pārdarśī moze
पारदर्शी मोजे

shoes
jūte
जूते

casual
rozmarrā ke vastr
रोज़मर्रा के वस्त्र

lingerie • adhovastr • अधोवस्त्र

wedding • vivāh • विवाह

strap
strep
स्ट्रेप

lace
les
लेस

veil
orhnī
ओढ़नी

bouquet
guldastā
गुलदस्ता

train
lambā
dupaṭṭā
लंबा दुपट्टा

negligée
gāun | गाउन

slip
slip | स्लिप

camisole
śamīz | शमीज़

suspenders
tanī
तनी

wedding dress
vivāh kī pośāk | विवाह की पोशाक

basque
aṅgiyā
अंगिया

stockings
lambī jurrāb
लंबी जुर्राब

tights
pārdarśī moze
पारदर्शी मोज़े

vest
śamīz
शमीज़

bra
brā | ब्रा

knickers
jāṅghiyā | जांघिया

nightdress
nāiṭī | नाइटी

vocabulary • śabdāvalī • शब्दावली

corset cholī चोली	**tailored** sile vastr सिले वस्त्र
garter geṭis गेटिस	**halter neck** ḍorī vālā galā डोरी वाला गला
shoulder pad śoldar paiḍ शोल्डर पैड	**underwired** aṅḍarvāyarḍ अंडरवायर्ड
waistband kamarband कमरबंद	**sports bra** sporṭs brā स्पोर्ट्स ब्रा

accessories • sahāyak vastuem̐ • सहायक वस्तुएं

buckle
baksuā
बकसुआ

handle
hatthā
हत्था

cap
ṭopī | टोपी

hat
ṭop | टोप

scarf
gulūband | गुलूबंद

belt
peṭī | पेटी

tip
nok
नोक

handkerchief
rūmāl | रूमाल

bow tie
bo-ṭāī | बो–टाई

tie-pin
ṭāī pin | टाई पिन

gloves
dastāne | दस्ताने

umbrella
chhātā | छाता

jewellery • zevar • ज़ेवर

pendant
locket | लॉकेट

brooch
jaṛāū pin | जड़ाऊ पिन

cufflink
kaflink | कफ़लिंक

string of pearls
motiyom̐ kī mālā
मोतियों की माला

clasp
baksuā
बकसुआ

link
kaṛī
कड़ी

earring
bunde
बुंदे

ring
aṅgūṭhī
अंगूठी

stone
k̄īmtī patthar
क़ीमती पत्थर

necklace
hār
हार

watch
ghaṛī
घड़ी

bracelet
bresleṭ | ब्रेसलेट

chain
chen | चेन

jewellery box
zevar peṭī | ज़ेवर पेटी

bags • baig • बैग

wallet
wallet | वॉलेट

purse
baṭuā | बटुआ

shoulder bag
baig | बैग

shoulder strap
baig kī tanī
बैग की तनी

handles
taniyām̐
तनियां

holdall
bistar band | बिस्तर बंद

briefcase
brīfkes | ब्रीफ़केस

handbag
haiṇḍ baig | हैंड बैग

backpack
piṭṭhū baig | पिट्ठू बैग

shoes • jūte-chappal • जूते–चप्पल

eyelet
chhed
छेद

lace
tasme/fīte
तस्मे/फ़ीते

tongue
jībh
जीभ

sole
talā
तला

heel
eṛī
एड़ी

lace-up
fīte vāle jūte | फ़ीते वाले जूते

walking boot
būṭ | बूट

trainer
ṭrenar | ट्रेनर

leather shoe
chamṛe ke jūte
चमड़े के जूते

flip-flop
chappal
चप्पल

high heel shoe
ūm̐chī eṛī ke jūte
ऊंची एड़ी के जूते

platform shoe
platform chappal
प्लेटफ़ॉर्म चप्पल

sandal
saiṇḍil
सैंडिल

slip-on
jūtiyām̐
जूतियां

brogue
brog
ब्रोग

hair • bāl • बाल

comb
kaṇghā
कंघा

comb (v)
kaṇghī karnā | कंघी करना

brush
braś
ब्रश

brush (v)
braś karnā | ब्रश करना

hairdresser
heyar ḍraisar
हेयर ड्रैसर

sink
besin
बेसिन

client
grāhak
ग्राहक

wash (v)
bāl dhonā | बाल धोना

robe
vastr
वस्त्र

rinse (v)
bāl dhonā | बाल धोना

cut (v)
bāl kāṭnā | बाल काटना

blow dry (v)
bāl sukhānā | बाल सुखाना

set (v) | bāl seṭ
karnā | बाल सेट करना

---

accessories • saundarya prasādhan • सौंदर्य प्रसाधन

hairdryer
heyar ḍrāyar
हेयर ड्रायर

shampoo
śaimpū | शैम्पू

conditioner
kaṇḍiśnar | कंडीशनर

gel
jail | जैल

hairspray
heyar spre | हेयर–स्प्रे

curling tongs
karliṅg chimṭī
कर्लिंग चिमटी

scissors
ḳaimchī | कैंची

hairband
heyar baiṇḍ | हेयर बैंड

curler
karlar | कर्लर

hairpin
bāl pin | बाल पिन

styles • keś sajjā • केश सज्जा

ponytail
ponī ṭel | पोनी टेल

ribbon
riban
रिबन
plait
choṭī | चोटी

french pleat
french jūṛā | फ़्रेंच जूड़ा

bun
jūṛā | जूड़ा

pigtails
do choṭī | दो चोटी

bob
bob | बॉब

crop
crop | क्रॉप

curly
ghuṅghrāle | घुंघराले

perm
parm | पर्म

straight
sidhe bāl | सीधे बाल

roots
jareṃ
जड़ें
highlights
haīlāiṭ | हाईलाइट

bald
ganjā | गंजा

wig
vig | विग

vocabulary • śabdāvalī • शब्दावली

trim (v) chhāṃṭnā छांटना	**greasy** tailīya तैलीय
straighten (v) sīdhā karnā सीधा करना	**dry** rūkhe रूखे
barber nāī नाई	**normal** sāmānya सामान्य
dandruff rūsī रूसी	**scalp** śirovalk शिरोवल्क
split ends domuṃhe bāl दोमुंहे बाल	**hairtie** bāloṃ kā fītā बालों का फ़ीता

colours • raṅg • रंग

blonde
sunahrā
सुनहरा

brunette
kālā-bhūrā
काला–भूरा

auburn
bhūrā | भूरा

ginger
lālī lie pīlā raṅg
लाली लिए पीला रंग

black
kālā | काला

grey
sleṭī | स्लेटी

white
safed | सफ़ेद

dyed | raṅge
hue | रंगे हुए

beauty • saundarya • सौंदर्य

hair dyer
heyar ḍāī
हेयर डाई

eye shadow
āī śaiḍo
आई शैडो

mascara
maskārā
मस्कारा

eyeliner
āī lāinar
आई लाइनर

blusher
blaśar
ब्लशर

foundation
fāunḍeśan
फ़ाउंडेशन

lipstick
lipsṭik
लिपस्टिक

make-up • sāj-śr̥ṅgār • साज–श्रृंगार

eyebrow pencil
āī bro pensil | आई ब्रो पेंसिल

eyebrow brush
āī bro braś | आई ब्रो ब्रश

tweezers
chimṭī | चिमटी

lip gloss
lip gloss
लिप ग्लॉस

lip brush
lip braś
लिप ब्रश

lip liner
lip lāinar | लिप लाइनर

brush
braś | ब्रश

concealer
kansīlar | कंसीलर

mirror
śīśā
शीशा

face powder
fes pāuḍar
फ़ेस पाउडर

powder puff
paf
पफ़

compact | pāuḍar | पाउडर

beauty treatments • sundarya upchār • सौंदर्य उपचार

face pack
fes paik
फ़ेस पैक

facial
feśiyal | फ़ेशियल

sunbed
san baiḍ | सन बैड

exfoliate (v)
mṛt tvachā utārnā
मृत त्वचा उतारना

wax
vaiks | वैक्स

pedicure
pairoṃ kī safāī
पैरों की सफ़ाई

manicure • hāthoṃ kī safāī • हाथों की सफ़ाई

nail varnish remover
nel polish rimūvar
नेल पॉलिश रिमूवर

nail file
nel fāilar
नेल फ़ाइलर

nail varnish
nel polish
नेल पॉलिश

nail scissors
nakh kaiṃchī
नख कैंची

nail clippers
nel kaṭar
नेल कटर

toiletries • saundarya prasādhan • सौंदर्य प्रसाधन

cleanser
klīnzar
क्लीज़र

toner
ṭonar
टोनर

moisturizer
moisturizer
मॉइश्चराइज़र

self-tanning cream
ṭain karne kī krīm
टैन करने की क्रीम

perfume
itr
इत्र

eau de toilette
parfyūm spre
परफ़्यूम स्प्रे

vocabulary • śabdāvalī • शब्दावली		
complexion raṅg rūp रंग–रूप	**oily** tailīya तैलीय	**dark** kālī काली
fair gorī गोरी	**sensitive** saṃvedanśīl संवेदनशील	**tattoo** gudnā गुदना
dry rūkhī रूखी	**shade** raṅg रंग	**cotton balls** rūī ke phāhe रूई के फाहे
anti-wrinkle jhurrī-nivārak झुर्री–निवारक	**hypoallergenic** elarjī rodhak एलर्जी रोधक	**tan** bhūre raṅg kā honā भूरे रंग का होना

health
svāsthya
स्वास्थ्य

illness • bīmārī • बीमारी

headache
sirdard
सिरदर्द

nosebleed
naksīr
नकसीर

cough
khāṃsī
खांसी

fever
buḳhār | बुखार

sneeze
chhīṃk | छींक

cold
zukām | जुकाम

flu
nazlā | नज़ला

inhaler
inhelar
इनहेलर

asthma
damā | दमा

cramps
maroṛ | मरोड़

nausea
mitlī | मितली

chickenpox
chhoṭī chechak | छोटी चेचक

rash
funsī | फुंसी

---

vocabulary • śabdāvalī • शब्दावली

heart attack dil kā daurā दिल का दौरा	**diabetes** madhumeh मधुमेह	**eczema** khāj खाज	**chill** sardī सर्दी	**vomit (v)** ulṭī karnā उल्टी करना	**diarrhoea** dast दस्त
stroke pakṣāghāt पक्षाघात	**allergy** elarjī एलर्जी	**infection** saṅkramaṇ संक्रमण	**stomach ache** peṭ kā dard पेट का दर्द	**epilepsy** mirgī मिरगी	**measles** khasrā खसरा
blood pressure raktchāp रक्तचाप	**hayfever** parāg jvar पराग ज्वर	**virus** viṣāṇu विषाणु	**faint (v)** behoś honā बेहोश होना	**migraine** ādhāsīsī आधासीसी	**mumps** kanpheṛe कनफेड़े

doctor • chikitsak • चिकित्सक
consultation • parāmarś • परामर्श

doctor
chikitsak
चिकित्सक

x-ray viewer
eksare dekhne
kā borḍ
एक्सरे देखने का बोर्ड

prescription
nuskhā
नुस्ख़ा

patient
marīz
मरीज़

height bar
kad-māpī
क़द–मापी

nurse
nars
नर्स

scales
vazan-māpī
वजन–मापी

blood pressure gauge
raktchāp māpak
रक्तचाप मापक

stethoscope
steṭhoskop | स्टेथोस्कोप

cuff
kaf | कफ़

vocabulary • śabdāvalī •
शब्दावली

appointment
milne kā samaya
मिलने का समय

inoculation
ṭīkā
टीका

surgery
śalya chikitsā
शल्य चिकित्सा

thermometer
tharmāmīṭar
थर्मामीटर

waiting room
pratīkṣā kakṣ
प्रतीक्षा कक्ष

**medical
examination**
śārīrik jāṃch
शारीरिक जांच

I need to see a doctor.
mujhe doctor ko dikhānā hai
मुझे डॉक्टर को दिखाना है।

It hurts here.
yahāṃ dard ho rahā hai
यहां दर्द हो रहा है।

injury • choṭ • चोट

sling
sling paṭṭī
स्लिंग पड्डी

neck brace
gardan kā
paṭṭā
गर्दन का पट्टा

sprain | moch | मोच

fracture | haḍḍī ṭūṭnā
हड्डी टूटना

whiplash | gale kī moch
गले की मोच

cut
kaṭnā | कटना

graze
ghisaṭ | घिसट

bruise
kharoṃch | खरोंच

splinter
khapchī | खपची

sunburn
dhūp se jalnā
धूप से जलना

burn
jalnā
जलना

bite
kāṭā huā
काटा हुआ

sting
ḍaṅk
डंक

---

vocabulary • śabdāvalī • शब्दावली

accident	**haemorrhage**	**poisoning**	**Will he be all right?**
durghaṭnā	raktsrāv	viṣpān	kyā vah ṭhīk ho jāegā?
दुर्घटना	रक्तस्राव	विषपान	क्या वह ठीक हो जाएगा?
emergency	**blister**	**electric shock**	**Where does it hurt?**
āpātkāl	chhālā	bijlī ke jhaṭke	kahāṃ dard ho rahā hai?
आपातकाल	छाला	बिजली के झटके	कहां दर्द हो रहा है?
wound	**concussion**	**head injury**	**Please call an ambulance!**
ghāv	manoghāt	sir kī choṭ	krpyā embulens bulāie!
घाव	मनोघात	सिर की चोट	कृपया एंबुलेंस बुलाइए!

first aid • prāthmik chikitsā • प्राथमिक चिकित्सा

ointment
marham
मरहम

plaster
plāstar
प्लास्तर

safety pin
sefṭī pin
सेफ्टी पिन

bandage
paṭṭī
पट्टी

painkillers
dardnāśak davā
दर्दनाशक दवा

antiseptic wipe
kīṭāṇunāśak paṭṭī
कीटाणुनाशक पट्टी

tweezers
chimṭī
चिमटी

scissors
kaimchī
कैंची

antiseptic
kīṭāṇunāśak
कीटाणुनाशक

gauze
gauze
गॉज़

first aid box | prāthmik chikitsā peṭī | प्राथमिक चिकित्सा पेटी

dressing
marham paṭṭī | मरहम पट्टी

splint | khapacchī | खपच्ची

adhesive tape
chipakne vālā ṭep
चिपकने वाला टेप

resuscitation
śvasan kriyā | श्वसन क्रिया

vocabulary • śabdāvalī • शब्दावली

shock	**pulse**	**choke (v)**
sadmā	nāṛī	dam ghuṭnā
सदमा	नाड़ी	दम घुटना
unconscious	**breathing**	**sterile**
behoś	sāṃs	saṅkramaṇ rahit
बेहोश	सांस	संक्रमण रहित

Can you help?
kyā āp madad
kar sakte haiṃ?
क्या आप मदद
कर सकते हैं?

hospital • aspatāl • अस्पताल

surgeon
śalya chikitsak
शल्य चिकित्सक

chart
chārṭ
चार्ट

nurse
nars
नर्स

anaesthetist
niśchetan
chikitsak
निश्चेतन
चिकित्सक

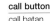

operating theatre
śalya kakṣ | शल्य कक्ष

blood test
k̲h̲ūn kī jāṃch
ख़ून की जांच

injection
ṭīkākaraṇ | टीकाकरण

x-ray
eks-re | एक्स–रे

trolley
trolley
ट्रॉली

call button
call baṭan
कॉल बटन

scan
skain | स्कैन

emergency room
āpātkālīn kakṣ
आपातकालीन कक्ष

ward
kakṣ | कक्ष

wheelchair
vhīlcheyar | व्हीलचेयर

---

vocabulary • śabdāvalī • शब्दावली

operation śalya chikitsā शल्य चिकित्सा	**discharged** chhuṭṭī denā छुट्टी देना	**visiting hours** milne kā samaya मिलने का समय	**children's ward** bacchoṃ kā ward बच्चों का वॉर्ड	**intensive care unit** saghan chikitsā kakṣ सघन चिकित्सा कक्ष
admitted bhartī भर्ती	**clinic** chikitsālaya चिकित्सालय	**maternity ward** prasūti kakṣ प्रसूति कक्ष	**private room** nijī kamrā निजी कमरा	**outpatient** anivāsī rogī अनिवासी रोगी

departments • vibhāg • विभाग

ENT | kān, nāk,
evam galā chikitsā
कान, नाक एवं गला चिकित्सा

cardiology
hṛdaya chikitsā
हृदय चिकित्सा

orthopaedy
asthi chikitsā
अस्थि चिकित्सा

gynaecology
strī rog chikitsā
स्त्री–रोग चिकित्सा

physiotherapy
vyāyām chikitsā
व्यायाम चिकित्सा

dermatology
tvachā chikitsā
त्वचा चिकित्सा

paediatrics
bāl chikitsā
बाल चिकित्सा

radiology
vikiraṇ chikitsā
विकिरण चिकित्सा

surgery
śalya chikitsā
शल्य चिकित्सा

maternity
prasūti
प्रसूति

psychiatry
manochikitsā
मनोचिकित्सा

ophthalmology
netr chikitsā
नेत्र चिकित्सा

vocabulary • śabdāvalī • शब्दावली

neurology snāyu vijñān स्नायु विज्ञान	**urology** mūtr vijñān मूत्र विज्ञान	**endocrinology** antrāsargikī अंतरासर्गिकी	**pathology** rog nidān रोग निदान	**result** pariṇām परिणाम
oncology kainsar vijñān कैंसर विज्ञान	**plastic surgery** plāsṭik sarjarī प्लास्टिक सर्जरी	**referral** sifāriś सिफ़ारिश	**test** jāṃch जांच	**consultant** parāmarśdātā परामर्शदाता

dentist • dant chikitsak • दंत चिकित्सक

tooth • dāṃt • दांत

enamel
dant valk
दंत वल्क

gum
masūṛā
मसूड़ा

nerve
snāyu
स्नायु

root
jaṛ
जड़

premolar
chhoṭī dāṛh
छोटी दाढ़

incisor
karttan
कर्त्तन
dāṃt
दांत

molar
dāṛh
दाढ़

canine
kīlā
कीला

check-up • jāṃch • जांच

reflector
riflekṭar
रिफ़्लेक्टर

probe
jāṃchne kī salāī
जांचने की सलाई

apron
epren
एप्रेन

basin
besin
बेसिन

dentist's chair
dant chikitsā kursī
दंत चिकित्सा–कुर्सी

---

vocabulary • śabdāvalī • शब्दावली

toothache
dāṃt kā dard
दांत का दर्द

drill
chhed karnā
छेद करना

plaque
plāk
प्लाक

extraction
dāṃt ukhāṛnā
दांत उखाड़ना

decay
saṛan
सड़न

crown
upri dant
उपरि दंत

filling
bharāvan
भरावन

floss (v)
dhāge se safāī karnā
धागे से सफ़ाई करना

brush
braś karnā
ब्रश करना

brace
tār kasnā
तार कसना

dental x-ray
dāṃtoṃ kā eksare
दांतों का एक्सरे

x-ray film
eksare film
एक्सरे फ़िल्म

dentures
naklī battīsī
नक़ली बत्तीसी

optician • dṛṣṭi parīkṣak • दृष्टि परीक्षक

case
kavar
कवर

lens
lains
लैंस

frame
frem
फ़्रेम

glasses
chaśmā | चश्मा

sunglasses
dhūp kā chaśmā | धूप का चश्मा

cleaning fluid
lains sāf karne kā dravya
लैंस साफ़ करने का द्रव्य

lens case
lains kavar
लैंस कवर

eye test | āṃkhoṃ kī jāṃch | आंखों की जांच

contact lenses | contact lains | कॉन्टेक्ट लैंस

---

eye • āṃkh • आंख

eyebrow
bhaumh
भौंह

eyelid
palak
पलक

pupil
putlī
पुतली

eyelash
baraunī
बरौनी

iris
uptārā
उपतारा

retina
dṛṣṭi paṭal
दृष्टि पटल

lens
lains
लैंस

cornea
korniyā
कोर्निया

optic nerve
dṛṣṭi tantrikā
दृष्टि तंत्रिका

vocabulary • śabdāvalī • शब्दावली	
vision dṛṣṭi दृष्टि	**astigmatism** dṛṣṭi vaiṣamya दृष्टि वैषम्य
long sight dīrgh dṛṣṭi दीर्घ दृष्टि	**tear** āṃsū आंसू
cataract motiyābind मोतियाबिंद	**short sight** alp dṛṣṭi अल्प दृष्टि
diopter śīśā parakhne kī ikāī शीशा परखने की इकाई	**bifocal** bāyafokal बायफ़ोकल

pregnancy • garbhāvasthā • गर्भावस्था

nurse
nars
नर्स

pregnancy test
garbhāvasthā jāṃch
गर्भावस्था जांच

scan
skain
स्कैन

ultrasound
alṭrāsāuṇḍ | अल्ट्रासाउंड

umbilical cord
nābhi-rajju
नाभि–रज्जु

placenta
garbhnāl
गर्भनाल

cervix
garbhaśaya dvār
गर्भाशय द्वार

uterus
garbhāśaya
गर्भाशय

foetus
bhrūṇ | भ्रूण

vocabulary • śabdāvalī • शब्दावली

ovulation bījjanan बीजजनन	**antenatal** janm pūrv जन्म पूर्व	**contraction** saṅkuchan संकुचन	**dilation** phailāv फैलाव	**delivery** prasav प्रसव	**breech** ulṭā bhrūṇ उल्टा भ्रूण
conception garbhādhān गर्भाधान	**womb** bacchedānī बच्चेदानी	**break waters (v)** pānī jānā पानी जाना	**epidural** epiḍyūral एपिड्यूरल	**birth** janm जन्म	**premature** samaya pūrv समय पूर्व
pregnant garbhvatī गर्भवती	**trimester** trimās त्रिमास	**amniotic fluid** ulv drav उल्व द्रव	**episiotomy** bhagacchhedan भगच्छेदन	**miscarriage** garbhpāt गर्भपात	**gynaecologist** strī rog viśeṣajñ स्त्री-रोग विशेषज्ञ
expectant garbhvatī गर्भवती	**embryo** aviksit bhrūṇ अविकसित भ्रूण	**amniocentesis** sīrinj se ulv drav nikālnā सीरिज से उल्व–द्रव निकालना	**caesarean section** operation prasav ऑपरेशन प्रसव	**stitches** ṭāṃke टांके	**obstetrician** prasav viśeṣajñ प्रसव विशेषज्ञ

childbirth • śiśu janm • शिशु जन्म

drip
drip
ड्रिप

monitor
monitor
मॉनीटर

midwife
dāī
दाई

catheter
mūtr nikāsī nalī
मूत्र निकासी
नली

induce labour (v)
kṛtrim prasav karānā | कृत्रिम प्रसव कराना

forceps
chimṭī
चिमटी

ventouse cup
prasav mem sahāyak upkaraṇ
प्रसव में सहायक उपकरण

assisted delivery
upkaraṇ dvārā prasav | उपकरण द्वारा प्रसव

identity tag
pahchān chihn
पहचान चिह्न

newborn baby
navjāt śiśu | नवजात शिशु

incubator | ūṣmak | ऊष्मक

scales
tarāzū
तराजू

birth weight
janm bhār | जन्म भार

nursing • stanpān • स्तनपान

breast pump
stan pamp
स्तन पंप

nursing bra
narsiṅg brā
नर्सिंग ब्रा

breastfeed (v)
stanpān karānā
स्तनपान कराना

pads
paid
पैड

alternative therapy • vaikalpik chikitsā • वैकल्पिक चिकित्सा

teacher
śikṣak
शिक्षक

massage
māliś | मालिश

shiatsu
śiyātsu | शियात्सु

yoga
yog | योग

mat
chaṭāī
चटाई

chiropractic
merudaṇḍ upchār
मेरुदंड उपचार

osteopathy | asthi
chikitsā | अस्थि चिकित्सा

reflexology | riflaiksolojī
रिफ्लैक्सोलोजी

meditation
dhyān | ध्यान

counsellor
parāmarśdātā
परामर्शदाता

reiki
rekī | रेकी

acupuncture
ekyūpaṅkchar
एक्यूपंक्चर

group therapy
samūh chikitsā | समूह चिकित्सा

ayurveda
āyurved | आयुर्वेद

hypnotherapy
sammohan chikitsā
सम्मोहन चिकित्सा

essential oils
sugandhit tel
सुगंधित तेल

herbalism | jarī-būṭī
sevan | जड़ी–बूटी सेवन

aromatherapy
sugandh chikitsā
सुगंध चिकित्सा

homeopathy
homyopaithī
होम्योपैथी

acupressure
ekyūpraiśar
एक्यूप्रैशर

therapist
chikitsak
चिकित्सक

psychotherapy
manochikitsā | मनोचिकित्सा

vocabulary • śabdāvalī • शब्दावली			
supplement	**feng shui**	**relaxation**	**naturopathy**
pūrak	feṅg śuī	tanāv mukti	prākṛtik chikitsā
पूरक	फेंग शुई	तनाव मुक्ति	प्राकृतिक चिकित्सा
hydrotherapy	**herb**	**stress**	**crystal healing**
jal chikitsā	jarī-būṭī	tanāv	kriṣṭal chikitsā
जल चिकित्सा	जड़ी–बूटी	तनाव	क्रिस्टल चिकित्सा

home
ghar
घर

house · makān · मकान

gutter
gaṭar
गटर

roof
chhat
छत

chimney
chimnī
चिमनी

wall
dīvār
दीवार

tile
ṭāil
टाइल

eaves
chhajjā
छज्जा

shutter
kapāṭ
कपाट

porch
dvārmaṇḍap
द्वारमंडप

window
khiṛkī
खिड़की

extension
atirikt bhāg
अतिरिक्त भाग

path
rāstā
रास्ता

front door
mukhyadvār
मुख्यद्वार

vocabulary · śabdāvalī · शब्दावली

detached ekal ghar एकल घर	**tenant** kirāedār किराएदार	**garage** gairej गैरेज	**letterbox** laiṭar box लैटर बॉक्स	**burglar alarm** chor ghaṇṭī चोर घंटी	**rent (v)** kirāe par lenā किराए पर लेना
townhouse śahrī makān शहरी मकान	**bungalow** baṅglā बंगला	**attic** aṭārī अटारी	**landlord** makān mālik मकान मालिक	**courtyard** āṅgan आंगन	**rent** kirāyā किराया
semidetached saṭā huā ghar सटा हुआ घर	**basement** tahḳhānā तहख़ाना	**room** kamrā कमरा	**porch light** dvārmaṇḍap battī द्वारमंडप बत्ती	**floor** manzil मंज़िल	**terraced** chhat vālā छत वाला

entrance • praveś dvār • प्रवेश द्वार

flat • flaiṭ • फ़्लैट

hand rail
reliṅg
रेलिंग

landing
chauṛī sīṛhī
चौड़ी सीढ़ी

banister
sīṛhiyoṃ
kā jaṅglā
सीढ़ियों
का जंगला

staircase
zīnā
जीना

hallway
galiyārā | गलियारा

balcony
bālkanī
बालकनी

block of flats
apārṭmenṭ | अपार्टमेंट

doorbell
darvāze kī ghanṭī
दरवाजे की घंटी

doormat
pāyadān
पायदान

door knocker
kunḍā
कुंडा

intercom
antaḥ sanchār | अंतः संचार

key
chābī
चाबी

door chain | darvāze
kī kaṛī | दरवाजे की कड़ी

lock
tālā | ताला

bolt
chaṭkhanī | चटखनी

lift
lifṭ | लिफ़्ट

internal systems • gharelū upkaraṇ • घरेलू उपकरण

blade
paṅkhṛī | पंखड़ी

fan | paṅkhā | पंखा

convector heater
bloar | ब्लोअर

radiator | reḍieṭar | रेडिएटर

heater | hīṭar | हीटर

---

electricity • bijlī • बिजली

filament
filāmeṇṭ
फ़िलामेंट

earthing
arthiṅg
अर्थिंग

neutral
nyūṭral | न्यूट्रल

pin
pin
पिन

bayonet fitting
beyoneṭ fiṭiṅg
बेयोनेट फ़िटिंग

light bulb
balb | बल्ब

live
lāiv
लाइव

plug
plag | प्लग

wires
tār | तार

---

vocabulary • śabdāvalī • शब्दावली

voltage volṭej वोल्टेज	**fuse** fyūz फ़्यूज़	**socket** socket सॉकेट	**mains supply** men saplāī मेन सप्लाई	**direct current** ḍāyarekṭ karaṇṭ डायरेक्ट करंट
amp ampīyar अंपीयर	**fuse box** fyūz box फ़्यूज़ बॉक्स	**switch** svich स्विच	**transformer** transformer ट्रांसफ़ॉर्मर	**alternating current** alternating karaṇṭ ऑल्टरनेटिंग करंट
power ūrjā ऊर्जा	**generator** jenreṭar जेनरेटर	**power cut** bijlī kaṭautī बिजली कटौती	**electricity meter** bijlī kā mīṭar बिजली का मीटर	

plumbing • nalsāzī • नलसाज़ी

inlet
inlet
इनलेट

outlet
āutleṭ
आउटलेट

pressure valve
preśar valve
प्रेशर वॉल्व

insulation
insuleśan
इंसुलेशन

overflow pipe
ovar flo pāip
ओवर फ्लो पाइप

tank
ṭaṅkī
टंकी

water chamber
water chaimbar
वॉटर चैम्बर

drain cock
nikāsī mārg
निकासी मार्ग

thermostat
tharmosṭeṭ
थर्मोस्टेट

gas burner
gais barnar
गैस बर्नर

boiler
boiler
बॉयलर

heating element
garm karne kī dhātu
गर्म करने की धातु

sink • siṅk • सिंक

tap
nal
नल

lever
uttolak
उत्तोलक

gasket
gāskeṭ
गास्केट

supply pipe
āpūrti nalī
आपूर्ति नली

shutoff valve
shutoff valve
शटऑफ़ वॉल्व

drain
nikās
निकास

waste disposal unit
kūṛā nikās ikāī
कूड़ा निकास इकाई

water closet • śauchālaya • शौचालय

float ball
floṭ ball
फ़्लोट बॉल

cistern
ṭaṅkī
टंकी

seat
sīṭ
सीट

bowl
bāul
बाउल

waste pipe
nikās pāip
निकास पाइप

waste disposal • kūṛe kā nipṭārā • कूड़े का निपटारा

bottle
botal
बोतल

recycling bin
punarchakravat pātr
पुनर्चक्रवत पात्र

pedal
paiḍal
पैडल

lid
ḍhakkan
ढक्कन

rubbish bin
kūredān
कूड़ेदान

sorting unit
chhamṭāī yūniṭ
छंटाई यूनिट

organic waste
jaivik kūrā
जैविक कूड़ा

living room • baiṭhak • बैठक

painting
chitr
चित्र

frame
frem
फ़्रेम

lamp
laimp
लैंप

wall light
lāiṭ
लाइट

clock
gharī
घड़ी

ceiling
chhat
छत

cabinet
almārī
अलमारी

sofa
sofā
सोफ़ा

cushion
gaddī
गद्दी

coffee table
coffee ṭebal
कॉफ़ी टेबल

floor
zamīn
ज़मीन

mirror
śīśā
शीशा

vase
guldān
गुलदान

mantelpiece
ātiśdān
आतिशदान

curtain
pardā | पर्दा

net curtain
jālīdār pardā
जालीदार पर्दा

fireplace
alāv
अलाव

venetian blind
veneśiyan blāiṇḍ
वेनेशियन ब्लाइंड

roller blind | rolar
blāiṇḍ | रोलर ब्लाइंड

screen
skrīn
स्क्रीन

candle
mombattī
मोमबत्ती

bookshelf
kitābom kī almārī
किताबों की अलमारी

sofabed
sofā-kam-beḍ
सोफ़ा–कम–बेड

rug
darī
दरी

moulding
paṭṭī | पट्टी

armchair
kursī
कुर्सी

study | paṛhne kā kamrā | पढ़ने का कमरा

dining room • bhojan kakṣ • भोजन कक्ष

table
mez
मेज़

pepper
kālī mirch
काली मिर्च

salt
namak
नमक

crockery
chīnī miṭṭī
ke bartan
चीनी मिट्टी
के बर्तन

cutlery
chhurī-kāmṭe
छुरी–कांटे

chair
kursī
कुर्सी

back
pīṭh
पीठ

seat
sīṭ
सीट

leg
pāyā
पाया

---

vocabulary • śabdāvalī • शब्दावली

serve (v) parosnā परोसना	**hungry** bhūkhā भूखा	**dinner** rāt kā bhojan रात का भोजन	**full** bharā huā भरा हुआ	**host** mezbān मेज़बान	**Can I have some more, please?** kyā maiṃ aur le saktā hūṃ? क्या मैं और ले सकता हूं?
eat (v) khānā खाना	**tablecloth** mezpoś मेज़पोश	**hostess** mahilā mezbān महिला मेज़बान	**portion** hissā हिस्सा	**guest** mehmān मेहमान	**I've had enough, thank you.** aur nahīṃ chāhie, dhanyavād. और नहीं चाहिए धन्यवाद।
lay the table (v) mez lagānā मेज़ लगाना	**breakfast** nāśtā नाश्ता	**lunch** dopahar kā bhojan दोपहर का भोजन	**meal** bhojan भोजन	**place mat** ṭebal maiṭ टेबल मैट	**That was delicious.** khānā svādiṣṭ thā. खाना स्वादिष्ट था।

crockery and cutlery • bartan aur chhurī-kāṃṭe • बर्तन और छुरी–कांटे

teaspoon
chhoṭā chammach
छोटा चम्मच

mug
mag
मग

coffee cup
coffee kā pyālā
कॉफ़ी का प्याला

teacup
chāya kā pyālā
चाय का प्याला

plate
pleṭ
प्लेट

bowl
kaṭorā
कटोरा

cafetière
coffee kī ketlī
कॉफ़ी की केतली

teapot
ketlī
केतली

jug
jag
जग

egg cup
aṇḍe kā kap
अंडे का कप

wine glass
vāin gilās
वाइन गिलास

tumbler
gilās
गिलास

glassware
kāṃch ke gilās
कांच के गिलास

napkin ring
naipkin riṅg
नैपकिन रिंग

side plate
chhoṭī pleṭ
छोटी प्लेट

dinner plate
baṛī pleṭ
बड़ी प्लेट

soup bowl
sūp kī pleṭ
सूप की प्लेट

soup spoon
sūp kā chammach
सूप का चम्मच

napkin
naipkin
नैपकिन

fork
kāṃṭā
कांटा

place setting
bartan lagāne kā tarīḵā
बर्तन लगाने का तरीक़ा

spoon
chammach
चम्मच

knife
chhurī
छुरी

---

english • hindī • हिन्दी

kitchen • rasoī • रसोई

shelves
k͟hāne
ख़ाने

extractor
chimnī
चिमनी

ceramic hob
sṭov
स्टोव

tap
nal
नल

worktop
k͟hānā banāne
kī jagah
खाना बनाने
की जगह

sink
siṅk
सिंक

oven
ovan
ओवन

drawer
darāz
दराज़

cabinet
almārī
अलमारी

appliances • upkaraṇ • उपकरण

microwave oven
māikrovev ovan | माइक्रोवेव ओवन

mixing bowl
miksiṅg bāul
मिक्सिंग बाउल

lid
ḍhakkan
ढक्कन

blade
bleḍ
ब्लेड

kettle
ketlī
केतली

toaster
ṭosṭar
टोस्टर

food processor
fūḍ prosesar
फ़ूड प्रोसेसर

blender
blenḍar
ब्लेंडर

dishwasher
bartan dhone kī maśīn
बर्तन धोने की मशीन

ice maker
baraf jamāne kī jagah
बर्फ़ जमाने की जगह

freezer
frīzar
फ़्रीज़र

fridge-freezer
frij | फ़्रिज

refrigerator
refrījareṭar
रेफ़्रीजरेटर

shelf
k̠hānā
ख़ाना

crisper
krispar
क्रिस्पर

vocabulary • śabdāvalī • शब्दावली	
burner barnar बर्नर	**freeze (v)** jamānā जमाना
hob sṭov स्टोव	**defrost (v)** pighlānā पिघलाना
rubbish bin kūṛedān कूड़ेदान	**sauté (v)** halkā bhūnnā हल्का भूनना
draining board dreniṅg borḍ ड्रेनिंग बोर्ड	**steam (v)** bhāp se pakānā भाप से पकाना

cooking • khānā pakānā • खाना पकाना

peel (v)
chhīlnā | छीलना

slice (v)
kāṭnā | काटना

grate (v)
ghisnā | घिसना

pour (v)
uṛelnā | उड़ेलना

mix (v)
milānā | मिलाना

whisk (v)
pheṃṭnā | फेंटना

boil (v)
ubālnā | उबालना

fry (v)
talnā | तलना

roll (v)
belnā | बेलना

stir (v)
chalānā | चलाना

simmer (v)
khadaknā
खदकना

poach (v)
pānī meṃ pakānā
पानी में पकाना

bake (v)
bek karnā
बेक करना

roast (v)
bhūnnā
भूनना

grill (v) | tandūr meṃ bhūnnā
तंदूर में भूनना

kitchenware • rasoī upkaraṇ • रसोई उपकरण

bread knife
breḍ kāṭne kī chhurī
ब्रेड काटने की छुरी

chopping board
sabzī kāṭne kā takhtā | सब्जी काटने का तख़्ता

kitchen knife
chākū
चाकू

cleaver
chāpaṛ
चापड़

knife sharpener
chākū tez karne vālā
चाकू तेज़ करने वाला

meat tenderizer
māms kūṭne kā auzār | मांस कूटने का औज़ार

skewer
sīkh | सीख

pestle
mūsal
मूसल

peeler | chhīlne vālā chākū
छीलने वाला चाकू

apple corer | bīj nikālne kī salāī
बीज निकालने की सलाई

grater
kaddūkas
कद्दूकस

mortar
kharal | खरल

masher
meśar | मेशर

can opener
kain opnar
कैन ओपनर

bottle opener
botal opnar
बोतल ओपनर

garlic press
lahsun kūṭne vālā
लहसुन कूटने वाला

serving spoon
parosne kā chammach
परोसने का चम्मच

fish slice
palṭā | पलटा

colander
chhalnā | छलना

spatula
speṭulā | स्पेटुला

wooden spoon
lakṛī kā chammach
लकड़ी का चम्मच

slotted spoon
kalchhī | कलछी

ladle
chamchā | चमचा

carving fork | ghumāvdār kāṃṭā | घुमावदार कांटा

scoop
chammach | चम्मच

whisk
pheṃṭnī | फेंटनी

sieve
chhannī | छन्नी

lid
ḍhakkan | ढक्कन

non-stick
non stick | नॉनस्टिक

frying pan
frāiṅg pain
फ़्राइंग पैन

saucepan
ḍegchī
डेगची

grill pan
gril pain
ग्रिल पैन

wok
karāhī
कड़ाही

earthenware dish
miṭṭī kā bartan
मिट्टी का बर्तन

glass
kāṁch
कांच

ovenproof
ovan rodhī | ओवन रोधी

mixing bowl
miksiṅg bāul
मिक्सिंग बाउल

soufflé dish
sūfle bartan
सूफ़्ले बर्तन

gratin dish
grāṭin ḍiś
ग्राटिन डिश

ramekin
remikīn
रेमिकीन

casserole dish
kaisrol
कैसरोल

baking cakes • kek banānā • केक बनाना

scales
tarāzū
तराज़ू

measuring jug
māpak jag
मापक जग

cake tin | kek
banāne kā sāṁchā |
केक बनाने का सांचा

pie tin | pāī banāne
kā sāṁchā | पाई
बनाने का सांचा

flan tin | flain
banāne kā sāṁchā |
फ़्लैन बनाने का सांचा

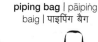

pastry brush
pesṭrī braś | पेस्ट्री ब्रश

rolling pin
belan | बेलन

piping bag | pāipiṅg
baig | पाइपिंग बैग

muffin tray
muffin ṭre
मॉफ़िन ट्रे

baking tray
bekiṅg ṭre
बेकिंग ट्रे

cooling rack
kūliṅg raik
कूलिंग रैक

oven glove
ovan ke dastāne
ओवन के दस्ताने

apron
epren
एप्रेन

bedroom • śayan kakṣ • शयन कक्ष

wardrobe
almārī
अलमारी

bedside lamp
sāiḍ laimp
साइड लैम्प

headboard
palaṅg kā sirhānā
पलंग का सिरहाना

bedside table
sāiḍ ṭebal
साइड टेबल

chest of drawers
darāzoṃ kī almārī
दराज़ों की अलमारी

drawer	**bed**	**mattress**	**bedspread**	**pillow**
darāz	palaṅg	gaddā	palaṅgpoś	takiyā
दराज़	पलंग	गद्दा	पलंगपोश	तकिया

**hot-water
bottle** | garm
panī kī thailī |
गर्म पानी की थैली

clock radio
reḍiyo ghaṛī
रेडियो घड़ी

alarm clock
alārm ghaṛī
अलार्म घड़ी

box of tissues
ṭiśyū box
टिश्यू बॉक्स

coat hanger
koṭ kā haiṅgar
कोट का हैंगर

bed linen • chādar va takiyā gilāf ādi • चादर व तकिया गिलाफ़ आदि

mirror
śīśā
शीशा

dressing table
śṛaṅgār mez
श्रृंगार मेज़

floor
farś
फ़र्श

pillowcase
gilāf
गिलाफ़

sheet
chādar
चादर

valance
jhālar
झालर

duvet
roeṃ se banī razāī
रोएं से बनी रजाई

quilt
razāī
रजाई

blanket
kambal
कंबल

---

vocabulary • śabdāvalī • शब्दावली

single bed	footboard	insomnia	wake up (v)	make the bed (v)
siṅgal palaṅg	pāyadān	anidrā	jāgnā	bistar lagānā
सिंगल पलंग	पायदान	अनिद्रा	जागना	बिस्तर लगाना
double bed	**spring**	**go to bed (v)**	**get up (v)**	**snore (v)**
ḍabal palaṅg	spriṅg	sone jānā	uṭhnā	kharrāṭe lenā
डबल पलंग	स्प्रिंग	सोने जाना	उठना	ख़र्राटे लेना
electric blanket	**carpet**	**go to sleep (v)**	**set the alarm (v)**	**built-in wardrobe**
vidyut kambal	kālīn	sonā	alārm lagānā	kapṛoṃ kī almārī
विद्युत कंबल	क़ालीन	सोना	अलार्म लगाना	कपड़ों की अलमारी

---

bathroom • snānghar • स्नानघर

cold tap
ṭhaṇḍe pānī kā nal
ठंडे पानी का नल

hot tap
garm pānī kā nal
गर्म पानी का नल

shower door
shower darvāzā
शॉवर–दरवाज़ा

towel rail
tauliyā haiṅgar
तौलिया हैंगर

shower head
phuhārā
फुहारा

washbasin
washbasin
वॉशबेसिन

shower
shower
शॉवर

plug
ḍāṭ
डाट

drain
nālī
नाली

toilet seat
toilet sīṭ
टॉयलेट सीट

bathtub
bāth ṭab | बाथ टब

toilet
toilet
टॉयलेट

bidet
biḍeṭ | बिडेट

toilet brush
toilet braś
टॉयलेट ब्रश

---

vocabulary • śabdāvalī • शब्दावली

medicine cabinet davāī kī almārī दवाई की अलमारी	**bath mat** snānghar kī chaṭāī स्नानघर की चटाई
toilet roll toilet rol टॉयलेट रोल	**shower curtain** shower kā pardā शॉवर का पर्दा
take a shower (v) phuhāre mem nahānā फुहारे में नहाना	**take a bath (v)** ṭab mem nahānā टब में नहाना

dental hygiene • dāṃtoṃ kī safāī • दांतों की सफाई

toothbrush
ṭūthbraś | टूथब्रश

dental floss
dental floss
डेंटल फ्लॉस

toothpaste
ṭūthpeṣṭ | टूथपेस्ट

mouthwash
mouthwash | माउथवॉश

loofah
jhāvāṃ
झावां

sponge
spañj | स्पंज

pumice stone
jhāmak | झामक

back brush | pīṭh
ragaṛne kā braś | पीठ
रगड़ने का ब्रश

deodorant
ḍiyoḍreṇṭ | डियोडरेंट

soap dish
sābundānī
साबुनदानी

shower gel
shower jail
शॉवर जेल

soap
sābun
साबुन

face cream
krīm
क्रीम

bubble bath
babbal bāth
बब्बल बाथ

hand towel
chhoṭā tauliyā
छोटा तौलिया

bath towel
baṛā tauliyā
बड़ा तौलिया

towels
taulie | तौलिए

body lotion
body lośan | बॉडी लोशन

talcum powder
ṭelkam pāuḍar
टेल्कम पाउडर

bathrobe | ḍresiṅg
gāun | ड्रेसिंग गाउन

shaving • hajāmat • हजामत

electric razor
ilekṭrik rezar
इलेक्ट्रिक रेजर

razor blade
rezar bleḍ
रेज़र ब्लेड

shaving foam
śeviṅg fom
शेविंग फ़ोम

disposable razor
ḍispozebal rezar
डिस्पोज़ेबल रेज़र

aftershave
āfṭar śev
आफ्टर शेव

nursery • śiśugr̥h • शिशुगृह

baby care • śiśu dekhbhāl • शिशु देखभाल

sponge
spañj
स्पंज

nappy rash cream
naipī reś krīm
नैपी रेश क्रीम

wet wipe
nam t̤iśyu
नम टिश्यु

baby bath
śiśu snān | शिशु स्नान

potty
potty | पॉटी

changing mat | kapr̥e badalne
kī gaddī | कपड़े बदलने की गद्दी

sleeping • sonā • सोना

mobile
jhūmar
झूमर

bars
sīṃkhche
सींख़चे

fleece
ūnī chādar
ऊनी चादर

sheet
chādar
चादर

blanket
kambal
कंबल

bedding
bichhaunā | बिछौना

bumper
bampar
बम्पर

mattress
gaddā | गद्दा

cot | khat̤olā | खटोला

rattle
jhunjhunā | झुनझुना

moses basket | mozes
bāsket̤ | मोजेस बास्केट

playing • khelnā • खेलना

doll
guṛiyā
गुड़िया

soft toy
mulāyam khilaune
मुलायम खिलौने

doll's house
guṛiyā ghar
गुड़िया घर

playhouse
khel ghar | खेल घर

safety • surakṣā • सुरक्षा

child lock
bacchoṃ kā tālā
बच्चों का ताला

baby monitor
bebī monitor
बेबी मॉनीटर

toy
khilaunā
खिलौना

toy basket | khilaune kī ṭokrī | खिलौने की टोकरी

ball
gend
गेंद

playpen
khel bāṛā | खेल बाड़ा

stair gate
siṛhiyoṃ kā geṭ
सीढ़ियों का गेट

eating • khānā • खाना

high chair
ūṃchī kursī | ऊंची कुर्सी

teat
nippal
निप्पल

drinking cup
pīne kā kap
पीने का कप

bottle
botal | बोतल

going out • bāhar jānā • बाहर जाना

pushchair | hāth gāṛī | हाथ गाड़ी

hood
chhatrī
छतरी

pram
bagghī | बग्घी

carrycot
pālnā | पालना

nappy
laṅgoṭī
लंगोटी

changing bag | bacchoṃ kā thailā | बच्चों का थैला

baby sling | śiśu paṭṭā
शिशु पट्टा

utility room • gharelū kārya kakṣ • घरेलू कार्य कक्ष

laundry • laundry • लॉन्ड्री

dirty washing
gande kapṛe
गंदे कपड़े

clean clothes
dhule kapṛe
धुले कपड़े

laundry basket
gande kaproṃ
kī ṭokrī | गंदे
कपड़ों की टोकरी

washing machine |
kapṛe dhone kī
maśīn | कपड़े धोने
की मशीन

washer-dryer
washer ḍrāyar
वॉशर–ड्रायर

tumble dryer
ḍrāyar
ड्रायर

linen basket
kaproṃ kī ṭokrī
कपड़ों की टोकरी

clothes line
alganī
अलगनी

clothes peg
chimṭī
चिमटी

dry (v)
sukhānā | सुखाना

iron
istrī | इस्त्री

ironing board
istrī kā taḵẖtā | इस्त्री का तख्ता

---

vocabulary • śabdāvalī • शब्दावली

rinse (v) khaṅgālnā खंगालना	**spin (v)** kapṛe nichoṛnā कपड़े निचोड़ना	**iron (v)** istrī karnā इस्त्री करना	**How do I operate the washing machine?** washing maśīn kaise chalānī hai? वॉशिंग मशीन कैसे चलानी है?
load (v) kapṛe maśīn meṃ ḍālnā कपड़े मशीन में डालना	**spin dryer** kapṛe nichorne vālā कपड़े निचोड़ने वाला	**conditioner** kanḍīśnar कंडीशनर	

cleaning equipment • safāī upkaraṇ • सफ़ाई उपकरण

suction hose
kūṛā khīṃchne kī nalī
कूड़ा खींचने की नली

brush
braś
ब्रश

dust pan | kūṛe kā
paṅjā | कूड़े का पंजा

bleach
blīch | ब्लीच

bucket
bālṭī
बाल्टी

powder
pāuḍar
पाउडर

liquid
dravya
द्रव्य

duster
jhāran
झाड़न

vacuum cleaner | vekyūm
klīnar | वेक्यूम क्लीनर

mop
pochhā | पोछा

detergent
ḍiṭarjenṭ | डिटर्जेंट

polish
polish | पॉलिश

activities • gatividhiyāṃ • गतिविधियां

clean (v)
safāī karnā | सफ़ाई करना

wash (v)
dhonā | धोना

wipe (v)
poṃchhnā | पोंछना

scrub (v)
ghisnā | घिसना

scrape (v)
khurachnā | खुरचना

broom
jhāṛū
झाड़ू

sweep (v)
jhāṛū lagānā | झाड़ू लगाना

dust (v)
dhūl jhāṛnā | धूल झाड़ना

polish (v)
chamkānā | चमकाना

workshop • kārk̲h̲ānā • कारख़ाना

chuck
chakkā
चक्का

drill bit
chhed karne kī sūī
छेद करने की सूई

battery pack
baiṭarī paik
बैटरी पैक

jigsaw
chhoṭā ārā
छोटा आरा

rechargeable drill
richārjebal ḍril
रिचार्जेबल ड्रिल

electric drill
vidyut ḍril/vedhnī
विद्युत ड्रिल/वेधनी

glue gun
gond gan | गोंद गन

clamp
śikanjā/paṭṭī
शिकंजा/पट्टी

blade
bleḍ
ब्लेड

vice
śikanjā | शिकंजा

sander
senḍar | सेंडर

circular saw
vṛttākār ārī | वृत्ताकार आरी

workbench
kām karne kī mez
काम करने की मेज़

wood glue
lakṛī kā gond
लकड़ी का गोंद

tool rack
auzār raik
औज़ार रैक

router
rūṭar
रूटर

bit brace
biṭ bres
बिट ब्रेस

wood shavings
lakṛī kī chhīlan
लकड़ी की छीलन

extension lead
atirikt tār
अतिरिक्त तार

techniques • vidhiyāṃ • विधियां

cut (v)
kāṭnā | काटना

saw (v)
chīrnā | चीरना

drill (v)
chhed karnā | छेद करना

hammer (v)
ṭhoknā | ठोकना

plane (v) | randā
karnā | रंदा करना

turn (v)
kharādnā | खरादना

solder
soldar karne kā tār
सोल्डर करने का तार

carve (v)
nakkāśī karnā | नक़्क़ाशी करना

solder (v) | ṭāṃkā
lagānā | टांका लगाना

materials • sāmān • सामान

MDF
em ḍī ef
एम डी एफ़

plywood
plāīvuḍ
प्लाईवुड

chipboard
chip borḍ
चिप बोर्ड

hardboard
hārḍ borḍ
हार्ड बोर्ड

softwood
mulāyam
lakṛī
मुलायम
लकड़ी

hardwood
kaṭhor lakṛī
कठोर लकड़ी

wire
tār
तार

cable
kebal | केबल

varnish
rogan
रोगन

stainless steel
ispāt
इस्पात

galvanised
ḵalaīdār
क़लईदार

woodstain
lakṛī ke dāg̱
लकड़ी के
दाग़

wood | lakṛī | लकड़ी

metal | dhātu | धातु

toolbox • auzār peṭī • औज़ार पेटी

spanner
pānā
पाना

adjustable spanner
parivartnīya pānā
परिवर्तनीय पाना

hammer
hathauṛā
हथौड़ा

needle-nose pliers
bārīk plās
बारीक प्लास

socket wrench
socket rinch
सॉकेट रिंच

screwdriver bits
pechkas vajr
पेचकस वज्र

spirit level
leval
लेवल

screwdriver
pechkas
पेचकस

washer
wāsar
वाशर

nut
purzā
पुर्ज़ा

tape measure
inch ṭep
इंच टेप

knife
chākū
चाकू

socket
socket
सॉकेट

bull-nose pliers
moṭā plās
मोटा प्लास

key
chābī
चाबी

drill bits • ḍriliṅg maśīn ke vajr • ड्रिलिंग मशीन के वज्र

metal bit
dhātu vajr
धातु वज्र

flat wood bit
samtal takhtā vajr | समतल तख़्ता वज्र

phillips screwdriver
filips pechkas
फ़िलिप्स पेचकस

reamer
barmā
बरमा

head
sirā
सिरा

nail
kīl | कील

security bit
surakṣā vajr
सुरक्षा वज्र

carpentry bits
baṛhaīgirī ke vajr
बढ़ईगिरी के वज्र

masonry bit
rājgirī ke vajr
राजगिरी के वज्र

screw
pech | पेच

wire strippers
tār chhīlne kā plās
तार छीलने का प्लास

wire cutters
tār kāṭne kā yantr
तार काटने का यंत्र

insulating tape
bijlī kā ṭep
बिजली का टेप

soldering iron
ṭāṃke kā upkaraṇ
टांके का उपकरण

scalpel
chhurī
छुरी

fretsaw
patlī ārī
पतली आरी

solder
ṭāṃkā lagāne kā tār
टांका लगाने का तार

tenon saw | chul ārā | चुल आरा

safety goggles
surakṣā chaśmā
सुरक्षा–चश्मा

plane
randā | रंदा

mitre block
mīṭar block
मीटर ब्लॉक

handsaw | ārī | आरी

hacksaw
dāṃtedār ārī | दांतेदार आरी

hand drill
hainḍ ḍril
हैंड ड्रिल

wire wool
tār
तार

sandpaper
regmāl
रेगमाल

wrench
rinch
रिंच

chisel
chhenī | छेनी

plunger
ḍaṭṭā
डट्टा

file
retī | रेती

sharpening stone
sān | सान

pipe cutter | pāip kaṭar | पाइप कटर

decorating • gṛh sajjā • गृह सज्जा

scissors
ḳaiṃchī | कैंची

craft knife
chhurī | छुरी

plumb line
sāhul ḍorī | साहुल डोरी

scraper
khurachnī | खुरचनी

decorator
prasādhak
प्रसाधक

wallpaper
wallpaper
वॉलपेपर

stepladder
sīṛhī
सीढ़ी

wallpaper brush
wallpaper
braś
वॉलपेपर ब्रश

pasting table
pesṭiṅg ṭebal
पेस्टिंग टेबल

pasting brush
pesṭiṅg braś
पेस्टिंग ब्रश

wallpaper paste
wallpaper pesṭ
वॉलपेपर पेस्ट

bucket
ṭokrī
टोकरी

wallpaper (v) | wallpaper lagānā | वॉलपेपर लगाना

strip (v) | khurachnā | खुरचना

fill (v) | bharnā | भरना

sand (v)
ghisāī karnā | घिसाई करना

plaster (v)
plastar karnā | प्लस्तर करना

hang (v)
laṭkānā | लटकाना

tile (v)
ṭāil lagānā | टाइल लगाना

roller
rolar
रोलर

paint tray
penṭ ṭre | पेंट ट्रे

paint
penṭ | पेंट

brush
braś
ब्रश

sponge
spañj
स्पंज

masking tape
apārdarśī ṭep
अपारदर्शी टेप

sandpaper
regmāl
रेगमाल

paint tin
penṭ kā ḍibbā
पेंट का डिब्बा

overalls
ūprī vastr
ऊपरी वस्त्र

turpentine
tārpīn
तारपीन

dustsheet
gandī darī
गंदी दरी

filler
filar | फ़िलर

white spirit
safed spriṭ | सफ़ेद स्प्रिट

paint (v)
raṅgnā | रंगना

vocabulary • śabdāvalī • शब्दावली

plaster	**gloss**	**embossed paper**	**undercoat**	**sealant**
plastar	lep	embosḍ pepar	bhītrī parat	sīlanṭ
प्लस्तर	लेप	एम्बोस्ड पेपर	भीतरी परत	सीलंट
varnish	**mat**	**lining paper**	**top coat**	**preservative**
rogan	chaṭāī	astar	ūprī parat	parirakṣak
रोग़न	चटाई	अस्तर	ऊपरी परत	परिरक्षक
emulsion	**stencil**	**primer**	**solvent**	**grout**
imalśan	sṭensil	prāimar	solvent	masālā
इमल्शन	स्टेंसिल	प्राइमर	सॉलवेंट	मसाला

garden • bagīchā • बग़ीचा

garden styles • bagīche kī śailiyāṃ • बग़ीचे की शैलियां

patio garden | upvan/bagīchī | उपवन/बग़ीची

formal garden | bagīchā | बग़ीचा

cottage garden
kuṭīr udyān
कुटीर उद्यान

herb garden
auṣadhi udyān
औषधि उद्यान

roof garden
chhat bagīchī
छत बग़ीची

rock garden
pathrīlā bāg | पथरीला बाग़

courtyard | āṅgan | आंगन

water garden
jal udyān
जल उद्यान

garden features • bagīche kī rūp sajjā • बग़ीचे की रूप सज्जा

hanging basket
jhūltī ṭokrī | झूलती टोकरी

trellis
bāṛā/jālī | बाड़ा/जाली

pergola
latāmaṇḍap
लतामंडप

soil • miṭṭī • मिट्टी

paving
khaṛañjā
खड़ंजा

flowerbed
kyārī
क्यारी

path
rāstā
रास्ता

compost heap
khād kā ḍher
खाद का ढेर

gate
geṭ
गेट

topsoil
ūprī miṭṭī | ऊपरी मिट्टी

sand
ret | रेत

shed
śeḍ
शेड

greenhouse
paudh ghar
पौध घर

lawn
udyān
उद्यान

fence
bāṛ
बाड़

chalk
khaṛiyā | खड़िया

pond
tālāb
तालाब

hedge
bāṛ/meṛ
बाड़/मेड़

arch
ārch
आर्च

vegetable garden
sabziyoṃ kā
bagīchā
सब्जियों का बगीचा

herbaceous border
hare-bhare paudhoṃ se
banā gherā
हरे–भरे पौधों से बना घेरा

silt
gād | गाद

decking
chabūtrā | चबूतरा

fountain | favvārā | फ़्व्वारा

clay | miṭṭī | मिट्टी

garden plants • bagīche ke paudhe • बग़ीचे के पौधे

types of plants • paudhoṃ ke prakār • पौधों के प्रकार

annual | vārṣikī paudh | वार्षिकी पौध

biennial | dvivārṣik paudh | द्विवार्षिक पौध

perennial
bārahmāsī | बारहमासी

bulb
balb | बल्ब

fern
parṇāṅg | पर्णांग्

rush
jalbeṃt | जलबेंत

bamboo
bāṃs | बांस

weeds
ghās-pāt | घास–पात

herb
jaṛī-būṭī | जड़ी–बूटी

water plant
jalīya paudh | जलीय पौध

tree
peṛ | पेड़

palm
tāṛ | ताड़

conifer
śaṅku vṛkṣ | शंकु वृक्ष

evergreen
sadābahār | सदाबहार

deciduous
parṇpātī | पर्णपाती

topiary
kaṭāī-chhaṃṭāī
कटाई–छंटाई

alpine
parvatīya paudhe
पर्वतीय पौधे

succulent
ārdr paudh
आर्द्र पौध

cactus
kaikṭas
कैक्टस

potted plant
gamle ke paudhe
गमले के पौधे

shade plant
chhāyādār paudhe
छायादार पौधे

climber
latā
लता

flowering shrub
phūloṃ kī jhāṛī
फूलों की झाड़ी

ground cover
grāuṇḍ kavar
ग्राउंड कवर

creeper
bel
बेल

ornamental
sajāvaṭī
सजावटी

grass
ghās
घास

garden tools • bagīche ke upkaraṇ • बग़ीचे के उपकरण

compost
khād | खाद

seeds
bīj | बीज

bone meal
asthi chūrṇ | अस्थि चूर्ण

gravel
bajrī | बजरी

lawn rake
jhārū
झाड़ू

spade
phāvṛā
फावड़ा

fork
kāṃṭā auzār
कांटा औज़ार

long-handled shears
lambe hatthe kī ḳaiṃchī
लंबे हत्थे की कैंची

rake
pāñchā
पांचा

hoe
khurpā | खुरपा

grass bag
ghās kā thailā
घास का थैला

motor
moṭar
मोटर

handle
hatthā
हत्था

trug | ṭre/ṭokrī | ट्रे/टोकरी

shield
pleṭ
प्लेट

stand
staiṇḍ
स्टैंड

trimmer | katarne kā auzār
कतरने का औज़ार

lawnmower | ghās kāṭne kī maśīn | घास काटने की मशीन

wheelbarrow
ṭhelā gāṛī | ठेला गाड़ी

hand fork
kuredni | कुरेदनी

trowel
khurpī | खुरपी

secateurs
kaṭar | कटर

gardening gloves
bāġbānī ke dastāne
बाग़बानी के दस्ताने

twine
ḍorī
डोरी

labels
lebal
लेबल

twist ties
chimṭiyām̐
चिमटियां

blade
phal
फल

seed tray
bīj ṭre | बीज ट्रे

ring ties
chhalle
छल्ले

canes
bemṭ | बेंत

shears
baṛī kaiṁchī
बड़ी कैंची

sieve
chhalnī
छलनी

hand saw
ārī | आरी

pesticide
kīṭnāśak
कीटनाशक

plant pot
gamlā
गमला

rubber boots | rabaṛ
ke jūte | रबड़ के जूते

watering • sīṁchnā • सींचना

spray gun
pichkārī | पिचकारी

sprinkler
hazārā
हज़ारा

nozzle
ṭomṭī
टोंटी

watering can
phuhārā
फुहारा

hosepipe
rabaṛ nalī
रबड़ नली

hose reel | huchkā | हुचका

---

english • hindī • हिन्दी

gardening • bāġbānī • बाग़बानी

lawn
udyān
उद्यान

flowerbed
kyārī | क्यारी

lawnmower
ghās kāṭne
kī maśīn
घास काटने
की मशीन

hedge
bāṛ
बाड़

stake
khūṃṭā
खूंटा

mow (v) | ghās kāṭnā | घास काटना

turf (v)
ghās bichhānā
घास बिछाना

spike (v)
khūṃṭā ṭhoknā
खूंटा ठोकना

rake (v)
buhārnā
बुहारना

trim (v)
chhāṃṭnā | छांटना

dig (v)
khodnā | खोदना

sow (v)
bonā | बोना

top dress (v)
khād ḍālnā | खाद डालना

water (v)
sīṃchnā | सींचना

cane
bemt
बेंत

train (v) | ākār denā |
आकार देना

deadhead (v) | sūkhe patte
nikālnā | सूखे पत्ते निकालना

spray (v)
chhiṛaknā | छिड़कना

cutting
kāṭnā
काटना

graft (v) | ḳalam bāṃ
dhnā | क़लम बांधना

propagate (v)
baṛhānā | बढ़ाना

prune (v)
chhāṃṭnā | छांटना

stake (v) | khūṃṭī se
bāṃdhnā | खूंटी से बांधना

transplant (v)
pratiropit karnā
प्रतिरोपित करना

weed (v)
nirānā
निराना

mulch (v)
ghās-pāt se ḍhaknā
घास–पात से ढकना

harvest (v)
fasal kāṭnā
फ़सल काटना

---

vocabulary • śabdāvalī • शब्दावली

cultivate (v) khetī karnā खेती करना	**fertilize (v)** urvar banānā उर्वर बनाना	**sieve (v)** chhānnā छानना	**organic** jaiv जैव	**seedling** paud पौद	**pot up (v)** gamle meṃ ḍālnā गमले में डालना	**subsoil** avmṛdā अवमृदा
tend (v) dekhbhāl karnā देखभाल करना	**pick (v)** chunnā/toṛnā चुनना/तोड़ना	**aerate (v)** havā lagānā हवा लगाना	**drainage** morī मोरी	**fertilizer** urvarak उर्वरक	**weedkiller** kharpatvār nāśak खरपतवार नाशक	

---

services
sevāeṃ
सेवाएं

emergency services • āpātkālīn sevāeṃ •
आपातकालीन सेवाएं

ambulance • embulens • एंबुलेंस

ambulance | embulens | एंबुलेंस

stretcher
strechar
स्ट्रेचर

paramedic
chikitsakīya sahāyak | चिकित्सकीय सहायक

---

police • pulis • पुलिस

badge
billā
बिल्ला

uniform
vardī
वर्दी

siren
sāyaran
सायरन

lights
battī
बत्ती

truncheon
bemt
बेंत

gun
bandūk
बंदूक

handcuffs
hathkaṛī
हथकड़ी

police officer
pulis adhikārī | पुलिस अधिकारी

police car
pulis kār | पुलिस कार

police station
pulis chaukī
पुलिस चौकी

vocabulary • śabdāvalī • शब्दावली

inspector	**suspect**	**complaint**	**arrest**
darogā	saṃdigdh	śikāyat	giraftār
दरोगा	संदिग्ध	शिकायत	गिरफ्तार
crime	**assault**	**investigation**	**police cell**
jurm	hamlā	jāṃch	havālāt
जुर्म	हमला	जांच	हवालात
detective	**fingerprint**	**burglary**	**charge**
jāsūs	uṃgliyoṃ kī	chorī	ārop
जासूस	chhāp	चोरी	आरोप
	उंगलियों की छाप		

fire brigade • damkal dastā • दमकल दस्ता

helmet
hailmeṭ
हैलमेट

smoke
dhuāṃ
धुआं

hose
pānī kī nalī
पानी की
नली

fire fighters
agniśāmak karmī
अग्निशामक कर्मी

cradle
kraiḍal
क्रैडल

water jet
pānī kī dhār
पानी की धार

boom
pāl daṇḍ
पाल दंड

ladder
sīṛhī
सीढ़ी

cab
gāṛī
गाड़ी

fire | āg | आग

fire station
damkal kendr
दमकल केंद्र

fire escape
āpātkālīn rakṣā mārg
आपातकालीन रक्षा मार्ग

fire engine
damkal | दमकल

smoke alarm
smok alārm
स्मोक अलार्म

fire alarm
fāyar alārm
फ़ायर अलार्म

axe
kulhāṛī
कुल्हाड़ी

fire extinguisher
agniśāmak upakaraṇ
अग्निशामक उपकरण

hydrant
nal kī ṭoṃṭī
नल की टोंटी

I need the ambulance.	There's a fire at…	There's been an accident.	Call the police!
mujhe embulens bulānī hai.	…meṃ āg lagī hai.	ek durghaṭnā huī hai.	pulis ko bulāo!
मुझे एंबुलेंस बुलानी है।	… में आग लगी है।	एक दुर्घटना हुई है।	पुलिस को बुलाओ!

bank • baink • बैंक

customer
grāhak
ग्राहक

window
khiṛkī
खिड़की

cashier
k̲h̲azānchī
ख़ज़ांची

leaflets
parchī
पर्ची

counter
kāuṇṭar
काउंटर

paying-in slips
jamā parchī
जमा पर्ची

bank manager
baink prabandhak
बैंक प्रबंधक

debit card
ḍebiṭ kārḍ
डेबिट कार्ड

credit card
kreḍiṭ kārḍ
क्रेडिट कार्ड

stub
parchī
पर्ची

account
number
khātā sankhyā
खाता संख्या

signature
hastākṣar
हस्ताक्षर

amount
raḳam
रक़म

chequebook
chek buk
चेक बुक

cheque
chek
चेक

---

vocabulary • śabdāvalī • शब्दावली

savings	mortgage	payment	pay in (v)	current account
bachat	rehan	bhugtān	jamā karnā	chālū khātā
बचत	रेहन	भुगतान	जमा करना	चालू खाता
tax	overdraft	direct debit	bank charge	savings account
kar	ovar ḍrāfṭ	pratyakṣ bhugtān	baink prabhār	bachat khātā
कर	ओवर ड्राफ्ट	प्रत्यक्ष भुगतान	बैंक प्रभार	बचत खाता
loan	interest rate	withdrawal slip	bank transfer	pin number
ṛiṇ	byāj dar	pratyāharaṇ parchī	baink dvārā antaraṇ	pin nambar
ऋण	ब्याज दर	प्रत्याहरण पर्ची	बैंक द्वारा अंतरण	पिन नंबर

---

coin
sikkā
सिक्का

note
noṭ
नोट

screen
skrīn
स्क्रीन

key pad
kuñjī paṭal
कुंजी पटल

card slot
kārḍ ḍālne kī jagah
कार्ड डालने की जगह

money
dhan | धन

cash machine
paise kī maśīn | पैसे की मशीन

currency • mudrā • मुद्रा

traveller's cheque
yātrī chek | यात्री चेक

bureau de change
videśī mudrā vinimaya kendr
विदेशी मुद्रा विनिमय केंद्र

exchange rate
vinimaya dar
विनिमय दर

finance • vitt • वित्त

share price
śeyar mūlya
शेयर मूल्य

stockbroker
śeyar dalāl
शेयर दलाल

financial advisor
vittīya salāhkār
वित्तीय सलाहकार

stock exchange
śeyar bāzār | शेयर बाज़ार

vocabulary • śabdāvalī • शब्दावली

cash (v)
naqad niḳālnā
नक़द निकालना

shares
śeyar
शेयर

denomination
abhidhān
अभिधान

dividends
lābhānś
लाभांश

commission
dalālī
दलाली

accountant
lekhākār
लेखाकार

investment
niveś
निवेश

portfolio
niveś vivaraṇikā
निवेश विवरणिका

stocks
stock
स्टॉक

equity
śeyar pūñjī
शेयर पूंजी

Can I change this please?
kyā maiṃ inheṃ badal saktā hūṃ?
क्या मैं इन्हें बदल सकता हूं?

What's today's exchange rate?
vartmān vinimaya dar kyā hai?
वर्तमान विनिमय दर क्या है?

communications • sañchār • संचार

postal worker
ḍāk karmī
डाक कर्मी

window
khiṛkī
खिड़की

scales
tarāzū
तराज़ू

counter
kāunṭar
काउंटर

post office
ḍākghar | डाकघर

postmark
mohar
मोहर

stamp
ḍāk ṭikaṭ
डाक टिकट

address
patā
पता

postal code
ḍāk koḍ
डाक कोड

envelope | lifāfā | लिफ़ाफ़ा

postman
ḍākiyā | डाकिया

---

vocabulary • śabdāvalī • शब्दावली

letter patr पत्र	**return address** vāpsī kā patā वापसी का पता	**delivery** vitraṇ वितरण	**fragile** nāzuk vastu नाजुक वस्तु	**do not bend (v)** kṛpyā moṛem nahīm कृपया मोड़ें नहीं
by airmail havāī ḍāk dvārā हवाई डाक द्वारा	**signature** hastākṣar हस्ताक्षर	**postal order** postal order पोस्टल ऑर्डर	**mailbag** ḍāk thailā डाक थैला	**this way up** is prakār rakhem इस प्रकार रखें।
registered post rajisṭarḍ ḍāk रजिस्टर्ड डाक	**collection** saṅgrah संग्रह	**postage** ḍāk vyaya डाक व्यय	**telegram** tār तार	**fax** faiks फ़ैक्स

---

postbox
ḍākpeṭī | डाकपेटी

letterbox
patrpeṭī | पत्रपेटी

parcel
pārsal | पार्सल

courier
kūriyar | कूरियर

telephone • dūrbhāṣ • दूरभाष

handset
hainḍ seṭ
हैंडसेट

base station
fon staind
फ़ोन स्टैंड

cordless phone
betār dūrbhāṣ
बेतार दूरभाष

answering machine
ānsaring maśīn
आंसरिंग मशीन

video phone
vīḍiyo fon
वीडियो फ़ोन

telephone box
ṭelifon box
टेलिफ़ोन बॉक्स

keypad
kī paiḍ
की–पैड

mobile phone
mobāil fon
मोबाइल फ़ोन

receiver
risīvar
रिसीवर

coin return
sikkā vāpsī
सिक्का वापसी

coin phone
sikke vālā fon
सिक्के वाला फ़ोन

card phone
kārḍ fon
कार्ड फ़ोन

---

vocabulary • śabdāvalī • शब्दावली

dial (v) nambar milānā नंबर मिलाना	**answer (v)** uttar denā उत्तर देना	**operator** prachālak प्रचालक
reverse charge call revars chārj call रिवर्स चार्ज कॉल	**text message** pāṭhya sandeś पाठ्य संदेश	**engaged/busy** vyast व्यस्त
directory enquiries ḍāyarekṭarī pūchhtāchh डायरेक्टरी पूछताछ	**voice message** dhvani sandeś ध्वनि संदेश	**disconnected** sampark ṭūṭnā संपर्क टूटना

Can you give me the number for...?
kyā āp mujhe ... kā nambar de sakte haiṃ?
क्या आप मुझे... का नंबर दे सकते हैं?

What is the dialling code for...?
... ke lie ḍāyaling koḍ kyā hai?
... के लिए डायलिंग कोड क्या है?

hotel • hoṭal • होटल
lobby • lobby • लॉबी

messages
sandeś
संदेश

guest
mehmān
मेहमान

room key
kamre kī chābī
कमरे की चाबी

pigeonhole
koṣṭh
कोष्ठ

receptionist
svāgat adhikārī
स्वागत अधिकारी

register
rajisṭar
रजिस्टर

counter
kāunṭar
काउंटर

reception | svāgat | स्वागत

luggage
sāmān
सामान

trolley
trolley
ट्रॉली

porter | darbān | दरबान

lift | lift | लिफ़्ट

room number
kamrā nambar
कमरा नंबर

rooms • kamre • कमरे

single room
siṅgal kamrā
सिंगल कमरा

double room
ḍabal kamrā
डबल कमरा

twin room
ṭvin kamrā
ट्विन कमरा

private bathroom
nijī snānghar
निजी स्नानघर

services • sevāeṃ • सेवाएं

maid service
parichārikā sevā
परिचारिका सेवा

laundry service
laundry sevā
लॉन्ड्री सेवा

breakfast tray
nāśte kī ṭre | नाश्ते की ट्रे

room service | rūm sarvis | रूम सर्विस

mini bar
minī bār | मिनी बार

restaurant
restrāṃ
रेस्तरां

gym
vyāyāmśālā
व्यायामशाला

swimming pool
taraṇtāl
तरणताल

---

vocabulary • śabdāvalī • शब्दावली

bed and breakfast
rahnā aur nāśtā
रहना और नाश्ता

full board
ful borḍ
फुल बोर्ड

half board
hāf borḍ
हाफ़ बोर्ड

Do you have any vacancies?
kyā āpke yahāṃ kamrā k̲h̲ālī hai?
क्या आपके यहां कमरा ख़ाली है?

I have a reservation.
maiṃne kamrā ārakṣit karāyā
huā hai
मैंने कमरा आरक्षित कराया हुआ है।

I'd like a single room.
mujhe ek siṅgal kamrā chāhie
मुझे एक सिंगल कमरा चाहिए।

I'd like a room for three nights.
mujhe tīn rātoṃ ke lie ek
kamrā chāhie
मुझे तीन रातों के लिए एक कमरा चाहिए।

What is the charge per night?
ek rāt kā kirāyā kitnā hai?
एक रात का किराया कितना है?

When do I have to vacate the room?
mujhe kab kamrā k̲h̲ālī karnā hai?
मुझे कब कमरा ख़ाली करना है?

---

shopping
kharīdārī
ख़रीदारी

shopping centre • k̲harīdārī kendr • ख़रीदारी केंद्र

atrium
parisar
परिसर

sign
nām
नाम

lift
lift
लिफ़्ट

second floor
dūsrī mañzil
दूसरी मंज़िल

first floor
pahlī mañzil
पहली मंज़िल

escalator
svachālit sīṛhiyāṃ
स्वचालित सीढ़ियां

ground floor
bhūtal
भूतल

customer
grāhak
ग्राहक

---

vocabulary • śabdāvalī • शब्दावली

luggage department
sāmān vibhāg
सामान विभाग

shoe department
jūtā chappal khaṇḍ
जूता चप्पल खंड

children's department
bāl vibhāg
बाल विभाग

store directory
sṭor nirdeśikā
स्टोर निर्देशिका

sales assistant
bikrī sahāyak
बिक्री सहायक

customer services
grāhak sevāeṃ
ग्राहक सेवाएं

changing rooms
chenjiṅg rūm
चेंजिंग रूम

toilets
prasādhan
प्रसाधन

baby changing facilities
bāl suvidhā kendr
बाल–सुविधा केंद्र

How much is this?
iskī kyā k̲īmat hai?
इसकी क्या क़ीमत है?

May I exchange this?
kyā maiṃ ise badal saktā hūṃ?
क्या मैं इसे बदल सकता हूं?

---

department store • ḍepārṭmenṭal sṭor • डिपार्टमेंटल स्टोर

men's wear
puruṣ paridhān
पुरुष परिधान

women's wear
mahilā paridhān
महिला परिधान

lingerie
adhovastr
अधोवस्त्र

perfumery
itr ityādi
इत्र इत्यादि

beauty
saundarya
सौंदर्य

linen
chādar takiyā ādi
चादर तकिया आदि

home furnishings
grh sāj-sajjā
गृह साज–सज्जा

haberdashery
janral sṭor
जनरल स्टोर

kitchenware
rasoī ke bartan
रसोई के बर्तन

china
chīnī miṭṭī ke bartan
चीनी मिट्टी के बर्तन

electrical goods
bijlī kā sāmān
बिजली का सामान

lighting
lāiṭiṅg
लाइटिंग

sports
sporṭs | स्पोर्ट्स

toys
khilaune | खिलौने

stationery | lekhan
sāmagrī | लेखन सामग्री

food hall
fūḍ hall | फ़ूड हॉल

supermarket • supar bāzār • सुपर बाज़ार

aisle
galiyārā
गलियारा

shelf
tāk
ताक़

conveyer belt
chal paṭṭī
चल पट्टी

cashier
khazānchī
ख़ज़ांची

offers
chhūṭ
छूट

checkout | ādāyagī paṭal | अदायगी पटल

customer
grāhak
ग्राहक

till
tijorī
तिजोरी

shopping bag
kharīdārī kā thailā
ख़रीदारी का थैला

groceries
kirānā vastuem
किराना वस्तुएं

handle
haiṇḍil
हैंडिल

bar code
bār koḍ | बार कोड

trolley | trolley | ट्रॉली

basket | ṭokrī | टोकरी

scanner | skainar |
स्कैनर

bakery
bekrī
बेकरी

dairy
dugdh utpād
दुग्ध उत्पाद

cereals
nāśtā sīriyal
नाश्ता सीरियल

tinned food
ḍibbāband
khādya padārth
डिब्बाबंद खाद्य पदार्थ

confectionery
mīṭhe khādya
मीठे खाद्य

vegetables
sāg-sabzī
साग–सब्ज़ी

fruit
phal
फल

meat and poultry
māṃsāhārī khādya padārth
मांसाहारी खाद्य पदार्थ

fish
machhlī
मछली

deli
viśiṣṭ khādya
विशिष्ट खाद्य

frozen food
frozan āhār
फ़्रोज़न आहार

convenience food
ḍibbāband āhār
डिब्बाबंद आहार

drinks
peya padārth
पेय पदार्थ

**household
products**
gharelū vastueṃ
घरेलू वस्तुएं

toiletries
saundarya
prasādhan
सौंदर्य प्रसाधन

baby products
śiśu utpād
शिशु उत्पाद

electrical goods
bijlī kī vastueṃ
बिजली की वस्तुएं

pet food
paśu āhār
पशु आहार

magazines | patrikāeṃ | पत्रिकाएं

chemist • davāī vikretā • दवाई विक्रेता

dental care
dant surakṣā
दंत सुरक्षा

feminine hygiene
strī svacchhatā sāmān
स्त्री–स्वच्छता सामान

vitamins
viṭāmin
विटामिन

dispensary
davākhānā
दवाख़ाना

pharmacist
auṣadh vitrak
औषध वितरक

cough medicine
khāṃsī kī davāī
खांसी की दवाई

herbal remedies
jarī-būṭī auṣadh
जड़ी–बूटी औषध

skin care
tvachā surakṣā
त्वचा सुरक्षा

aftersun
āfṭarsan
आफ्टरसन

sunscreen
sanskrīn | सनस्क्रीन

sunblock
sunblock
सनब्लॉक

insect repellent
macchhar avrodhak
मच्छर अवरोधक

wet wipe
namīyukt ṭiśyū
नमीयुक्त टिश्यू

tissue
ṭiśyū | टिश्यू

sanitary towel | sainiṭarī
paid | सैनिटरी पैड

tampon
ṭempon | टेम्पोन

panty liner | painṭī
lāinar | पैंटी लाइनर

capsule
kaipsūl | कैप्सूल

pill
goliyāṃ | गोलियां

measuring spoon
māpak chammach
मापक चम्मच

syrup
sirap | सिरप

instructions
nirdeś
निर्देश

inhaler | śvās yantr |
श्वास यंत्र

cream
krīm | क्रीम

ointment
marham | मरहम

gel
jail | जैल

suppository
guhyavarti | गुह्यवर्ति

dropper
dropper
ड्रॉपर

drops | drops | ड्रॉप्स

needle
sūī
सूई

syringe
siriṅj | सिरिंज

spray
spre | स्प्रे

powder
pāuḍar | पाउडर

---

vocabulary • śabdāvalī • शब्दावली

iron āyaran आयरन	**insulin** insulin इंसुलिन	**disposable** ḍispozebal डिस्पोज़ेबल	**medicine** davāī दवाई	**painkiller** dardnāśak दर्दनाशक
calcium kailśiyam कैल्शियम	**side-effects** viprīt prabhāv विपरीत प्रभाव	**soluble** ghulanśīl घुलनशील	**laxative** k͟abz͟kuśā क़ब्ज़कुशा	**sedative** praśāmak प्रशामक
magnesium maignīśiyam मैग्नीशियम	**expiry date** samāpti tithi समाप्ति तिथि	**dosage** k͟hurāk ख़ुराक	**diarrhoea** dast दस्त	**sleeping pill** nīṃd kī golīyāṃ नींद की गोलियां
multivitamins bahu viṭāmin बहु विटामिन	**travel sickness pills** mitlī kī davā मितली की दवा	**medication** upchār उपचार	**throat lozenge** k͟harāś kī davā ख़राश की दवा	**anti-inflammatory** sūjan rodhī सूजन रोधी

---

florist • phūl vikretā • फूल विक्रेता

flowers
phūl
फूल

lily
lilī
लिली

acacia
babūl
बबूल

carnation
kārneśan
कार्नेशन

pot plant
gamle kā
paudhā
गमले का पौधा

gladiolus
glediyolas
ग्लेडियोलस

iris
āyaris
आयरिस

daisy
dezī
डेजी

chrysanthemum
guldāūdī
गुलदाऊदी

gypsophila
jipsofilā
जिप्सोफ़िला

stocks
stocks | स्टॉक्स

gerbera
jarberā | जरबेरा

foliage
phūl-patte | फूल–पत्ते

rose
gulāb | गुलाब

freesia
frīziyā | फ़्रीजिया

arrangements • sajāvaṭ • सजावट

vase
phūldān
फूलदान

orchid
orchid | ऑर्किड

peony
piyoni | पियोनि

bunch
gucchhā
गुच्छा

stem
ḍaṇḍī
डंडी

daffodil
ḍaifoḍil
डैफ़ोडिल

bud
kalī
कली

wrapping
gift pepar
गिफ़्ट पेपर

tulip | ṭyūlip | ट्यूलिप

ribbon
riban
रिबन

bouquet
guldastā | गुलदस्ता

dried flowers | sūkhe
phūl | सूखे फूल

pot-pourri
sūkhe phūl | सूखे फूल

wreath
puṣp chakr | पुष्प चक्र

garland
phūlmālā
फूलमाला

---

vocabulary • śabdāvalī • शब्दावली

Can I have them wrapped?
āp inhem kagaz meṃ lapeṭ deṇge?
आप इन्हें काग़ज़ में लपेट देंगे?

Can I have a bunch of... please.
kyā mujhe ... kā gucchhā mil saktā hai?
क्या मुझे ... का गुच्छा मिल सकता है?

Can I attach a message?
kyā maiṃ ek sandeś lagā saktā hūṃ?
क्या मैं एक संदेश लगा सकता हूं?

Can you send them to...?
kyā āp unheṃ ... ko bhej sakte haiṃ?
क्या आप उन्हें... को भेज सकते हैं?

newsagent • samāchār patr vikretā • समाचार पत्र विक्रेता

cigarettes
sigreṭ
सिगरेट

packet of cigarettes
sigreṭ kī ḍibbī
सिगरेट की डिब्बी

matches
māchis
माचिस

lottery tickets
lottery ṭikṭeṃ
लॉटरी टिकटें

stamps
ḍāk ṭikaṭ
डाक टिकट

postcard
posṭ kārḍ | पोस्ट कार्ड

comic
chitrkathā | चित्रकथा

magazine
patrikā | पत्रिका

newspaper
aḵhbār | अख़बार

smoking • dhūmrpān • धूम्रपान

tobacco
tambākū | तंबाकू

lighter
lāiṭar | लाइटर

stem
nalī
नली

bowl
pyālī
प्याली

pipe
pāip | पाइप

cigar
sigār | सिगार

confectioner • kanfekśnar • कनफ़ेक्शनर

box of chocolates	snack bar	crisps
chocolate box	snaiks bār	krisps
चॉकलेट बॉक्स	स्नैक्स बार	क्रिस्प्स

sweet shop | toffee kī dukān | टॉफ़ी की दुकान

vocabulary • śabdāvalī • शब्दावली

milk chocolate	**caramel**
dūdh kī chocolate	toffee
दूध की चॉकलेट	टॉफ़ी
plain chocolate	**truffle**
sādī chocolate	ṭrafal
सादी चॉकलेट	ट्रफ़ल
white chocolate	**biscuit**
safed chocolate	biskuṭ
सफ़ेद चॉकलेट	बिस्कुट
pick and mix	**boiled sweets**
manpasand	mīṭhī goliyāṃ
goliyāṃ	मीठी गोलियां
मनपसंद गोलियां	

confectionery • kanfekśnarī • कनफ़ेक्शरी

chocolate
chocolate | चॉकलेट

chocolate bar
chocolate kī paṭṭī
चॉकलेट की पट्टी

sweets
kaindī | कैंडी

lollipop
lollipop | लॉलीपॉप

toffee | toffee | टॉफ़ी

nougat | girī kī chocolate |
गिरी की चॉकलेट

marshmallow
mārśmailo
मार्शमैलो

mint
mint toffee | मिंट टॉफ़ी

chewing gum
chuingam | चुइंगम

jellybean
jailībīn | जैलीबीन

fruit gum
frūṭ gam | फ़्रूट गम

licquorice
muleṭhī kaindī
मुलेठी कैंडी

other shops • anya dukānem • अन्य दुकानें

baker's
bekrī
बेकरी

cake shop
kek kī dukān
केक की दुकान

butcher's
ḳasaī kī dukān
क़साई की दुकान

fishmonger's
machhlī kī dukān
मछली की दुकान

greengrocer's | phal
evam sabziyom kī dukān |
फल एवं सब्जियों की दुकान

grocer's
pansārī kī dukān
पंसारी की दुकान

shoe shop
jūte kī dukān
जूते की दुकान

hardware shop
hārḍveyar shop
हार्डवेयर शॉप

antiques shop | prāchīn
vastuom kī dukān
प्राचीन वस्तुओं की दुकान

gift shop
uphārom kī dukān
उपहारों की दुकान

travel agent's
ṭreval ejensī
ट्रेवल एजेंसी

jeweller's
sunār kī dukān
सुनार की दुकान

english • hindī • हिन्दी

book shop
kitābom̐ kī dukān
किताबों की दुकान

record shop
record kī dukān
रिकॉर्ड की दुकान

off licence
śarāb kī dukān
शराब की दुकान

pet shop
pāltū jānvarom̐ kī dukān
पालतू जानवरों की दुकान

furniture shop
farnīchar kī dukān
फ़र्नीचर की दुकान

boutique
buṭīk
बुटीक

vocabulary • śabdāvalī • शब्दावली

estate agent's property ḍīlar प्रॉपर्टी डीलर	**camera shop** kaimre kī dukān कैमरे की दुकान
garden centre bagbānī kī dukān बाग़बानी की दुकान	**art shop** ārṭ shop आर्ट शॉप
dry cleaner's ḍraī klīnar ड्राई क्लीनर	**second-hand shop** saikaṇḍ haiṇḍ shop सैकंड हैंड शॉप
launderette laundry लॉन्ड्री	**health food shop** svāsthya āhār kī dukān स्वास्थ्य आहार की दुकान

tailor's | darzī kī
dukān | दर्ज़ी की दुकान

hairdresser's | nāī kī
dukān | नाई की दुकान

market | bāzār | बाज़ार

food
khādya padārth
खाद्य पदार्थ

meat • māṃs • मांस

butcher
kasāī
क़साई

knife sharpener
chākū/chhurī tez
karne kā upkaraṇ
चाकू/छुरी तेज़
करने का उपकरण

meat hook
mīṭ huk
मीट हुक

scales
tarāzū
तराज़ू

lamb
maṭan | मटन

bacon
bekan | बेकन

sausages
sausages | सॉसेजेस

liver
kalejī | कलेजी

vocabulary • śabdāvalī • शब्दावली

pork sūar kā māṃs सूअर का मांस	**venison** mṛg māṃs मृग मांस	**offal** chhīchhṛe छीछड़े	**free range** jaṅglī जंगली	**red meat** lāl māṃs लाल मांस
beef go māṃs गो मांस	**rabbit** khargoś ख़रगोश	**cured** sanrakṣit संरक्षित	**organic** jaivik जैविक	**lean meat** binā charbī kā māṃs बिना चर्बी का मांस
veal bachhṛe kā māṃs बछड़े का मांस	**tongue** jībh जीभ	**smoked** dhūmrit धूम्रित	**white meat** safed māṃs सफ़ेद मांस	**cooked meat** pakā huā māṃs पका हुआ मांस

cuts • māṃs ke ṭukṛe • मांस के टुकड़े

ham
haim
हैम

rind
bāhrī parat
बाहरी परत

slice
ḳatlā | क़तला

rasher
jaṅghā kā māṃs
जंघा का मांस

mince
ḳīmā | क़ीमा

fillet
machhlī kā ṭukṛā
मछली का टुकड़ा

rump steak | kamar kā
māṃs | कमर का मांस

fat
vasā
वसा

bone
haḍḍī
हड्डी

kidney
gurdā
गुर्दा

sirloin steak | puṭṭhe
kā māṃs | पुट्ठे का मांस

rib
paslī | पसली

chop
chop | चॉप

joint
joṛ | जोड़

heart
dil | दिल

poultry • pakṣī-māṃs • पक्षी–मांस

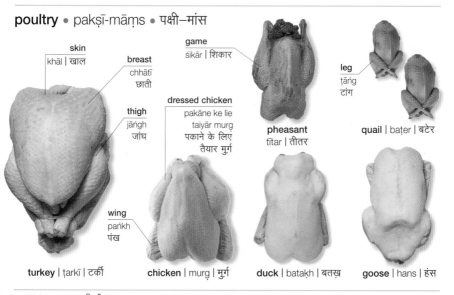

skin
khāl | खाल

breast
chhātī
छाती

game
śikār | शिकार

leg
ṭāṅg
टांग

dressed chicken
pakāne ke lie
taiyār murg
पकाने के लिए
तैयार मुर्ग

thigh
jāṅgh
जांघ

pheasant
tītar | तीतर

quail | baṭer | बटेर

wing
paṅkh
पंख

turkey | ṭarkī | टर्की

chicken | murg | मुर्ग

duck | bataḳh | बतख़

goose | hans | हंस

fish • machhlī • मछली

peeled prawns
chhile hue jhīṅge
छिले हुए झींगे

ice
baraf
बर्फ़

red mullet
chhoṭī machhlī
छोटी मछली

halibut fillets
hailibaṭ ḳatlī
हैलिबट क़तली

rainbow trout
renbo ṭrāuṭ
machhlī
रेनबो ट्राउट
मछली

skate wings
skeṭ machhlī
स्केट मछली

fishmonger's
machhlī kī dukān | मछली की दुकान

monkfish
maṅk fiś | मंक फ़िश

mackerel | maikral
machhlī | मैकरल मछली

trout | ṭrāuṭ machhlī
ट्राउट मछली

swordfish
khaṅg mīn
खंग मीन

Dover sole
sol machhlī
सोल मछली

lemon sole
laiman sol
लैमन सोल

haddock
haddock | हैडॉक

sardine
sārḍin | सार्डिन

skate | śaṅkuchi
machhlī | शंकुचि मछली

whiting | viṭīṅg | विटींग

sea bass | sī bās | सी बास

salmon | sāman machhlī | सामन मछली

cod | cod machhlī | कॉड मछली

sea bream
sī brīm | सी ब्रीम

tuna | ṭyūnā machhlī | ट्यूना मछली

seafood • samudrī bhojan • समुद्री भोजन

scallop
paṅkhā sīpī
पंखा सीपी

lobster
samudrī jhīṅgā
समुद्री झींगा

crab
kekṛā
केकड़ा

king prawn
jhīṅgā
झींगा

mussel
śambūk
शंबूक

crayfish
krefiś
क्रेफ़िश

razor-shell | ek
prakār kā samudrī
jīv | एक प्रकार का
समुद्री जीव

oyster
sīpī
सीपी

cockle | cockle
sīpī | कॉकल सीपी

octopus
aṣṭbhuj | अष्टभुज

cuttlefish
kaṭal fiś | कटल फ़िश

squid
skivaḍ | स्किवड

clam
baṛī sīpī | बड़ी सीपी

---

vocabulary • śabdāvalī • शब्दावली

fresh tāzā ताज़ा	**cleaned** svacchh स्वच्छ	**smoked** dhūmrit धूम्रित	**tail** pūñchh पूंछ	**fillet** kaṭlā क़तला	**salted** lavaṇit लवणित	**loin** śroṇik māṃs श्रोणिक मांस
frozen saṃśītit संशीतित	**filleted** kaṭle kiyā huā क़तले किया हुआ	**skinned** khāl rahit खाल रहित	**bone** kāṃṭe कांटे	**scale** mīn śalk मीन शल्क	**Will you clean it for me?** kyā āp ise sāf kar deṅge? क्या आप इसे साफ़ कर देंगे?	

---

vegetables 1 • sabziyāṃ • सब्ज़ियां

seed
bīj
बीज

broad bean
bāklā
बाकला

runner bean
guār kī phalī
गुआर की फली

french bean
frānsbīn
फ़्रांसबीन

garden pea
maṭar
मटर

bean sprout
aṅkurit phalī
अंकुरित फली

bamboo
bāṃs
बांस

pod
phalī
फली

okra
bhiṇḍī
भिंडी

sweetcorn
makaī
मकई

chicory
chikorī
चिकोरी

fennel
soā
सोआ

palm hearts
tāṛ kī gāṃṭheṃ
ताड़ की गांठें

celery
selerī
सेलेरी

---

vocabulary • śabdāvalī • शब्दावली

leaf	**floret**	**tip**	**organic**	**Do you sell organic vegetables?**
pattī	chhoṭā phūl	nok	jaivik	āp jaivik sabziyāṃ bechte haiṃ?
पत्ती	छोटा फूल	नोक	जैविक	आप जैविक सब्ज़ियां बेचते हैं?
stalk	**kernel**	**heart**	**plastic bag**	**Are these grown locally?**
ḍanṭhal	girī	bhītrī gāṃṭh	plāsṭik baig	kyā ye āspās ugāī jātī haiṃ?
डंठल	गिरी	भीतरी गांठ	प्लास्टिक बैग	क्या ये आसपास उगाई जाती हैं?

rocket
rocket salād
रॉकेट सलाद

watercress
watercress
वॉटरक्रेस

radicchio
lāl pattāgobhī
लाल पत्तागोभी

brussel sprout
gāṃṭh gobhī
गांठ गोभी

swiss chard
svis chārḍ | स्विस चार्ड

kale
kel pattī | केल पत्ती

sorrel
sorrel pattī | सॉरेल पत्ती

endive | enḍāiv
pattī | एनडाइव पत्ती

dandelion
ḍenḍiliyan
डेंडिलियन

spinach
pālak
पालक

kohlrabi
śalgam
शलग़म

pak-choi
pāk-choī
पाक–चोई

lettuce
salād pattā | सलाद पत्ता

broccoli
broklī | ब्रोकली

cabbage
bandgobhī | बंदगोभी

spring greens
harā salād pattā | हरा
सलाद पत्ता

vegetables 2 • sabziyāṃ • सब्ज़ियां

artichoke
artichoke
आर्टीचॉक

radish
chhoṭī mūlī
छोटी मूली

cauliflower
phūlgobhī
फूलगोभी

turnip
śalgam
शलग़म

potato
ālū
आलू

onion
pyāz
प्याज़

pepper
śimlā mirch
शिमला मिर्च

chilli
harī mirch
हरी मिर्च

marrow
harā kaddū
हरा कद्दू

vocabulary • śabdāvalī • शब्दावली

cherry tomato bebī ṭamāṭar बेबी टमाटर	**taro root** kachālū कचालू	**frozen** saṃśītit संशीतित	**bitter** karvā कड़वा	**What's the price per kilo?** ek kilo kitne kā hai? एक किलो कितने का है?
carrot gājar गाजर	**cassava** kasāvā कसावा	**raw** kacchā कच्चा	**firm** sakht सख़्त	**What are those called?** inheṃ kyā kahte haiṃ? इन्हें क्या कहते हैं?
breadfruit breḍfrūṭ ब्रेडफ्रूट	**water chestnut** siṅghāṛā सिंघाड़ा	**hot (spicy)** tīkhā तीखा	**flesh** gūdā गूदा	**Can I have one kilo of potatoes please?** kyā mujhe ek kilo ālū deṅge? क्या मुझे एक किलो आलू देंगे?
new potato nayā ālū नया आलू	**celeriac** ek prakār kā kand एक प्रकार का कंद	**sweet** mīṭhā मीठा	**root** jaṛ जड़	

sweet potato
śakarkandī
शकरकंदी

yam
jimīkand
जिमीकंद

beetroot
chukandar
चुकंदर

swede
svīḍan kā śalgam
स्वीडन का शलग़म

jerusalem artichoke
yerūśalam artichoke
येरूशलम आर्टीचॉक

horseradish
tīkhī mūlī
तीखी मूली

parsnip
pīlī gājar
पीली गाजर

ginger
adrak
अदरक

aubergine
baingan
बैंगन

tomato
ṭamāṭar
टमाटर

spring onion
harā pyāz
हरा प्याज़

leek
līk
लीक

shallot
pyāz
प्याज़

garlic
lahsun
लहसुन

clove
kalī
कली

truffle
gucchhī
गुच्छी

mushroom
maśrūm
मशरूम

cucumber
khīrā
खीरा

courgette
toraī
तोरई

butternut squash
peṭhā
पेठा

acorn squash
banjuphal
बंजुफल

pumpkin
kaddū
कद्दू

fruit 1 • phal • फल

citrus fruit • khaṭṭe phal • खट्टे फल

orange
santrā | संतरा

clementine
mālṭā | माल्टा

ugli fruit
aglī frūṭ | अगली फ्रूट

pith
bhītrī
chhilkā
भीतरी
छिलका

grapefruit
chakotrā | चकोतरा

segment
phāṃk
फाँक

satsuma
jāpānī santrā
जापानी संतरा

tangerine
nāraṅgī | नारंगी

zest
chhilkā
छिलका

lime
nībū | नीबू

lemon
khaṭṭā | खट्टा

kumquat
kummkāṭ | कुम्मकाट

stoned fruit • guṭhlīdār phal • गुठलीदार फल

peach
āṛū | आड़ू

nectarine
śaftālū | शफ़तालू

apricot
ḳhubānī
ख़ुबानी

plum
ālū buḳhārā
आलू बुख़ारा

cherry
cherī
चेरी

pear
nāśpātī
नाशपाती

apple
seb | सेब

basket of fruit
phaloṃ kī ṭokrī | फलों की टोकरी

berries and melons • ber aur sardā • बेर और सर्दा

strawberry
strawberry | स्ट्रॉबेरी

raspberry
rasbharī | रसभरी

melon
sardā
सर्दा

grapes
āṃgūr | अंगूर

blackberry
blaikberī | ब्लैकबेरी

redcurrant
reḍ karaṇṭ | रेड करंट

blackcurrant
blaik karaṇṭ
ब्लैक करंट

rind
chhilkā
छिलका

seed
bīj
बीज

flesh
gūdā
गूदा

cranberry
krainberī
क्रैनबेरी

white currant
vhāiṭ karaṇṭ
व्हाइट करंट

watermelon
tarbūz
तरबूज़

blueberry
jāmun | जामुन

loganberry
loganberī
लोगनबेरी

gooseberry
jharberī
झरबेरी

---

vocabulary • śabdāvalī • शब्दावली

rhubarb revāchīnī रेवाचीनी	**sour** khaṭṭā खट्टा	**crisp** kurkurā कुरकुरा	**juice** jūs जूस	**Are they ripe?** kyā ye pake hue haiṃ? क्या ये पके हुए हैं?
fibre reśedār रेशेदार	**fresh** tāzā ताज़ा	**rotten** saṛā huā सड़ा हुआ	**core** bīj बीज	**Can I try one?** kyā maiṃ ek chakh lūṃ? क्या मैं एक चख लूं?
sweet mīṭhā मीठा	**juicy** rasīlā रसीला	**pulp** gūdā गूदा	**seedless** bīj rahit बीज रहित	**How long will they keep?** ye kab tak ṭhīk raheṅge? ये कब तक ठीक रहेंगे?

fruit 2 • phal 2 • फल 2

mango
ām | आम

pineapple
anannās
अन्नास

avocado
avokāḍo
अवोकाडो

papaya
papītā
पपीता

peach
āṛū
आड़ू

lychee
līchī
लीची

kiwifruit
kīvī | कीवी

cape gooseberry
rasbharī
रसभरी

pip
bīj | बीज

skin
chhilkā
छिलका

quince
kīns | कीन्स

passion fruit
paiśan frūṭ
पैशन फ्रूट

banana
kelā | केला

guava
amrūd | अमरूद

pomegranate
anār | अनार

persimmon
tendū phal
तेंदू फल

feijoa
fehoā | फ़ेहोआ

prickly pear
nākh | नाख

starfruit
kamrakh
कमरख

mangosteen
maṅguṣṭh
मंगुष्ठ

nuts and dried fruit • meve aur girī • मेवे और गिरी

pine nut
chilgozā | चिलगोज़ा

pistachio
pistā | पिस्ता

cashewnut
kājū | काजू

peanut
mūṅgphalī | मूंगफली

hazelnut
pahāṛī bādām
पहाड़ी बादाम

brazilnut
brāzīlnaṭ | ब्राज़ीलनट

pecan
pīkan | पीकन

almond
bādām | बादाम

walnut
akhroṭ | अख़रोट

chestnut
chesṭnaṭ | चेस्टनट

macadamia
maikāḍemiyā
मैकाडेमिया

fig
añjīr | अंजीर

date
khajūr | खजूर

prune
sūkhā alūchā
सूखा अलूचा

shell
khol
ख़ोल

sultana
bījrahit kiśmiś
बीजरहित किशमिश

raisin
kiśmiś
किशमिश

currant
munakkā
मुनक्का

flesh
girī
गिरी

coconut
nāriyal | नारियल

vocabulary • śabdāvalī • शब्दावली

green harā हरा	**hard** sakht सख़्त	**kernel** girī गिरी	**salted** lavaṇit लवणित	**roasted** bhunā भुना	**tropical fruit** uṣṇdeśīya phal उष्णदेशीय फल	**shelled** chhilkā rahit छिलका रहित
ripe pakā पका	**soft** narm नर्म	**desiccated** sukhāyā huā सुखाया हुआ	**raw** kacchā कच्चा	**seasonal** mausmī मौसमी	**candied fruit** page phal पगे फल	**whole** sābut साबुत

grains and pulses • anāj evam dāleṃ • अनाज एवं दालें

grains • anāj • अनाज

wheat
gehūṃ | गेहूं

oats
jaī | जई

barley
jau | जौ

millet
jvār | ज्वार

corn
makkā | मक्का

quinoa
kinoyā | किनोया

vocabulary • śabdāvalī • शब्दावली		
seed bīj बीज	**fragranced** ḳhuśbūdār ख़ुशबूदार	**long-grain** baṛā dānā बड़ा दाना
husk bhūsī भूसी	**cereal** khādyānn खाद्यान्न	**short-grain** chhoṭā dānā छोटा दाना
kernel girī गिरी	**wholegrain** sābut साबुत	**fresh** tāzā ताज़ा
dry sukhā सूखा	**soak (v)** bhigonā भिगोना	**easy cook** jaldī pakne vālā जल्दी पकने वाला

rice • chāval • चावल

white rice | safed
chāval | सफ़ेद चावल

brown rice | brāun
rāis | ब्राउन राइस

wild rice | jaṅglī
chāval | जंगली चावल

pudding rice | puḍiṅg
rāis | पुडिंग राइस

processed grains • sansādhit anāj • संसाधित अनाज

couscous
khaskhas | खसखस

cracked wheat
daliyā | दलिया

semolina
sūjī | सूजी

bran
chokar | चोकर

beans and peas • dālem• दालें

butter beans
sem
सेम

haricot beans
safed rājmā
सफ़ेद राजमा

red kidney beans
rājmā
राजमा

aduki beans
aḍukī bīn
अडुकी बीन

broad beans
bāklā
बाकला

soya beans
soyābīn
सोयाबीन

black-eyed beans
lobiyā
लोबिया

pinto beans
chitrā rājmā
चितरा राजमा

mung beans
sābut mūṅg
साबुत मूंग

flageolet beans
sūkhī frānsbīn
सूखी फ़ांसबीन

brown lentils
kālī masūr
काली मसूर

red lentils
lāl masūr
लाल मसूर

green peas
maṭar
मटर

chick peas
kābulī chane
काबुली चने

split peas
maṭrā
मटरा

seeds • bīj • बीज

pumpkin seed
kaddū ke bīj
कद्दू के बीज

mustard seed
rāī | राई

caraway
safed zīrā
सफ़ेद ज़ीरा

sunflower seed
sūrajmukhī ke bīj | सूरजमुखी के बीज

sesame seed
til | तिल

herbs and spices • auṣadhi evam masāle • औषधि एवं मसाले

spices • masāle • मसाले

vanilla | vainilā
(paudhā) | वैनिला (पौधा)

nutmeg
jāyaphal
जायफल

mace
jāvitrī | जावित्री

turmeric
haldī | हल्दी

cumin
zīrā | ज़ीरा

bouquet garni
masāloṃ kī poṭlī
मसालों की पोटली

allspice
lavaṅg badar
लवंग बदर

peppercorn | kālī
mirch | काली मिर्च

fenugreek
methī | मेथी

chilli
mirch | मिर्च

saffron
kesar | केसर

cardamom
ilāyachī | इलायची

curry powder
śorbe kā masālā
शोरबे का मसाला

whole
sābut
साबुत

crushed
kuṭā
कुटा

ground
pisā
पिसा

paprika
pisī mirch
पिसी मिर्च

flakes
dardarā
दरदरा

garlic
lahsun | लहसुन

english • hindī • हिन्दी

herbs • auṣadhi • औषधि

sticks
chhāl
छाल

cinnamon
dālchīnī | दालचीनी

fennel | soā | सोआ

fennel seeds
moṭī saumf
मोटी सौंफ़

bay leaf
tezpattā | तेज़पत्ता

parsley
pārsli | पारस्लि

lemon grass
leman grās
लेमन ग्रास

chives
jambū | जंबू

mint
pudīnā | पुदीना

thyme
ajvāyan | अजवायन

sage | kapūr kā
pattā | कपूर का पत्ता

cloves
lauṅg
लौंग

tarragon
ṭairāgan | टैरागन

marjoram
marūvā | मरूवा

basil
tulsī | तुलसी

star anise
sṭār enīs
स्टार एनीस

oregano
oregano | ऑरिगानो

coriander
dhaniyā | धनिया

dill
śatpuṣpikā
शतपुष्पिका

ginger
adrak
अदरक

rosemary
rozmerī | रोज़मेरी

bottled foods • botalband khādya padārth • बोतलबंद खाद्य पदार्थ

cork
ḍhakkan
ढक्कन

sunflower oil
sūrajmukhī kā tel
सूरजमुखी का तेल

walnut oil
akhroṭ kā tel
अख़रोट का तेल

grapeseed oil
amgūr ke bīj kā tel
अंगूर के बीज का तेल

almond oil
bādām kā tel
बादाम का तेल

**sesame
seed oil**
til kā tel
तिल का तेल

hazelnut oil
hezalnaṭ tel
हेजलनट तेल

olive oil
zaitūn kā tel
ज़ैतून का तेल

herbs
jaṛī-būṭī
जड़ी–बूटी

flavoured oil
sugandhit tel
सुगंधित तेल

oils | tel | तेल

sweet spreads • jaim, śahad ityādi • जैम, शहद इत्यादि

jar
jār | जार

honeycomb
chhattā | छत्ता

set honey
kārtik śahad
कार्तिक शहद

lemon curd
leman karḍ
लेमन कर्ड

raspberry jam
rasbharī jaim
रसभरी जैम

marmalade
mārmleḍ
मार्मलेड

clear honey
śahad
शहद

maple syrup
mepal sirap
मेपल सिरप

condiments and spreads • chaṭnī sauce ityādi
चटनी, सॉस इत्यादि

cider vinegar
seb sirkā
सेब सिरका

balsamic vinegar
bolsam sirkā
बॉल्सम सिरका

bottle
botal
बोतल

english mustard
iṅgliś masṭarḍ
इंगलिश मस्टर्ड

mayonnaise
myonīz
म्योनीज़

ketchup
ṭamāṭar sauce
टमाटर सॉस

french mustard
french masṭarḍ
फ़्रेंच मस्टर्ड

chutney
chaṭnī
चटनी

malt vinegar
mālṭ kā sirkā
माल्ट का सिरका

wine vinegar
vāin sirkā
वाइन सिरका

sauce
sauce
सॉस

wholegrain mustard
sābut sarsoṃ
साबुत सरसों

vinegar | sirkā | सिरका

---

sealed jar
sīlband jār
सीलबंद जार

peanut butter
pīnaṭ baṭar
पीनट बटर

chocolate spread
chocolate spraiḍ
चॉकलेट स्प्रैड

preserved fruit
sanrakṣit phal
संरक्षित फल

vocabulary • śabdāvalī • शब्दावली

corn oil
makaī kā tel
मकई का तेल

rapeseed oil
tilhan kā tel
तिलहन का तेल

groundnut oil
mūṅgphalī kā tel
मूंगफली का तेल

cold-pressed oil
kolḍ-praisḍ tel
कोल्ड–प्रैस्ड तेल

vegetable oil
vanaspati tel
वनस्पति तेल

dairy produce • ḍeyarī utpād • डेयरी उत्पाद

cheese • chīz • चीज़

rind
paprī
पपड़ी

semi-hard cheese
ardh saḳht chīz
अर्ध सख़्त चीज़

grated cheese
kaddūkas kiyā chīz
कद्दूकस किया चीज़

hard cheese
ṭhos chīz | ठोस चीज़

semi-soft cheese
ardh mulāyam chīz
अर्ध मुलायम चीज़

cottage cheese
panīr
पनीर

cream cheese
krīm chīz
क्रीम चीज़

blue cheese
nīlī chīz
नीली चीज़

soft cheese
mulāyam chīz
मुलायम चीज़

fresh cheese | tāzī chīz | ताज़ी चीज़

milk • dūdh • दूध

whole milk
ful krīm dūdh
फुल क्रीम दूध

semi-skimmed milk
krīmyukt dūdh
क्रीमयुक्त दूध

skimmed milk
krīm rahit dūdh
क्रीम रहित दूध

milk carton
dūdh kā ḍibbā
दूध का डिब्बा

goat's milk
bakrī kā dūdh
बकरी का दूध

condensed milk
kaṇḍensḍ milk
कंडेंस्ड मिल्क

cow's milk | gāya kā dūdh | गाय का दूध

butter
makkhan | मक्खन

margarine
kṛtrim makkhan
कृत्रिम मक्खन

cream
krīm | क्रीम

single cream
patlī krīm | पतली क्रीम

double cream
gaṛhī krīm
गाढ़ी क्रीम

whipped cream
phemṭī huī krīm
फेंटी हुई क्रीम

sour cream
sār krīm | सार क्रीम

yoghurt
dahī | दही

ice-cream
āiskrīm |आइसक्रीम

eggs · aṇḍe · अंडे

yolk
zardī
ज़र्दी

egg white
safed bhāg
सफ़ेद भाग

shell
chhilkā
छिलका

egg cup
aṇḍe
rakhne
kā kap
अंडे रखने
का कप

boiled egg | ublā aṇḍā | उबला अंडा

goose egg
hans kā aṇḍā
हंस का अंडा

quail egg
baṭer kā aṇḍā
बटेर का अंडा

hen's egg
murgī kā aṇḍā
मुर्गी का अंडा

duck egg
batakh kā aṇḍā
बतख़ का अंडा

vocabulary · śabdāvalī · शब्दावली

pasteurized pāscharīkṛt पास्चरीकृत	**milkshake** milkśek मिल्कशेक	**salted** lavaṇit लवणित	**sheep's milk** bheṛ kā dūdh भेड़ का दूध	**lactose** dugdh śarkarā दुग्ध शर्करा	**homogenised** samāṅgīkṛt dūdh समांगीकृत दूध
unpasteurized apāscharīkṛt अपास्चरीकृत	**frozen yoghurt** dahī kī āiskrīm दही की आइसक्रीम	**unsalted** lavaṇ rahit लवण रहित	**buttermilk** chhāchh छाछ	**fat free** vasā rahit वसा रहित	**powdered milk** pāuḍar dūdh पाउडर दूध

breads and flours • breḍ evam āṭā • ब्रेड एवं आटा

sliced bread
breḍ slāis
ब्रेड स्लाइस

poppy seeds
khaskhas
खसखस

rye bread
rāī breḍ
राई ब्रेड

baguette
french breḍ
फ्रेंच ब्रेड

bakery | bekrī | बेकरी

making bread • breḍ banānā • ब्रेड बनाना

white flour
maidā | मैदा

brown flour
gehūṃ kā āṭā | गेहूं का आटा

wholemeal flour
āṭā | आटा

yeast
khamīr | खमीर

sift (v)
chhānnā | छानना

mix (v)
milānā | मिलाना

dough
loī
लोई

knead (v)
gūṃdhnā | गूंधना

bake (v)
bek karnā | बेक करना

crust
kinārā
किनारा

white bread
maidā breḍ | मैदा ब्रेड

loaf
sābut
breḍ
साबुत ब्रेड

brown bread
brāun breḍ | ब्राउन ब्रेड

wholemeal bread
āṭe kī breḍ | आटे की ब्रेड

slice
ṭukṛā
टुकड़ा

granary bread
miśrit anāj breḍ
मिश्रित अनाज ब्रेड

corn bread
makaī breḍ | मकई ब्रेड

soda bread
soḍā breḍ | सोडा ब्रेड

sourdough bread
khamīrī breḍ
खमीरी ब्रेड

flatbread
chapṭī breḍ | चपटी ब्रेड

bagel
begal ban | बेगल बन

bap
safed ban | सफ़ेद बन

roll
rol | रोल

fruit bread
frūṭ breḍ | फ्रूट ब्रेड

seeded bread
bījyukt breḍ | बीजयुक्त ब्रेड

naan bread
nān | नान

pitta bread
piṭā breḍ | पीटा ब्रेड

crispbread
kurkurī breḍ | कुरकुरी ब्रेड

---

vocabulary • śabdāvalī • शब्दावली

strong flour moṭā āṭā मोटा आटा	**rise (v)** phūlnā फूलना	**prove (v)** ūpar uṭhnā ऊपर उठना	**breadcrumbs** breḍ kā chūrā ब्रेड का चूरा	**slicer** slāisar स्लाइसर
self-raising flour mahīn āṭā महीन आटा	**plain flour** āṭā आटा	**glaze (v)** chamak ānā चमक आना	**flute** flūṭ फ्लूट	**baker** bekar बेकर

---

cakes and desserts • kek aur miṣṭānn • केक और मिष्टान्न

éclair
ekleyar
एक्लेयर

cream
krīm
क्रीम

filling
bharāv
भराव

choux pastry
śūz pesṭrī
शूज पेस्ट्री

puff pastry
paf pesṭrī
पफ़ पेस्ट्री

filo pastry
filo pesṭrī
फ़िलो पेस्ट्री

fruit cake
frūṭ kek
फ्रूट केक

fruit tart
frūṭ ṭārṭ
फ्रूट टार्ट

meringue
mīraiṅg
मिरैंग

chocolate coated
chocolate parat
चॉकलेट परत

muffin
mafin
मफ़िन

sponge cake
spañj kek
स्पंज केक

cakes | kek | केक

---

vocabulary • śabdāvalī • शब्दावली

rice pudding khīr खीर	**bun** ban बन	**pastry** pesṭrī पेस्ट्री	**crème patisserie** krīm pesṭrī क्रीम पेस्ट्री	**May I have a slice please?** kyā maiṁ ek ṭukṛā le saktā hūṁ? क्या मैं एक टुकड़ा ले सकता हूं?
celebration samāroh समारोह	**custard** kasṭarḍ कस्टर्ड	**slice** ṭukṛā टुकड़ा	**chocolate cake** chocolate kek चॉकलेट केक	

chocolate chip
chocolate chip biskuṭ
चॉकलेट चिप बिस्कुट

sponge fingers
spañj fiṅgar
स्पंज फ़िंगर

florentine
florenṭāin
फ़्लोरेन्टाइन

trifle
ṭrāifal
ट्राइफ़ल

biscuits | biskuṭ | बिस्कुट

mousse
mūs puḍiṅg | मूस पुडिंग

sorbet
sorbet | सॉर्बेट

cream pie
krīm pāī | क्रीम पाई

crème caramel | krīm
kairāmal | क्रीम कैरामल

celebration cakes • samāroh kek • समारोह केक

top tier
ūprī chakr
ऊपरी चक्र

decoration
sajāvaṭ
सजावट

ribbon
riban
रिबन

bottom tier
nichlā chakr
निचला चक्र

icing
āisiṅg
आइसिंग

marzipan
bādām
parat
बादाम परत

wedding cake | śādī kā kek | शादी का केक

birthday candles
mombattī
मोमबत्ती

blow out (v)
phūṃk se
bujhānā
फूंक से बुझाना

birthday cake | janmdin kā kek | जन्मदिन का केक

delicatessen • kek peṣṭrī dukān • केक पेस्ट्री दुकान

spicy sausage
masāledār
sausage
मसालेदार सॉसेज

oil
tel
तेल

vinegar
sirkā
सिरका

uncooked meat
kacchā māṃs
कच्चा मांस

counter
kāuṇṭar
काउंटर

flan
flen
फ़्लेन

salami
salāmī
सलामी

pepperoni
tīkhī sausages
तीखी सॉसेजेस

pâté
paiṭī
पैटी

mozzarella
mozerelā | मोज़ेरेला

brie
brī chīz | ब्री चीज़

goat's cheese | bakrī
ke dūdh kā panīr |
बकरी के दूध का पनीर

cheddar
cheḍar chīz | चेडर चीज़

rind
paprī
पपड़ी

parmesan | pārmā meṃ
banā panīr | पारमा में बना पनीर

camembert
panīr | पनीर

edam | eḍām
chīz | एडाम चीज़

manchego | manchego
chīz | मनचेगो चीज़

pies
pāī
पाई

black olive
kālā zaitūn
काला जैतून

chili
mirch
मिर्च

sauce
chaṭnī
चटनी

bread roll
breḍ rol
ब्रेड रोल

cooked meat
pakā huā māṃs
पका हुआ मांस

green olive
harā zaitūn
हरा जैतून

ham
haim
हैम

sandwich counter
saiṇḍvich kāuṇṭar | सैंडविच काउंटर

smoked fish
parirakṣit machhlī
परिरक्षित मछली

capers
kaipars
कैपर्स

chorizo
speniś
sausage
स्पेनिश सॉसेज

prosciutto | iṭeliyan
haim | इटेलियन हैम

stuffed olive | bharvāṃ
zaitūn | भरवां जैतून

vocabulary • śabdāvalī • शब्दावली		
in oil	**marinated**	**in brine**
tel meṃ pakā	masāle meṃ liptā	namkīn pānī meṃ rakhā
तेल में पका	मसाले में लिपटा	नमकीन पानी में रखा
smoked	**salted**	**cured**
dhūmrit	lavaṇit	sanrakṣit
धूम्रित	लवणित	संरक्षित

Take a number please.
kṛpyā nambar le leṃ
कृपया नंबर ले लें।

Can I try some of that please?
kyā maiṃ chakh saktā hūṃ?
क्या मैं चख सकता हूं?

May I have six slices of that please?
kyā mujhe iske chhah pīs deṇge?
क्या मुझे इसके छह पीस देंगे?

drinks • peya • पेय

water • pānī • पानी

bottled water
botalband pānī
बोतलबंद पानी

sparkling
gaisvālā pānī
गैसवाला पानी

still
gaisrahit pānī
गैसरहित पानी

tap water | nal kā pānī | नल का पानी

tonic water
tonic water
टॉनिक वॉटर

soda water
soḍā | सोडा

mineral water
minral water | मिनरल वॉटर

hot drinks • garm peya • गर्म पेय

teabag
ṭī baig
टी बैग

loose leaf tea
khulī chāya pattī
खुली चाय पत्ती

tea | chāya | चाय

beans
coffee ke bīj
कॉफ़ी के बीज

ground coffee
pisī coffee
पिसी कॉफ़ी

coffee | coffee | कॉफ़ी

hot chocolate
hot chocolate
हॉट चॉकलेट

malted drink
mālṭ vāle peya
माल्ट वाले पेय

soft drinks • śītal peya • शीतल पेय

straw
straw
स्ट्रॉ

tomato juice
ṭamāṭar kā jūs
टमाटर का जूस

grape juice
aṃgūr kā jūs
अंगूर का जूस

lemonade
śikanjī
शिकंजी

orangeade
santare kā jūs
संतरे का जूस

cola
kolā
कोला

alcoholic drinks • madya peya • मद्य पेय

can
kain
कैन

beer
bīyar | बीयर

cider | eppal
vāin | एप्पल वाइन

bitter | ḍārk
bīyar | डार्क बीयर

stout
sṭāuṭ | स्टाउट

gin
jin | जिन

vodka
vodkā | वोदका

whisky
vhiskī | व्हिस्की

rum
ram | रम

brandy
brānḍī | ब्रांडी

port
porṭ | पोर्ट

dry
sādī
सादी

sherry
śerī | शेरी

rosé
gulābī
गुलाबी

campari
kampārī | कमपारी

white
safed
सफ़ेद

red
lāl
लाल

liqueur
likar | लिकर

tequila
ṭakīlā | टकीला

champagne
śaimpen | शैम्पेन

wine
vāin | वाइन

eating out
bāhar khānā
बाहर खाना

café • kaife • कैफ़े

menu
vyañjan
sūchī
व्यंजन सूची

awning
sāyabān
सायबान

umbrella
chhātā
छाता

terrace café | khulā kaife | खुला कैफ़े

waiter
bairā
बैरा

coffee machine
coffee masīn
कॉफ़ी मशीन

table
mez
मेज़

pavement café | roḍ sāiḍ kaife | रोड साइड कैफ़े

snack bar | snaik bār | स्नैक बार

coffee • coffee • कॉफ़ी

white coffee
coffee
कॉफ़ी

black coffee
blaik coffee
ब्लैक कॉफ़ी

cocoa powder
koko pāuḍar
कोको पाउडर

froth
jhāg
झाग

filter coffee
filṭar coffee | फ़िल्टर कॉफ़ी

espresso
espraiso | एस्प्रैसो

cappuccino
kepyūchino | केप्यूचिनो

iced coffee
āisḍ coffee | आइस्ड कॉफ़ी

tea • chāya • चाय

herbal tea
auṣadhīya chāya
औषधीय चाय

camomile tea | babūnā kī chāya |
बबूना की चाय

green tea | harī chāya |
हरी चाय

tea with milk
dūdh vālī chāya
दूध वाली चाय

black tea
kālī chāya
काली चाय

tea with lemon
nībū vālī chāya
नीबू वाली चाय

mint tea
pudīne kī chāya
पुदीने की चाय

iced tea
ṭhaṇḍī chāya
ठंडी चाय

juices and milkshakes • jūs evam milkśek • जूस एवं मिल्कशेक

chocolate milkshake
chocolate milkśek
चॉकलेट मिल्कशेक

strawberry milkshake
strawberry milkśek
स्ट्रॉबेरी मिल्कशेक

orange juice
santare kā jūs
संतरे का जूस

apple juice
seb kā jūs
सेब का जूस

pineapple juice
anannās kā jūs
अनन्नास का जूस

tomato juice
ṭamāṭar kā jūs
टमाटर का जूस

coffee milkshake
coffee milkśek
कॉफ़ी मिल्कशेक

food • khādya padārth • खाद्य पदार्थ

brown bread
brāun breḍ
ब्राउन ब्रेड

scoop
skūp
स्कूप

toasted sandwich | ṭosṭeḍ
saiṇḍvich | टोस्टेड सैंडविच

salad
salād | सलाद

ice cream
āiskrīm | आइसक्रीम

pastry
pesṭrī | पेस्ट्री

bar • bār • बार

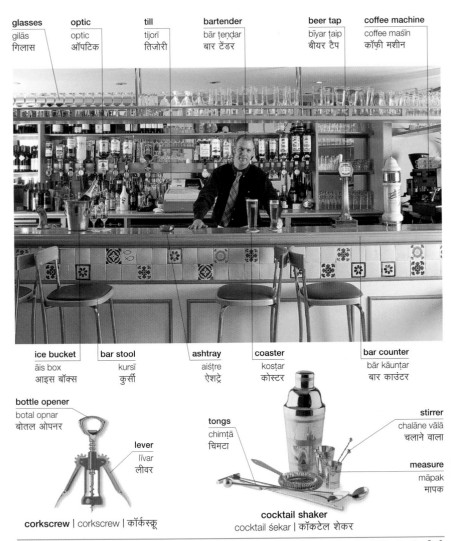

glasses
gilās
गिलास

optic
optic
ऑप्टिक

till
tijorī
तिजोरी

bartender
bār ṭenḍar
बार टेंडर

beer tap
bīyar ṭaip
बीयर टैप

coffee machine
coffee maśīn
कॉफ़ी मशीन

ice bucket
āis box
आइस बॉक्स

bar stool
kursī
कुर्सी

ashtray
aiśtre
ऐशट्रे

coaster
kosṭar
कोस्टर

bar counter
bār kāunṭar
बार काउंटर

bottle opener
botal opnar
बोतल ओपनर

lever
līvar
लीवर

corkscrew | corkscrew | कॉर्कस्क्रू

tongs
chimṭā
चिमटा

stirrer
chalāne vālā
चलाने वाला

measure
māpak
मापक

cocktail shaker
cocktail śekar | कॉकटेल शेकर

gin and tonic
jin aur tonic
जिन और टॉनिक

pitcher
jag
जग

scotch and water
scotch aur pānī
स्कॉच और पानी

ice cube
baraf
बर्फ़

rum and coke
ram aur kok
रम और कोक

vodka and orange
vodkā aur santrā
वोदका और संतरा

martini
mārṭinī | मार्टिनी

cocktail
cocktail | कॉकटेल

wine
vāin | वाइन

beer
bīyar | बीयर

a shot
ek shot | एक शॉट

single
siṅgal
सिंगल

double
ḍabal
डबल

measure
māp | माप

without ice | baraf
rahit | बर्फ़ रहित

ice and lemon
baraf va śikaṅjī
बर्फ़ व शिकंजी

with ice | baraf ke
sāth | बर्फ़ के साथ

bar snacks • bār snaiks • बार स्नैक्स

crisps | kurkurā | कुरकुरा

cashewnuts
kājū
काजू

peanuts
chīnā bādām
चीना बादाम

almonds
bādām
बादाम

nuts | meve | मेवे

olives | zaitūn | ज़ैतून

restaurant • restrām̐ • रेस्तरां

non-smoking section
dhūmrapān niṣedh sthān
धूम्रपान निषेध स्थान

napkin
naipkin
नैपकिन

commis chef
sahāyak rasoiyā
सहायक रसोइया

table setting
mez sajjā
मेज सज्जा

chef
rasoiyā
रसोइया

glass
gilās
गिलास

tray
ṭre
ट्रे

kitchen
rasoī | रसोई

waiter
bairā | बैरा

vocabulary • śabdāvalī • शब्दावली

receipt rasīd रसीद	**specials** viśeṣ विशेष	**price** mūlya मूल्य	**customer** grāhak ग्राहक	**service included** sevā sammilit सेवा सम्मिलित	**à la carte** menyu ke mutābik मेन्यु के मुताबिक
wine list vāin sūchī वाइन सूची	**sweet trolley** pestrī trolley पेस्ट्री ट्रॉली	**bill** bil बिल	**salt** namak नमक	**service not included** sevā sammilit nahīṃ सेवा सम्मिलित नहीं	**smoking section** dhūmrapān kṣetr धूम्रपान क्षेत्र
tip bakhśīś बख्शीश	**pepper** kālī mirch काली मिर्च	**bar** bār बार	**buffet** bufe बुफ़े	**evening menu** sandhyākālīn vyañjan sūchī संध्याकालीन व्यंजन सूची	**lunch menu** dopahar kī vyañjan sūchī दोपहर की व्यंजन सूची

menu

vyañjan sūchī
व्यंजन सूची

child's meal
bāl āhār | बाल–आहार

order (v)
order denā | ऑर्डर देना

pay (v)
dām chukānā | दाम चुकाना

courses • bhojan kā daur • भोजन का दौर

apéritif
ārambh peya | आरंभ पेय

starter
sṭārṭar | स्टार्टर

soup
sūp | सूप

main course
men kors | मेन कोर्स

side order
sāiḍ order | साइड ऑर्डर

fork
kāṃṭā
कांटा

coffee spoon
coffee kā
chammach
कॉफ़ी का चम्मच

dessert
miṣṭānn | मिष्टान्न

coffee
coffee | कॉफ़ी

vocabulary • śabdāvalī •
शब्दावली

A table for two please.
kṛpyā do logoṃ ke lie ṭebal batāeṃ.
कृपया दो लोगों के लिए टेबल बताएं।

Can I see the menu/winelist please?
kyā menyu/vāin lisṭ dikhāeṇge?
क्या मेन्यु/वाइन लिस्ट दिखाएंगे?

Is there a fixed price menu?
kyā yah ekdām menyu hai?
क्या यह एकदाम मेन्यु है?

Do you have any vegetarian dishes?
kyā yahāṃ śākāhārī khānā haï?
क्या यहां शाकाहारी खाना है?

Could I have the bill/a receipt please?
kyā mujhe bil/rasīd mil saktī hai?
क्या मुझे बिल/रसीद मिल सकती है?

Can we pay separately?
kyā ham alag-alag bil de sakte haiṃ?
क्या हम अलग–अलग बिल दे सकते हैं?

Where are the toilets, please?
śauchālaya kahāṃ hai?
शौचालय कहां है?

fast food • fāsṭ fūḍ • फ़ास्ट फ़ूड

straw
straw
स्ट्रॉ

burger
bargar
बर्गर

soft drink
sītal peya
शीतल पेय

french fries
french frāī
फ़्रेंच फ़्राई

paper napkin
pepar naipkin
पेपर नैपकिन

tray
ṭre
ट्रे

burger meal | bargar mīl | बर्गर मील

pizza
pītsā
पीत्सा

price list
mūlya sūchī
मूल्य सूची

canned drink
ḍibbāband peya
डिब्बाबंद पेय

home delivery
hom ḍilīvarī | होम डिलीवरी

street stall
sṭrīṭ stall | स्ट्रीट स्टॉल

bun
ban
बन

mustard
mastarḍ
मस्टर्ड

sausage
sausage
सॉसेज

hamburger
haim bargar
हैम बर्गर

chicken burger
chikan bargar
चिकन बर्गर

veggie burger
vej bargar
वेज बर्गर

hot dog
hot dog | हॉट डॉग

filling
bharāvan
भरावन

sandwich
saiṇḍvich
सैंडविच

club sandwich
klab saiṇḍvich
क्लब सैंडविच

open sandwich
khulā saiṇḍvich
खुला सैंडविच

wrap
rol | रोल

sauce
sauce
सॉस

savoury
namkīn
नमकीन

sweet
mīṭhā
मीठा

topping
topping
टॉपिंग

crêpes
maide kā chīlā
मैदे का चीला

kebab
kabāb | कबाब

chicken nuggets | chikan
nageṭs | चिकन नगेट्स

fish and chips
talī machhlī aur chips
तली मछली और चिप्स

ribs
chāmp
चांप

fried chicken
frāiḍ chikan
फ़्राइड चिकन

pizza
pītsā
पीत्सा

breakfast • subah kā nāśtā • सुबह का नाश्ता

milk
dūdh
दूध

cereal
sīriyal
सीरियल

jam
jaim
जैम

dried fruit
meve
मेवे

ham
haim
हैम

cheese
chīz
चीज़

crispbread
kurkurī breḍ
कुरकुरी ब्रेड

breakfast buffet
brekfāsṭ bufe | ब्रेकफ़ास्ट बुफ़े

marmalade
mārmleḍ
मार्मलेड

pâté
mīṭ kā pesṭ
मीट का पेस्ट

butter
makkhan
मक्खन

fruit juice
phalom̐ kā ras
फलों का रस

coffee
coffee
कॉफ़ी

hot chocolate
hot chocolate
हॉट चॉकलेट

croissant
krosām̐ ban
क्रोसां बन

tea
chāya
चाय

breakfast table
nāśte kī mez | नाश्ते की मेज़

drinks
peya padārth | पेय पदार्थ

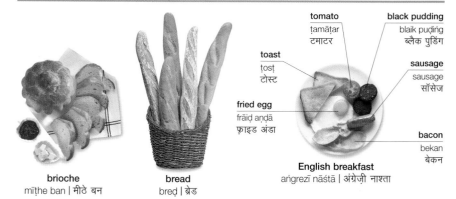

tomato
ṭamāṭar
टमाटर

black pudding
blaik puḍiṅg
ब्लैक पुडिंग

toast
ṭosṭ
टोस्ट

sausage
sausage
सॉसेज

fried egg
frāiḍ aṇḍā
फ़्राइड अंडा

bacon
bekan
बेकन

English breakfast
aṅgrezī nāśtā | अंग्रेज़ी नाश्ता

brioche
mīṭhe ban | मीठे बन

bread
breḍ | ब्रेड

kippers
kipars | किपर्स

french toast
french ṭosṭ
फ़्रेंच टोस्ट

yolk
zardī
ज़र्दी

boiled egg
ublā aṇḍā
उबला अंडा

scrambled eggs
aṇḍe kī bhurjī | अंडे की भुर्जी

cream
krīm
क्रीम

fruit yoghurt
frūṭ dahī
फ़्रूट दही

pancakes
painkek | पैनकेक

waffles
waffles | वॉफ़ल्स

porridge
daliyā | दलिया

fresh fruit
tāze phal | ताज़े फल

dinner • ḍinar • डिनर

soup
sūp | सूप

broth
śorbā | शोरबा

stew
dampuḵẖt | दमपुख़्त

curry
rasedār | रसेदार

roast
bhunā | भुना

pie
pāī | पाई

soufflé
sūfle | सूफ़ले

kebab
kabāb | कबाब

meatballs
kofte | कोफ़्ते

omelette
omelette | ऑमलेट

stir fry | kam tel meṃ
bhunā | कम तेल में भुना

noodles
nūḍals
नूडल्स

pasta
pāstā | पास्ता

rice
chāval | चावल

mixed salad | miśrit
salād | मिश्रित सलाद

green salad
harā salād | हरा सलाद

dressing
ḍresiṅg | ड्रेसिंग

techniques • vidhiyāṃ • विधियां

stuffed
bharvāṃ | भरवां

in sauce | sauce meṃ
सॉस में

grilled
bhunā huā | भुना हुआ

marinated | masāle meṃ
lipṭā | मसाले में लिपटा

poached
pochaḍ | पोच्ड

mashed
maslā huā | मसला हुआ

baked | bek kiyā
huā | बेक किया हुआ

pan fried | kam tel meṃ
pakā | कम तेल में पका

fried
talā huā | तला हुआ

pickled
achārit | अचारित

smoked
dhūmrit | धूम्रित

deep fried
talā huā | तला हुआ

syrup | sirap meṃ
banā | सिरप में बना

dressed | ḍresiṅg kiyā
huā | ड्रेसिंग किया हुआ

steamed | bhāp meṃ
pakā | भाप में पका

cured
sanrakṣit | संरक्षित

study
adhyayan
अध्ययन

school • vidyālaya • विद्यालय

teacher
adhyāpikā
अध्यापिका

blackboard
śyāmpaṭ
श्यामपट

schoolboy
skūlī chhātr | स्कूली छात्र

pupil
chhātr
छात्र

school uniform
skūlī vardī
स्कूली वर्दी

desk
beñch
बेंच

school bag
skūlī bastā
स्कूली बस्ता

chalk
chalk
चॉक

classroom | kakṣā | कक्षा

schoolgirl
skūlī chhātrā | स्कूली छात्रा

---

vocabulary • śabdāvalī • शब्दावली		
history itihās इतिहास	**science** vijñān विज्ञान	**physics** bhautikī भौतिकी
languages bhāṣāeṁ भाषाएं	**art** kalā कला	**chemistry** rasāyan śāstr रसायन शास्त्र
literature sāhitya साहित्य	**music** saṅgīt संगीत	**biology** jīv vijñān जीव विज्ञान
geography bhūgol भूगोल	**maths** gaṇit गणित	**physical education** śārīrik śikṣā शारीरिक शिक्षा

activities • gatividhiyāṁ • गतिविधियां

read (v) | paṛhnā | पढ़ना

write (v) | likhnā | लिखना

spell (v) | vartanī likhnā
वर्तनी लिखना

draw (v)
chitr banānā | चित्र बनाना

nib
nib
निब

colouring pencil
raṅgīn pensil
रंगीन पेंसिल

pencil sharpener
sharpener
शॉपनर

overhead projector
ovarheḍ projekṭar
ओवरहेड प्रोजेक्टर

pen
pen | पेन

pencil
pensil | पेंसिल

rubber
rabaṛ | रबड़

notebook
copy | कॉपी

textbook | pāṭhya pustak | पाठ्य पुस्तक

pencil case
pensil kes | पेंसिल केस

ruler
paimānā | पैमाना

question (v) | praśan
pūchhnā | प्रश्न पूछना

answer (v)
uttar denā | उत्तर देना

discuss (v) | vichār-vimarś
karnā | विचार–विमर्श करना

learn (v)
sīkhnā | सीखना

vocabulary • śabdāvalī • शब्दावली		
head teacher mukhyādhyāpikā मुख्याध्यापिका	**answer** uttar उत्तर	**grade** śreṇī श्रेणी
lesson adhyāya अध्याय	**homework** gṛhkārya गृहकार्य	**year** varṣ वर्ष
question praśan प्रश्न	**examination** parīkṣā परीक्षा	**dictionary** śabdkoś शब्दकोश
take notes (v) noṭs lenā नोट्स लेना	**essay** nibandh निबंध	**encyclopaedia** viśvakoś विश्वकोश

maths • gaṇit • गणित

shapes • ākṛtiyāṃ • आकृतियां

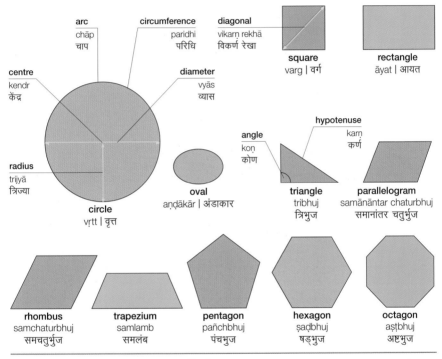

arc
chāp
चाप

circumference
paridhi
परिधि

diagonal
vikarṇ rekhā
विकर्ण रेखा

square
varg | वर्ग

rectangle
āyat | आयत

centre
kendr
केंद्र

diameter
vyās
व्यास

hypotenuse
karṇ
कर्ण

angle
koṇ
कोण

radius
trijyā
त्रिज्या

circle
vṛtt | वृत्त

oval
aṇḍākār | अंडाकार

triangle
tribhuj
त्रिभुज

parallelogram
samānāntar chaturbhuj
समानांतर चतुर्भुज

rhombus
samchaturbhuj
समचतुर्भुज

trapezium
samlamb
समलंब

pentagon
pañchbhuj
पंचभुज

hexagon
ṣaḍbhuj
षड्भुज

octagon
aṣṭbhuj
अष्टभुज

solids • ghanākṛtiyāṃ • घनाकृतियां

side
bhujā
भुजा

apex
śīrṣ
शीर्ष

base
ādhār
आधार

cone
śaṅku | शंकु

cylinder
belan | बेलन

cube
ghan | घन

pyramid
pirāmiḍ | पिरामिड

sphere
golā | गोला

lines • rekhāeṃ • रेखाएं

straight
sīdhī | सीधी

parallel
samānāntar | समानांतर

perpendicular
lamb | लंब

curved
vakr | वक्र

measurements • māpak • मापक

volume
parimāṇ | परिमाण

numerator
aṃś
अंश

denominator
har
हर

fraction
bhinn | भिन्न

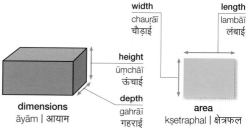

dimensions
āyām | आयाम

width
chaurāī
चौड़ाई

height
ūṃchāī
ऊंचाई

depth
gahrāī
गहराई

length
lambāī
लंबाई

area
kṣetraphal | क्षेत्रफल

equipment • upkaraṇ • उपकरण

set square
samkoṇak
समकोणक

protractor
koṇmāpak/ḍī
कोणमापक/डी

ruler
paimānā
पैमाना

compass
parkār
परकार

calculator
kailkyuleṭar
कैलक्युलेटर

---

vocabulary • śabdāvalī • शब्दावली

geometry	plus	times	equals	add (v)	multiply (v)	equation
rekhāgaṇit	jamā	guṇā	barābar	joṛnā	guṇā karnā	samīkaraṇ
रेखागणित	जमा	गुना	बराबर	जोड़ना	गुणा करना	समीकरण

arithmetic	minus	divided by	count (v)	subtract (v)	divide (v)	percentage
aṅkgaṇit	ghaṭā	bhājak	ginnā	ghaṭānā	bhāg denā	pratiśat
अंकगणित	घटा	भाजक	गिनना	घटाना	भाग देना	प्रतिशत

science • vijñān • विज्ञान

laboratory
prayogśālā | प्रयोगशाला

scales
tarāzū | तराजू

weight
vazan
वज़न

spring balance
spring tulā | स्प्रिंग तुला

crucible
kuṭhālī
कुठाली

bunsen burner
bansan barnar
बनसन बर्नर

tripod
tipāī | तिपाई

glass bottle
kāṃch kī botal
कांच की बोतल

lamp stand
laimp staiṇḍ
लैंप स्टैंड

clamp
kīlak
कीलक

funnel
kīp
कीप

flask
jār
जार

stopper
stopper
स्टॉपर

test tube
parakhnalī
परखनली

rack
raik | रैक

timer
ṭaimar | टाइमर

petri dish
peṭrī ḍiś | पेट्री डिश

experiment | prayog | प्रयोग

thermometer
tharmāmīṭar | थर्मामीटर

syringe
siriṅj | सिरिंज

tweezers
chhoṭī chimṭī | छोटी चिमटी

scalpel
chāḳū | चाकू

dropper
dropper | ड्रॉपर

forceps
forceps | फ़ॉरसेप

tongs
baṛī chimṭī | बड़ी चिमटी

spatula
spaiṭyūlā | स्पैट्यूला

pestle
mūsal
मूसल

eyepiece
dūrbīn kā śīśā
दूरबीन का शीशा

mortar
kharal | खरल

filter paper
filṭar pepar | फ़िल्टर पेपर

safety goggles | surakṣā
chaśmā | सुरक्षा चश्मा

focusing knob
fokas knob
फ़ोकस नॉब

glass rod
kāmch kī chhaṛ
कांच की छड़

objective lens
lains
लैंस

stage
tal
तल

pipette
nalikā | नलिका

beaker
bīkar | बीकर

slide
slāiḍ
स्लाइड

magnet
chumbak
चुंबक

crocodile clip
daṃtedār chimṭī
दांतेदार चिमटी

mirror
śīśā
शीशा

negative electrode
negeṭiv electrode
नेगेटिव इलेक्ट्रॉड

positive electrode
positive electrode
पॉज़ीटिव इलेक्ट्रॉड

microscope
sūkṣamdarśī | सूक्ष्मदर्शी

battery
baiṭrī | बैटरी

college • mahāvidyālaya • महाविद्यालय

admissions
praveś
प्रवेश

sports field
khel kā
maidān
खेल का मैदान

refectory
bhojan kakṣ
भोजन कक्ष

hall of residence
chhātrāvās
छात्रावास

health centre
svāsthya kendr
स्वास्थ्य केंद्र

campus | parisar | परिसर

catalogue
sūchī
सूची

librarian
pustakālaya adhyakṣ
पुस्तकालय अध्यक्ष

loans desk
pustak prāpti
पुस्तक प्राप्ति

bookshelf
pustakoṃ kī almārī
पुस्तकों की अलमारी

periodical
patrikāeṃ
पत्रिकाएं

journal
patrikāeṃ
पत्रिकाएं

library | pustakālaya | पुस्तकालय

vocabulary • śabdāvalī • शब्दावली

library card pustakālaya kārḍ पुस्तकालय कार्ड	**enquiries** pūchhtāchh पूछताछ	**loan** udhār उधार
reading room adhyayan kakṣ अध्ययन कक्ष	**borrow (v)** udhār lenā उधार लेना	**book** pustak पुस्तक
reading list adhyayan sūchī अध्ययन सूची	**reserve (v)** surakṣit karnā सुरक्षित करना	**title** śīrṣak शीर्षक
return date deya tithi देय तिथि	**renew (v)** navīkṛt karvānā नवीकृत करवाना	**aisle** galiyārā गलियारा

undergraduate
snātak vidyārthī
स्नातक विद्यार्थी

lecturer
prādhyāpak
प्राध्यापक

graduate
snātak
स्नातक

robe
chogā | चोग़ा

lecture theatre
lekchar thiyeṭar | लेक्चर थियेटर

graduation ceremony
snātak samāroh | स्नातक समारोह

schools • vidyālaya • विद्यालय

model
model
मॉडल

art college | kalā
mahāvidyālaya | कला महाविद्यालय

music school
saṅgīt vidyālaya | संगीत विद्यालय

dance academy
nṛtya akādmī | नृत्य अकादमी

vocabulary • śabdāvalī • शब्दावली

scholarship
chhātrvṛtti
छात्रवृत्ति

research
anusaṅdhān
अनुसंधान

dissertation
śodh nibandh
शोध निबंध

medicine
āyurvijñān
आयुर्विज्ञान

philosophy
darśan śāstr
दर्शन शास्त्र

diploma
ḍiplomā
डिप्लोमा

masters
viśārad
विशारद

department
vibhāg
विभाग

zoology
prāṇī vijñān
प्राणी विज्ञान

literature
sāhitya
साहित्य

degree
upādhi
उपाधि

doctorate
doctorate
डॉक्ट्रेट

law
ḳānūn
क़ानून

physics
bhautikī
भौतिकी

history of art
kalā kā itihās
कला का इतिहास

postgraduate
snātakottar
स्नातकोत्तर

thesis
śodh prabandh
शोध प्रबंध

engineering
abhiyāntrikī
अभियांत्रिकी

politics
rājnīti
राजनीति

economics
arthśāstr
अर्थशास्त्र

work
kārya
कार्य

office • kāryālaya • कार्यालय
office • kāryālaya • कार्यालय

monitor
monitor
मॉनीटर

computer
kampyūṭar
कंप्यूटर

keyboard
kī borḍ
की–बोर्ड

telephone
dūrbhāṣ
दूरभाष

desk
mez
मेज़

desktop organizer
desktop organizer
डेस्कटॉप ऑर्गेनाइज़र

file
fāil
फ़ाइल

in-tray
in-ṭre
इन–ट्रे

out-tray
āuṭ-ṭre
आउट–ट्रे

notebook
copy
कॉपी

label
chiṭ
चिट

wastebasket
raddī kī ṭokrī
रद्दी की टोकरी

swivel chair
ghumāū kursī
घुमाऊ कुर्सी

drawer
darāz
दराज़

filing cabinet
fāil-darāz
फ़ाइल–दराज़

---

office equipment • kāryālayī upkaraṇ • कार्यालयी उपकरण

paper tray
pepar ṭre
पेपर ट्रे

paper guide
pepar gāiḍ
पेपर गाइड

fax
faiks
फ़ैक्स

printer
priṇṭar | प्रिंटर

fax machine
faiks maśīn | फ़ैक्स मशीन

172

office supplies • kāryālayī vastuem • कार्यालयी वस्तुएं

compliments slip
preṣak chiṭ
प्रेषक चिट

letterhead
laiṭar haiḍ
लैटर हैड

envelope
lifāfā | लिफ़ाफ़ा

box file
box fāil
बॉक्स फ़ाइल

tab
ṭaib
टैब

divider
vibhājak
विभाजक

clipboard
klip borḍ
क्लिप बोर्ड

note pad
noṭ paiḍ
नोट पैड

hanging file
haiṅgiṅg fāil
हैंगिंग फाइल

concertina file
concertina fāil
कॉनसर्टीना फ़ाइल

lever arch file
ārch fāil
आर्च फ़ाइल

staples
sṭaipals
स्टैपल्स

sticky tape
ṭep
टेप

ink pad
syāhī paiḍ
स्याही पैड

personal organizer
nijī organizer
निजी ऑर्गेनाइज़र

stapler
sṭeplar
स्टेप्लर

tape dispenser
ṭep ḍispeńsar
टेप डिस्पेंसर

hole punch
hol pañch
होल पंच

rubber stamp
rabar kī mohar
रबड़ की मोहर

rubber band
rabar baiṇḍ
रबड़ बैंड

bulldog clip
barī klip
बड़ी क्लिप

paper clip
pepar klip
पेपर क्लिप

drawing pin
drawing pin
ड्रॉइंग पिन

notice board
sūchnāpaṭ | सूचनापट

office • kāryālaya • कार्यालय

flipchart
flip chārt
फ़्लिप चार्ट

minutes
kāryavr̥tt
कार्यवृत्त

easel
chitrādhār
चित्राधार

manager
prabandhak
प्रबंधक

proposal
prastāv
प्रस्ताव

report
prativedan
प्रतिवेदन

executive
ekzīkyūṭiv
एक्ज़ीक्यूटिव

meeting | sabhā/mīṭiṅg | सभा/मीटिंग

vocabulary • śabdāvalī • शब्दावली

meeting room sabhā kakṣ सभा कक्ष	**attend (v)** upasthit rahnā उपस्थित रहना
agenda kāryasūchī कार्यसूची	**chair (v)** adhyakṣtā karnā अध्यक्षता करना

What time is the meeting?
mīṭiṅg kis samaya hai?
मीटिंग किस समय है?

What are your office hours?
tumhāre kāryālaya kā kyā samaya hai?
तुम्हारे कार्यालय का क्या समय है?

projector
projekṭar
प्रोजेक्टर

speaker
vaktā
वक्ता

presentation | prastutīkaraṇ | प्रस्तुतीकरण

business • vyavsāya • व्यवसाय

laptop
laptop
लैपटॉप

notes
noṭs
नोट्स

businessman
vyavsāyī
व्यवसायी

businesswoman
mahilā vyavsāyī
महिला व्यवसायी

business lunch | biznes lanch | बिज़नेस लंच

business trip | biznes ṭrip | बिज़नेस ट्रिप

diary | ḍāyarī | डायरी

appointment
milne kā samaya
मिलने का समय

client
grāhak
ग्राहक

palmtop
palmtop
पामटॉप

managing director
prabandh nideśak
प्रबंध निदेशक

business deal
vyāvsāyik saudā | व्यावसायिक सौदा

---

vocabulary • śabdāvalī • शब्दावली

company
kampnī
कंपनी

head office
pradhān kāryālaya
प्रधान कार्यालय

branch
śākhā
शाखा

staff
karmchārī varg
कर्मचारी वर्ग

salary
vetan
वेतन

payroll
vetanbhogī sūchī
वेतनभोगी सूची

accounts department
lekhā vibhāg
लेखा विभाग

marketing department
vipṇan vibhāg
विपणन विभाग

sales department
bikrī vibhāg
बिक्री विभाग

legal department
kānūnī vibhāg
क़ानूनी विभाग

customer service department
grāhak sevā vibhāg
ग्राहक सेवा विभाग

personnel department
kārmik vibhāg
कार्मिक विभाग

---

computer • kampyūṭar • कंप्यूटर

printer
prinṭar
प्रिंटर

monitor
monitor
मॉनीटर

screen
skrīn
स्क्रीन

central processing unit
senṭral prosesiṅg yūniṭ
सेंट्रल प्रोसेसिंग यूनिट

scanner
skainar
स्कैनर

speaker
spīkar | स्पीकर

key
kī | की

KEYBOARD
kī paiḍ | की पैड

mouse
māus | माउस

hardware | hārḍveyar | हार्डवेयर

disk
ḍisk | डिस्क

laptop
laptop | लैपटॉप

hard drive
hārḍ ḍrāiv
हार्ड ड्राइव

modem
moḍem
मोडेम

vocabulary • śabdāvalī • शब्दावली		
memory memorī मेमोरी	**software** software सॉफ़्टवेयर	**server** sarvar सर्वर
RAM raim रैम	**application** eplīkeśan एप्लीकेशन	**port** porṭ पोर्ट
bytes bāiṭs बाइट्स	**program** progrām प्रोग्राम	**processor** prosesar प्रोसेसर
system sisṭam सिस्टम	**network** neṭvark नेटवर्क	**power cable** vidyut tār विद्युत तार

desktop • desktop • डेस्कटॉप

menubar
menyu bār
मेन्यु बार

toolbar
ṭūlbār
टूलबार

wallpaper
wallpaper
वॉलपेपर

font
font
फ़ॉन्ट

icon
āikan
आइकन

scrollbar
scrollbar
स्क्रॉलबार

window
vinḍo
विंडो

file | fāil | फ़ाइल

folder | folḍar | फ़ोल्डर

trash | ṭrais | ट्रैश

internet • inṭarneṭ • इंटरनेट

email • ī-mel • ई–मेल

browser
brāuzar
ब्राउज़र

inbox
inbox
इनबॉक्स

website
vebsāiṭ
वेबसाइट

browse (v)
brāuz | ब्राउज़

email address
ī-mel patā
ई–मेल पता

vocabulary • śabdāvalī • शब्दावली

connect (v) sampark karnā संपर्क करना	**service provider** sevā pradātā सेवा प्रदाता	**log on (v)** log on karnā लॉग ऑन करना	**download (v)** ḍāunloḍ karnā डाउनलोड करना	**send (v)** bhejnā भेजना	**save (v)** surakṣit karnā सुरक्षित करना
instal (v) instal karnā इनस्टॉल करना	**email account** ī-mel akāunṭ ई–मेल अकाउंट	**on-line** on lāin ऑन लाइन	**attachment** aṭaichmenṭ अटैचमेंट	**receive (v)** prāpt karnā प्राप्त करना	**search (v)** ḍhūṃṛhnā ढूंढ़ना

media • mīḍiyā • मीडिया

television studio • ṭelīvizan stūḍiyo • टेलीविज़न स्टूडियो

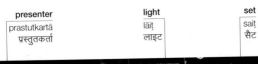

presenter	light	set
prastutkartā	lāiṭ	saiṭ
प्रस्तुतकर्ता	लाइट	सैट

camera	camera crane	cameraman
kaimrā	kaimrā kren	kaimrāmain
कैमरा	कैमरा क्रेन	कैमरामैन

vocabulary • śabdāvalī • शब्दावली

channel	news	press	soap	cartoon	live
chainal	samāchār	prais	nāṭak	kārṭūn	sīdhā prasāraṇ
चैनल	समाचार	प्रैस	नाटक	कार्टून	सीधा प्रसारण

programming	documentary	television series	game show	prerecorded	broadcast (v)
progrāmiṅg	vṛttchitr	ṭelīvizan sṛṅkhlā	gem śo	pūrv recorded	prasārit karnā
प्रोग्रामिंग	वृत्तचित्र	टेलीविज़न शृंखला	गेम शो	पूर्व रिकॉर्डेड	प्रसारित करना

interviewer
sākṣātkārkartā
साक्षात्कारकर्ता

reporter
patrakār | पत्रकार

autocue
teli promter | टेली प्रॉमटर

newsreader | samāchār
vāchak | समाचार वाचक

actors
abhinetā | अभिनेता

sound boom
sāuṇḍ būm | साउंड बूम

clapper board | klaipar
borḍ | क्लैपर बोर्ड

film set
film saiṭ | फ़िल्म सैट

radio • reḍiyo • रेडियो

vocabulary • śabdāvalī • शब्दावली	
radio station reḍiyo steśan रेडियो स्टेशन	**frequency** āvṛtti आवृत्ति
broadcast prasāraṇ प्रसारण	**volume** dhvani star ध्वनि स्तर
wavelength vevlenth वेवलेंथ	**DJ** ḍīje डीजे
long wave long vev लॉन्ग वेव	**short wave** short vev शॉर्ट वेव
tune (v) chainal lagānā चैनल लगाना	**medium wave** mīḍiyam vev मीडियम वेव

mixing desk
miksing ḍesk
मिक्सिंग डेस्क

microphone
māikrofon
माइक्रोफ़ोन

sound technician
sāuṇḍ taknīśiyan
साउंड तकनीशियन

recording studio | recording sṭūḍiyo | रिकॉर्डिंग स्टूडियो

law • k̤ānūn • क़ानून

court officer
nyāyālaya adhikārī
न्यायालय अधिकारी

witness
gavāh
गवाह

judge
jaj | जज

lawyer
vakīl
वकील

jury
jūrī
जूरी

jury box
jūrī box
जूरी बॉक्स

courtroom
nyāyālaya | न्यायालय

prosecution
abhiyojan
अभियोजन

court official
nyāyālaya karmchārī
न्यायालय कर्मचारी

---

vocabulary • śabdāvalī • शब्दावली

lawyer's office vakīl kā kāryālaya वकील का कार्यालय	**summons** saman समन	**writ** riṭ रिट	**court case** muk̤addmā मुक़द्दमा
legal advice k̤ānūnī salāh क़ानूनी सलाह	**statement** bayān बयान	**court date** nyāyālaya kī tārīk̤h न्यायालय की तारीख़	**charge** abhiyog अभियोग
client muvakkil मुवक्किल	**warrant** vāraṇṭ वारंट	**plea** pairavī पैरवी	**accused** abhiyukt अभियुक्त

---

defendant
prativādī
प्रतिवादी

stenographer
āśulipik
आशुलिपिक

suspect
sandigdh
संदिग्ध

photofit
anumānit tasvīr
अनुमानित तस्वीर

criminal
aprādhī
अपराधी

criminal record
āprādhik record
आपराधिक रिकॉर्ड

defence
bachāv pakṣ
बचाव पक्ष

prison guard | jel kā
pahredār | जेल का पहरेदार

cell | jel kī
koṭhrī | जेल की कोठरी

prison
jel | जेल

vocabulary • śabdāvalī • शब्दावली

evidence	**guilty**	**bail**	**I want to see a lawyer.**
sabūt	doṣī	zamānat	mujhe ek vakīl chāhie.
सबूत	दोषी	ज़मानत	मुझे एक वकील चाहिए
verdict	**acquitted**	**appeal**	**Where is the courthouse?**
faislā	abhimukt	apīl	nyāyālaya kahāṃ hai?
फ़ैसला	अभिमुक्त	अपील	न्यायालय कहां है?
innocent	**sentence**	**parole**	**Can I post bail?**
bekasūr	daṇḍādeś	pairol	kyā maiṃ zamānat bhar saktā hūṃ?
बेक़सूर	दंडादेश	पैरोल	क्या मैं ज़मानत भर सकता हूं?

farm • khet • खेत

farmland
kr̥ṣi bhūmi
कृषि भूमि

farmyard
ahātā
अहाता

outbuilding
āuṭ hāus
आउट हाउस

farmhouse
fārm hāus
फ़ार्म हाउस

field
khet
खेत

barn
khalihān
खलिहान

farmer
kisān
किसान

vegetable plot
śāk khet
शाक खेत

gate
darvāzā
दरवाज़ा

hedge
meṛ
मेड़

fence
bāṛ
बाड़

pasture
charāgāh
चरागाह

livestock
paśudhan
पशुधन

cultivator
phāl
फाल

tractor | ṭrekṭar | ट्रेक्टर

combine harvester | kaṭāī maśīn | कटाई मशीन

types of farm · khetoṃ ke prakār · खेतों के प्रकार

crop
fasal
फ़सल

arable farm
khetī yogya bhūmi
खेती योग्य भूमि

dairy farm
ḍerī fārm
डेरी फ़ार्म

flock
jhuṇḍ
झुंड

sheep farm
bheroṃ kā bāṛā
भेड़ों का बाड़ा

poultry farm | murgī pālan
kendr | मुर्गी पालन केंद्र

pig farm
śūkar pālan kendr
शूकरपालन केंद्र

fish farm
machhlī pālan kṣetr
मछली पालन क्षेत्र

fruit farm
phaloṃ kā bāġ
फलों का बाग़

vineyard
aṃgūr kā bāġ
अंगूर का बाग़

actions · khetoṃ ke kāmkāj · खेतों के कामकाज

furrow
hal rekhā
हल रेखा

plough (v)
jotnā | जोतना

sow (v)
bonā | बोना

milk (v)
dūdh duhnā | दूध दुहना

feed (v)
charnā | चरना

water (v)
sīṃchnā | सींचना

harvest (v)
fasal kāṭnā | फ़सल काटना

vocabulary · śabdāvalī · शब्दावली		
herbicide	**herd**	**trough**
vanaspatināśak	jhuṇḍ	nāṃd
वनस्पतिनाशक	झुंड	नांद
pesticide	**silo**	**plant (v)**
kīṭnāśak	khattī	ropnā
कीटनाशक	खत्ती	रोपना

farm • khet • खेत

crops • fasal • फ़सल

wheat
gehūṃ | गेहूं

corn
makaī | मकई

barley
jau | जौ

rapeseed | safed
sarsoṃ | सफ़ेद सरसों

sunflower
sūrajmukhī | सूरजमुखी

bale
gaṭṭhā | गट्ठा

hay
sūkhī ghās | सूखी घास

alfalfa
alfālfā | अल्फ़ाल्फ़ा

tobacco
tambākū | तंबाकू

rice
dhān | धान

tea
chāya | चाय

coffee
coffee | कॉफ़ी

flax
alsī
अलसी

sugarcane
gannā
गन्ना

cotton
kapās
कपास

scarecrow
bijūkā
बिजूका

livestock · paśudhan · पशुधन

piglet
śiśu sūar
शिशु सूअर

pig
sūar | सूअर

calf
bachhṛā
बछड़ा

cow
gāya | गाय

bull
bail | बैल

sheep
bheṛ | भेड़

lamb
meṛhā | मेढ़ा

kid
memnā | मेमना

goat
bakrī | बकरी

foal
śiśu aśv
शिशु अश्व

horse
ghoṛā | घोड़ा

donkey
gadhā | गधा

chick
chūzā | चूज़ा

chicken
murgī | मुर्गी

cockerel
murgā | मुर्गा

turkey
ṭarkī | टर्की

duckling
śiśu bataḳh
शिशु बतख़

duck
bataḳh | बतख़

stable
astabal | अस्तबल

pen
bāṛā | बाड़ा

chicken coop
darbā | दड़बा

pigsty
sūarbāṛā | सूअरबाड़ा

construction • nirmāṇ kārya • निर्माण कार्य

scaffolding
pāṛ | पाड़

pallet
takhte
तख़्ते

ladder
sīṛhī
सीढ़ी

window
khiṛkī
खिड़की

rafter
kaṛī/śahtīr
कड़ी/शहतीर

fork-lift truck
kren
क्रेन

building site
nirmāṇ sthal
निर्माण स्थल

lintel
chaukhaṭ
चौखट

wall
dīvār
दीवार

girder
garḍar
गर्डर

hard hat
ṭop
टोप

toolbelt
auzār peṭī
औज़ार पेटी

beam
śahtīr
शहतीर

cement
sīmenṭ
सीमेंट

build (v)
nirmāṇ karnā | निर्माण करना

builder
rājgīr | राजगीर

cement mixer | sīmenṭ
miksar | सीमेंट मिक्सर

materials • sāmān • सामान

brick
īṃṭ | ईंट

timber
imāratī lakṛī | इमारती लकड़ी

roof tile
paṭiyā | पटिया

concrete block
concrete block | कॉन्क्रीट ब्लॉक

tools • auzār • औज़ार

mortar
gārā | गारा

handle
hatthā
हत्था

trowel
kannī | कन्नी

spirit level
talmāpī | तलमापी

sledgehammer
hathaurā | हथौड़ा

pickaxe
kudāl | कुदाल

shovel
belchā | बेलचा

machinery • maśīnarī • मशीनरी

roller
rolar | रोलर

dumper truck
ḍampar | डम्पर

support
ādhār stambh
आधार स्तंभ

hook
huk
हुक

crane | kren | क्रेन

roadworks • saṛak nirmāṇ kārya • सड़क निर्माण कार्य

tarmac
tārkol
तारकोल

cone
kon
कोन

pneumatic drill
nyūmaiṭik ḍril
न्यूमैटिक ड्रिल

resurfacing
punaḥ parat lagānā
पुनः परत लगाना

occupations 1 • vyavasāya 1 • व्यवसाय

carpenter
baṛhaī | बढ़ई

electrician | bijlī mistrī |
बिजली मिस्त्री

plumber
nalkār | नलकार

builder
rājgīr | राजगीर

gardener
mālī | माली

vacuum cleaner
vekyūm klīnar
वेक्यूम क्लीनर

cleaner
safaī karmī | सफ़ाई कर्मी

mechanic
mistrī | मिस्त्री

butcher
ḳasāī | क़साई

scissors
kaiṃchī
कैंची

hairdresser | keś
prasādhak | केश प्रसाधक

fishmonger
machhlī vikretā
मछली विक्रेता

greengrocer
sabzī vikretā
सब्ज़ी विक्रेता

florist
phool vikretā
फूल विक्रेता

barber
nāī | नाई

jeweller
sunār | सुनार

shop assistant | dukān
sahāyak | दुकान सहायक

estate agent | bhūsam-
patti dalāl | भूसंपत्ति दलाल

optician | dṛṣṭi
parīkṣak | दृष्टि परीक्षक

mask
naḳāb
नक़ाब

dentist | dant
chikitsak | दंत चिकित्सक

doctor
chikitsak | चिकित्सक

pharmacist
auṣadhkārak | औषधकारक

nurse
nars | नर्स

vet | paśu chikitsak |
पशु चिकित्सक

farmer
kisān | किसान

fisherman
machhuārā | मछुआरा

machine-
gun
maśīngan
मशीनगन

identity badge
pahchān paṭṭikā
पहचान–पट्टिका

uniform
vardī
वर्दी

security guard |
surakṣā karmī | सुरक्षा
कर्मी

sailor
nāvik | नाविक

soldier
sainik | सैनिक

policeman | pulis
karmī | पुलिस कर्मी

fireman
fāyarmain | फ़ायरमैन

occupations 2 • vyavasāya 2 • व्यवसाय

lawyer
vakīl | वकील

accountant
lekhākār | लेखाकार

model
namūnā
नमूना

architect
vāstukār | वास्तुकार

scientist
vaijñānik | वैज्ञानिक

teacher
adhyāpak | अध्यापक

librarian
pustakālaya adhyakṣ
पुस्तकालय अध्यक्ष

receptionist
svāgatkartā | स्वागतकर्ता

mailbag
ḍāk thailā
डाक–थैला

postman
ḍākiyā | डाकिया

bus driver
bas chālak | बस चालक

lorry driver
ṭrak chālak | ट्रक चालक

taxi driver | ṭaiksī
chālak | टैक्सी चालक

pilot | vimān
chālak | विमान चालक

air stewardess | vimān
parichārikā | विमान परिचारिका

travel agent | ṭreval
ejenṭ | ट्रेवल एजेंट

chef's hat
rasoie kī ṭopī
रसोइए की
टोपी

chef
rasoiyā | रसोइया

tutu
baile skarṭ
बैले स्कर्ट

musician
saṅgītkār | संगीतकार

dancer
nartakī | नर्तकी

actor
abhinetā | अभिनेता

singer
gāyikā | गायिका

waitress
parichārikā | परिचारिका

barman
bārmain | बारमैन

sportsman
khilāṛī | खिलाड़ी

sculptor
mūrtikār | मूर्तिकार

notes
noṭs
नोट्स

painter
chitrakār | चित्रकार

photographer
chhāyākār | छायाकार

newsreader | samāchār
vāchak | समाचार वाचक

journalist
patrakār | पत्रकार

editor
sampādak | संपादक

designer
ḍizāinar | डिज़ाइनर

seamstress
darzin | दर्ज़िन

tailor
darzī | दर्ज़ी

transport
parivahan
परिवहन

roads • saṛkeṁ • सड़कें

motorway
moṭar mārg
मोटर मार्ग

toll booth
ṭol būth
टोल बूथ

road markings
mārg chihn
मार्ग चिह्न

slip road
sāiḍ kī sarak
साइड की सड़क

one-way
iktarfā rāstā
इकतरफ़ा रास्ता

divider
vibhājak
विभाजक

junction
jaṅkśan
जंक्शन

traffic light
yātāyāt battī
यातायात बत्ती

inside lane
bhītrī len
भीतरी लेन

middle lane
madhya len
मध्य लेन

outside lane
bāhrī len
बाहरी लेन

exit ramp
nikās ḍhalān
निकास ढलान

traffic
yātāyāt
यातायात

flyover
flāī ovar
फ्लाईओवर

hard shoulder
sarak kā kinārā
सड़क का किनारा

lorry
ṭrak
ट्रक

central reservation
kendrīya ārakṣaṇ
केंद्रीय आरक्षण

underpass
bhūmigat mārg
भूमिगत मार्ग

emergency phone
āpātkālīn dūrbhāṣ
आपातकालीन दूरभाष

disabled parking
viklāṅg
pārkiṅg sthal
विकलांग
पार्किंग स्थल

traffic jam
yātāyāt jām | यातायात जाम

**pedestrian
crossing**
paidal pārpath
पैदल पारपथ

map
mānchitr
मानचित्र

parking meter
pārkiṅg mīṭar
पार्किंग मीटर

traffic policeman
yātāyāt puliskarmī
यातायात पुलिसकर्मी

vocabulary • śabdāvalī • शब्दावली		
roundabout gol chakkar गोल चक्कर	**park (v)** pārk karnā पार्क करना	**roadworks** saṛak nirmāṇ kārya सड़क निर्माण कार्य
tow away (v) ṭo karnā टो करना	**overtake (v)** āge nikālnā आगे निकालना	**Is this the road to...?** kyā... jāne kā yahī mārg hai? क्या... जाने का यही मार्ग है?
diversion parivartit mārg परिवर्तित मार्ग	**drive (v)** gāṛī chalānā गाड़ी चलाना	**dual carriageway** dvaya vāhan mārg द्वय वाहन मार्ग
crash barrier ṭakkar avrodh टक्कर अवरोध	**reverse (v)** pīchhe karnā पीछे करना	**Where can I park?** maiṃ kahāṃ pārk kar saktā hūṃ? मैं कहां पार्क कर सकता हूं?

road signs • yātāyāt saṅket • यातायात संकेत

no entry
praveś niṣedh
प्रवेश निषेध

speed limit
gati sīmā
गति सीमा

hazard
sāvdhān
सावधान

no stopping
ruknā manā hai
रुकना मना है

no right turn
dāeṃ muṛnā niṣedh
दाएं मुड़ना निषेध

bus · bas · बस

driver's seat
chālak sīṭ
चालक सीट

handrail
haindrel
हैंडरेल

automatic door
svachālit darvāzā
स्वचालित दरवाज़ा

front wheel
āge kā pahiyā
आगे का पहिया

luggage hold
sāmān kakṣ
सामान कक्ष

door | darvāzā | दरवाज़ा

coach | bas | बस

types of buses · basoṃ ke prakār · बसों के प्रकार

route number
rūṭ nambar
रूट नंबर

driver
chālak
चालक

double-decker bus
ḍabal-ḍekar bas
डबल–डेकर बस

tram
ṭrām | ट्राम

trolley bus
trolley bas | ट्रॉली बस

school bus | skūl bas | स्कूल बस

rear wheel
pichhlā pahiyā
पिछला पहिया

window
khiṛkī
खिड़की

stop button
stop baṭan
स्टॉप बटन

bus ticket
bas ṭikaṭ | बस टिकट

bell
ghaṇṭī | घंटी

bus station
bas aḍḍā | बस अड्डा

bus stop
bas stop
बस स्टॉप

vocabulary • śabdāvalī • शब्दावली		
timetable samaya sūchī समय सूची	**fare** kirāyā किराया	**wheelchair access** vhīlcheyar suvidhā व्हीलचेयर सुविधा
bus shelter bas khaṛī karne kī jagah बस खड़ी करने की जगह	**Do you stop at…?** kyā āp … par rokeṅge? क्या आप … पर रोकेंगे? **Which bus goes to…?** … ke lie kaun sī bas jātī hai? … के लिए कौन सी बस जाती है?	

minibus
minī bas | मिनी बस

tourist bus | paryaṭak bas | पर्यटक बस

shuttle bus | śaṭal bas | शटल बस

car 1 • kār • कार

exterior • bāhrī svarūp • बाहरी स्वरूप

wing mirror
viṅg mirar
विंग मिरर

windscreen
sāmne kā śīśā
सामने का शीशा

rearview mirror
riyarvyū mirar
रियरव्यू मिरर

windscreen wiper
vinḍskrīn vāipar
विंडस्क्रीन वाइपर

door
darvāzā
दरवाज़ा

bonnet
bonaṭ
बोनट

boot
ḍikkī
डिक्की

indicator
saṅketak
संकेतक

licence plate
nambar pleṭ
नंबर प्लेट

bumper
bampar
बम्पर

headlight
āge kī battī
आगे की बत्ती

wheel
pahiyā
पहिया

tyre
ṭāyar
टायर

luggage
sāmān
सामान

roofrack
kairiyar | कैरियर

tailgate | ḍikkī kā darvāzā |
डिक्की का दरवाज़ा

seat belt
sīṭ belṭ | सीट बेल्ट

child seat
bālak-sīṭ | बालक–सीट

types • prakār • प्रकार

small car
chhoṭī kār | छोटी कार

hatchback
haichbaik | हैचबैक

saloon
salūn | सलून

estate
vaigan | वैगन

convertible
kanvarṭibal
कन्वर्टीबल

sports car
sporṭs kār
स्पोर्ट्स कार

people carrier
pīpul kairiyar
पीपुल कैरियर

four-wheel drive
for-vhīl ḍrāiv
फ़ोर–व्हील ड्राइव

vintage
vinṭej kār | विंटेज कार

limousine
limozīn | लिमोज़ीन

petrol station • peṭrol sṭeśan • पेट्रोल स्टेशन

petrol pump
peṭrol pamp
पेट्रोल पंप

price
mūlya
मूल्य

forecourt
dālān
दालान

air supply
havā saplāī
हवा सप्लाई

vocabulary • śabdāvalī • शब्दावली		
oil tel तेल	**leaded** sīsā yukt सीसा युक्त	**car wash** kār dhulāī कार धुलाई
petrol peṭrol पेट्रोल	**diesel** ḍīzal डीज़ल	**antifreeze** enṭī frīz एंटी फ़्रीज़
unleaded sīsā rahit सीसा रहित	**garage** gairej गैरेज	**screenwash** screenwash स्क्रीनवॉश

Fill the tank, please.
kṛpyā pūrī ṭankī bhar dem
कृपया पूरी टंकी भर दें ।

car 2 • kār 2 • कार

interior • inṭīriyar • इंटीरियर

door lock
darvāze kā lock
दरवाज़े का लॉक

armrest
ārmresṭ
आर्मरेस्ट

handle
haiṇḍil
हैंडिल

back seat
pichhlī sīṭ | पिछली सीट

headrest
sirhānā | सिरहाना

---

vocabulary • śabdāvalī • शब्दावली

two-door do-darvāzā दो–दरवाज़ा	**four-door** chār-darvāzā चार–दरवाज़ा	**automatic** svachālit स्वचालित	**brake** brek ब्रेक	**accelerator** aiksīlreṭar ऐक्सीलरेटर
three-door tīn-darvāzā तीन–दरवाज़ा	**manual** mānav-chālit मानव–चालित	**ignition** igniīśan इग्नीशन	**clutch** klach क्लच	**air conditioning** vātānukūlan वातानुकूलन

Can you tell me the way to...?
kyā āp mujhe... jāne kā rāstā
batāeṅge?
क्या आप मुझे... जाने का रास्ता बताएंगे?

Where is the car park?
kār pārkiṅg kahām̐ hai?
कार पार्किंग कहां है?

Can I park here?
kyā maim̐ yahām̐ gāṛī khaṛī kar
saktā hūm̐?
क्या मैं यहां गाड़ी खड़ी कर सकता हूं?

---

controls • niyantraṇ • नियंत्रण

steering wheel
stīyariṅg
स्टीयरिंग

horn
horn
हॉर्न

dashboard
ḍaisborḍ
डैशबोर्ड

hazard lights
saṅkaṭ sūchak battī
संकट सूचक बत्ती

satellite navigation
upgrah mārgdarśan
उपग्रह मार्गदर्शन

left-hand drive | bāīṃ or kī ḍrāiv | बाईं ओर की ड्राइव

temperature gauge
tāpmān māpak
तापमान मापक

rev counter
parikramaṇ gaṇak
परिक्रमण गणक

speedometer
spīḍ mīṭar
स्पीड मीटर

fuel gauge
īndhan māpī
ईंधन मापी

car stereo
stīriyo
स्टीरियो

lights switch
lāiṭ baṭan
लाइट बटन

heater controls
hīṭar kaṇṭrol
हीटर कंट्रोल

odometer
pathmāpak yantr
पथमापक यंत्र

gearstick
gīyar
गीयर

air bag
eyar baig
एयर बैग

right-hand drive | dāīṃ or kī ḍrāiv | दाईं ओर की ड्राइव

car 3 • kār 3 • कार

mechanics • yāntrikī • यांत्रिकी

screen wash reservoir
screen wash ḍibbā
स्क्रीन वॉश डिब्बा

dipstick
ḍipasṭik
डिपस्टिक

air filter
vāyu chhalnī
वायु छलनी

brake fluid reservoir
brek dravya ḍibbā
ब्रेक द्रव्य डिब्बा

battery
baiṭrī
बैटरी

bodywork
bodywork
बॉडीवर्क

coolant reservoir
kūlenṭ ḍibbā
कूलेंट डिब्बा

cylinder head
silenḍar
सिलेंडर

pipe
pāip
पाइप

sunroof
kār kī chhat
कार की छत

radiator
reḍieṭar
रेडिएटर

fan
paṅkhā
पंखा

engine
injan
इंजन

hubcap
dhurī kā
ḍhakkan
धुरी का ढक्कन

gearbox
garārī baksā
गरारी बक्सा

transmission
ṭrānsmiśan
ट्रांसमिशन

driveshaft
ḍrāiv śāfṭ
ड्राइव शाफ्ट

puncture • paṅkchar • पंक्चर

spare tyre
atirikt ṭāyar
अतिरिक्त टायर

wrench
pānā
पाना

wheel nuts
ṭāyar ke pech
टायर के पेच

jack
jaik
जैक

change a wheel (v)
ṭāyar badalnā | टायर बदलना

roof
chhat
छत

suspension
ālamban chhaṛ
आलंबन छड़

silencer
dhvanirodhak
ध्वनिरोधक

exhaust pipe
dhuāṃ nikās nalī
धुआं निकास नली

vocabulary • śabdāvalī • शब्दावली

car accident
kār durghaṭnā
कार दुर्घटना

breakdown
brek ḍāun
ब्रेक डाउन

insurance
bīmā
बीमा

tow truck
ṭo ṭrak
टो ट्रक

mechanic
maikenik
मैकेनिक

tyre pressure
ṭāyar preśar
टायर प्रेशर

fuse box
fyūz baksā
फ्यूज़ बक्सा

spark plug
spārk plag
स्पार्क प्लग

fan belt
fain belṭ
फ़ैन बेल्ट

turbocharger
ṭarbo chārjar
टर्बो चार्जर

distributor
vitrak
वितरक

chassis
chesis
चेसिस

handbrake
haiṇḍ brek
हैंड ब्रेक

alternator
pratyāvartak
प्रत्यावर्तक

cam belt
kem belṭ
केम बेल्ट

timing
ṭāimiṅg
टाइमिंग

petrol tank
peṭrol ṭaṅkī
पेट्रोल टंकी

My car won't start.
merī kār sṭārṭ nahīṃ
ho rahī.
मेरी कार स्टार्ट नहीं हो रही।

My car has broken down.
merī gāṛī kharāb ho
gaī hai.
मेरी गाड़ी ख़राब हो गई है।

motorbike • moṭarbāik • मोटरबाइक

helmet
hailmeṭ
हैलमेट

indicator
saṅketak
संकेतक

speedometer
gatimāpak
गतिमापक

brake
brek
ब्रेक

clutch
klach
क्लच

horn
horn
हॉर्न

throttle
gati niyantrak
गति नियंत्रक

controls
niyantraṇ yantr | नियंत्रण यंत्र

carrier
samvāhak
संवाहक

reflector
parāvartak
परावर्तक

pillion
pichhlī sīṭ
पिछली सीट

seat
sīṭ
सीट

engine
injan
इंजन

fuel tank
īndhan ṭaiṅk
ईंधन टैंक

tail light
pichhlī lāiṭ
पिछली लाइट

exhaust pipe
dhuāṃ nikās nalī
धुआं निकास नली

silencer
dhvanirodhak
ध्वनिरोधक

oil tank
tel kī ṭaṅkī
तेल की टंकी

gearbox
garārī baksā
गरारी बक्सा

air filter
vāyu chhalnī
वायु छलनी

visor
hailmeṭ kā śīśā
हैलमेट का शीशा

leathers
laidar vastr
लैदर वस्त्र

reflector strap
parāvartak paṭṭī
परावर्तक पड्डी

knee pad
nī paiḍ
नी पैड

clothing | vastr | वस्त्र

headlight
sāmne kī lāiṭ
सामने की लाइट

suspension
ālamban chhaṛ
आलंबन छड़

mudguard
miṭṭī rodhak
मिट्टी रोधक

brake pedal
brek paiḍal
ब्रेक पैडल

axle
dhurī
धुरी

tyre
pahiyā
पहिया

types • prakār • प्रकार

racing bike | resiṅg bāik | रेसिंग बाइक

windshield
vinḍśīlaḍ
विंडशील्ड

tourer | moṭar sāikil | मोटर साइकिल

dirt bike | ḍarṭ bāik | डर्ट बाइक

stand
sṭainḍ | स्टैंड

scooter | skūṭar | स्कूटर

bicycle • sāikil • साइकिल

saddle
gaddī
गद्दी

seat post
sīṭ post
सीट पोस्ट

water bottle
pānī kī botal
पानी की बोतल

frame
frem
फ़्रेम

brake
brek
ब्रेक

hub
dhurī
धुरी

gears
gīyar
गीयर

rim
rim
रिम

tyre
ṭāyar
टायर

chain
chen
चेन

cog
dāṃtā
दांता

pedal
paiḍal
पैडल

tandem | do sīṭoṃ vālī sāikil
दो सीटों वाली साइकिल

racing bike
resiṅg bāik
रेसिंग बाइक

mountain bike
māunṭen bāik
माउंटेन बाइक

touring bike
ṭūriṅg bāik | टूरिंग बाइक

helmet
hailmeṭ
हैलमेट

road bike
roḍ bāik | रोड बाइक

cycle lane | sāikil len | साइकिल लेन

crossbar
crossbar
कॉसबार

handlebar
haiṇḍal
हैंडल

gear lever
gīyar līvar
गीयर लीवर

brake lever
brek līvar
ब्रेक लीवर

tyre lever
ṭāyar līvar
टायर लीवर

patch
thiglī
थिगली

repair kit
marammat kā sāmān | मरम्मत का सामान

fork
chimṭā
चिमटा

key
chābī
चाबी

spoke
tīlī
तीली

pump
pamp
पंप

lock
tālā
ताला

wheel
pahiyā
पहिया

valve
vālv
वाल्व

tread
ṭāyar par ḍizāin
टायर पर डिजाइन

inner tube
bhītrī ṭyūb
भीतरी ट्यूब

child seat
bālak sīṭ
बालक–सीट

---

vocabulary • śabdāvalī • शब्दावली

lamp	**kickstand**	**brake block**	**basket**	**toe clip**	**brake (v)**
laimp	kiksṭaiṇḍ	brek block	ṭokrī	ṭo klip	roknā
लैंप	किकस्टैंड	ब्रेक ब्लॉक	टोकरी	टो क्लिप	रोकना
rear light	**bike rack**	**cable**	**dynamo**	**toe strap**	**cycle (v)**
pichhe kī lāiṭ	bāik raik	tār	ḍāyanemo	ṭo sṭrep	sāikil chalānā
पीछे की लाइट	बाइक रैक	तार	डायनेमो	टो स्ट्रेप	साइकिल चलाना
reflector	**stabilisers**	**sprocket**	**puncture**	**pedal (v)**	**change gear (v)**
parāvartak	sṭeblāizars	chakradant	paṅkchar	paiḍal mārnā	gīyar badalnā
परावर्तक	स्टेबलाइजर्स	चक्रदंत	पंक्चर	पैडल मारना	गीयर बदलना

train · relgāṛī · रेलगाड़ी

carriage
relgāṛī
ḍibbā
रेलगाड़ी
डिब्बा

platform number
platform saṃkhyā
प्लेटफ़ॉर्म संख्या

commuter
yātrī
यात्री

trolley
trolley
ट्रॉली

platform
platform
प्लेटफ़ॉर्म

train station | relve sṭeśan | रेलवे स्टेशन

types of train · relgāṛī ke prakār · रेलगाड़ी के प्रकार

engine
injan
इंजन

driver's cab
chālak kakṣ
चालक कक्ष

rail
paṭrī
पटरी

steam train
bhāp chālit rel | भाप चालित रेल

diesel train | ḍīzal rel | डीज़ल रेल

electric train
vidyut rel | विद्युत रेल

high-speed train
tez gati rel | तेज़ गति रेल

monorail
ekpaṭrī rel | एकपटरी रेल

underground train
bhūmigat rel | भूमिगत रेल

tram
ṭrām gāṛī | ट्राम गाड़ी

freight train
mālgāṛī | मालगाड़ी

english · hindi · हिन्दी

luggage rack
sāmān kī jagah
सामान की जगह

window
khiṛkī
खिड़की

track
paṭrī
पटरी

door
darvāzā
दरवाज़ा

seat
sīṭ
सीट

ticket barrier
ṭikaṭ bairiyar | टिकट बैरियर

compartment | ḍibbā | डिब्बा

41213
KUPONG 7.00 kr

ticket
ṭikaṭ | टिकट

public address
system
jan sūchnā praṇālī
जन सूचना प्रणाली

timetable
samaya sāriṇī
समय–सारिणी

dining car | bhojanyān | भोजनयान

sleeping compartment
śayan yān | शयन यान

concourse | relve parisar | रेलवे परिसर

---

vocabulary • śabdāvalī • शब्दावली

rail network
relgāṛī tantr
रेलगाड़ी तंत्र

underground map
bhūmigat nakśā
भूमिगत नक्शा

ticket office
ṭikaṭ ghar
टिकट घर

live rail
chālū paṭrī
चालू पटरी

inter-city train
antar nagarīya relgāṛī
अंतर नगरीय रेलगाड़ी

delay
vilamb
विलंब

ticket inspector
ṭikaṭ nirīkṣak
टिकट निरीक्षक

signal
signal
सिग्नल

rush hour
vyast samaya
व्यस्त समय

fare
kirāyā
किराया

change (v)
badalnā
बदलना

emergency lever
āpātkālīn līvar
आपातकालीन लीवर

---

aircraft • vāyuyān • वायुयान

airliner • yātrī vimān • यात्री विमान

cockpit	exit	engine	fuselage	wing	tail
chālak kakṣ	nikās dvār	injan	fyūzilej	paṅkh	pūṃchh
चालक कक्ष	निकास द्वार	इंजन	फ्यूज़िलेज	पंख	पूंछ

rudder
raḍar | रडर

nose	nosewheel	landing gear	aileron	fin	tailplane
agra bhāg	āge kā pahiyā	lenḍiṅg gīyar	pichhlī patvār	paṅkh	pichhlā samtal paṅkh
अग्र भाग	आगे का पहिया	लेंडिंग गीयर	पिछली पतवार	पंख	पिछला समतल पंख

cabin • kebin • केबिन

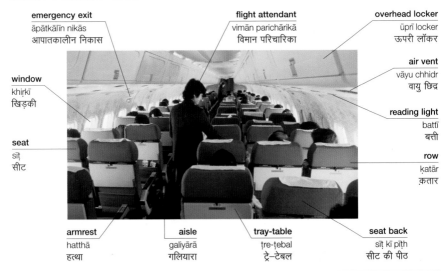

emergency exit
āpātkālīn nikās
आपातकालीन निकास

flight attendant
vimān parichārikā
विमान परिचारिका

overhead locker
ūprī locker
ऊपरी लॉकर

air vent
vāyu chhidr
वायु छिद्र

reading light
battī
बत्ती

window
khiṛkī
खिड़की

row
kaṭār
क़तार

seat
sīṭ
सीट

armrest	aisle	tray-table	seat back
hatthā	galiyārā	ṭre-ṭebal	sīṭ kī pīṭh
हत्था	गलियारा	ट्रे–टेबल	सीट की पीठ

microlight
māikrolāiṭ
माइक्रोलाइट

glider
glāiḍar
ग्लाइडर

biplane
bāiplen
बाइप्लेन

propeller
chālak yantr
चालक यंत्र

hot-air balloon
garm havā kā gubbārā
गर्म हवा का गुब्बारा

light aircraft
halkā vayuyān
हल्का वायुयान

sea plane
naukā vimān
नौका विमान

private jet
nijī vimān | निजी विमान

supersonic jet
supersonic vimān
सुपरसॉनिक विमान

rotor blade
roṭar bleḍ
रोटर ब्लेड

missile
misāil | मिसाइल

helicopter
helicopter | हैलीकॉप्टर

bomber
bamvarṣak | बमवर्षक

fighter plane
laṛākū vimān | लड़ाकू विमान

---

vocabulary • śabdāvalī • शब्दावली

pilot vimān chālak विमान चालक	**take off (v)** uṛān bharnā उड़ान भरना	**land (v)** utarnā उतरना	**economy class** sāmānya śreṇī सामान्य श्रेणी	**hand luggage** halkā sāmān हल्का सामान
co-pilot sah-vimān chālak सह–विमान चालक	**fly (v)** uṛnā उड़ना	**altitude** ūmchāī ऊंचाई	**business class** vyāvasāyik śreṇī व्यावसायिक श्रेणी	**seat belt** sīṭ belṭ सीट बेल्ट

airport · havāī aḍḍā · हवाई अड्डा

apron
epran
एप्रन

baggage trailer
sāmān gāṛī
सामान गाड़ी

terminal
ṭarminal
टर्मिनल

service vehicle
sevā vāhan
सेवा वाहन

walkway
mārg
मार्ग

airliner | vāyuyān | वायुयान

vocabulary · śabdāvalī · शब्दावली

runway
havāī paṭṭī
हवाई पट्टी

international flight
antarrāṣṭrīya uṛān
अंतरराष्ट्रीय उड़ान

domestic flight
gharelū uṛān
घरेलू उड़ान

connection
saṃyojī
संयोजी

flight number
uṛān nambar
उड़ान नंबर

immigration
āpravās
आप्रवास

customs
sīmā śulk
सीमा शुल्क

excess baggage
atirikt sāmān
अतिरिक्त सामान

carousel
sāmān kī chal paṭṭī
सामान की चल पट्टी

security
surakṣā
सुरक्षा

x-ray machine
eksare maśīn
एक्सरे मशीन

holiday brochure
paryaṭan sūchnā pustikā
पर्यटन सूचना पुस्तिका

holiday
chhuṭṭiyāṃ
छुट्टियां

check in (v)
chek in
चेक इन

control tower
niyantraṇ tower
नियंत्रण टॉवर

book a flight (v)
uṛān buk karnā
उड़ान बुक करना

visa
vīzā
वीज़ा

passport | pāsporṭ | पासपोर्ट

hand luggage
halkā sāmān
हल्का सामान

luggage
sāmān
सामान

trolley
trolley
ट्रॉली

check-in desk
chek in ḍesk
चेक इन डेस्क

passport control
pāsporṭ kanṭrol
पासपोर्ट कंट्रोल

boarding pass
borḍing pās
बोर्डिंग पास

ticket
ṭikaṭ
टिकट

gate number
dvār saṃkhyā
द्वार संख्या

departures
prasthān
प्रस्थान

departure lounge
prasthān kakṣ | प्रस्थान कक्ष

destination
gantavya
sthān
गंतव्य स्थान

arrivals
āgman
आगमन

information screen
sūchnā skrīn | सूचना स्क्रीन

duty-free shop
śulk mukt dukān
शुल्क मुक्त दुकान

baggage reclaim
sāmān vāpsī
सामान वापसी

taxi rank
ṭaiksī ḳatār
टैक्सी–क़तार

car hire
kirāe kī kār
किराए की कार

ship • jahāz • जहाज़

radar
rāḍār
राडार

radio antenna
reḍiyo enṭīnā
रेडियो एंटीना

deck
ḍaik
डैक

funnel
chimnī
चिमनी

quarterdeck
kvārṭar ḍaik
क्वार्टर डैक

prow
potāgr
पोताग्र

plimsoll line
tal rekhā
तल रेखा

porthole
gavākṣ
गवाक्ष

hull
peṭā
पेटा

lifeboat
rakṣā naukā
रक्षा नौका

keel
nautal
नौतल

propeller
chālak yantr
चालक यंत्र

ocean liner | samudrī jahāz | समुद्री जहाज़

bridge
potādhikārī kakṣ
पोताधिकारी कक्ष

engine room
injan kakṣ
इंजन कक्ष

cabin
kaibin | कैबिन

galley
pot | पोत

vocabulary • śabdāvalī • शब्दावली

dock	**windlass**
dock	charkhī
डॉक	चरखी
port	**captain**
bandargāh	kaptān
बंदरगाह	कप्तान
gangway	**speedboat**
mārgikā	moṭar naukā
मार्गिका	मोटर नौका
anchor	**rowing boat**
laṅgar	chappū vālī nāv
लंगर	चप्पू वाली नाव
bollard	**canoe**
rakṣā stambh	ḍoṅgī
रक्षा–स्तंभ	डोंगी

other ships • anya jahāz • अन्य जहाज़

ferry | yātrī vāhak jahāz | यात्री वाहक जहाज़

outboard motor
āuṭborḍ moṭar
आउटबोर्ड मोटर

inflatable dinghy | havā bharī ḍoṅgī | हवा भरी डोंगी

hydrofoil | jal patrak
जल पत्रक

yacht
krīṛā naukā | क्रीड़ा नौका

catamaran
ḍonāvā | दोनावा

tug boat
karṣ naukā | कर्ष नौका

hovercraft
hover krāft | हॉवर क्राफ़्ट

container ship
māl pot | माल पोत

rigging
sāj sāmān
साज सामान

sailboat
pāl naukā | पाल नौका

hold
māl kakṣ
माल कक्ष

freighter | mālvāhak
मालवाहक

oil tanker
tel pot | तेल पोत

aircraft carrier | vāyuyān vāhak | वायुयान वाहक

battleship
jaṅgī jahāz | जंगी जहाज़

conning tower
chālak kakṣ
चालक कक्ष

submarine
panḍubbī | पनडुब्बी

port • bandargāh • बंदरगाह

warehouse	crane	fork-lift truck	access road	customs house
mālgodām	kren	kren	praveś mārg	sīmā śulk chaukī
मालगोदाम	क्रेन	क्रेन	प्रवेश मार्ग	सीमा शुल्क चौकी

dock	container	quay	cargo
godī	māl ḍibbā	jahāz ghāṭ	kārgo
गोदी	माल डिब्बा	जहाज़ घाट	कार्गो

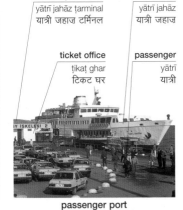

ferry terminal
yātrī jahāz ṭarminal
यात्री जहाज़ टर्मिनल

ferry
yātrī jahāz
यात्री जहाज

ticket office
ṭikaṭ ghar
टिकट घर

passenger
yātrī
यात्री

container port | māl vāhak bandargāh
माल वाहक बंदरगाह

passenger port
yātrī bandargāh | यात्री बंदरगाह

net
jāl
जाल

fishing boat
machhuārī nāv
मछुआरी नाव

mooring
laṅgargāh
लंगरगाह

marina | taṭvartī ḳasbā | तटवर्ती क़स्बा

fishing port | matsya bandargāh | मत्स्य बंदरगाह

harbour | bandargāh | बंदरगाह

pier | potghāṭ | पोतघाट

jetty | jeṭī | जेटी

shipyard | pot nirmāṇ ghāṭ | पोत निर्माण घाट

lamp
laimp
लैंप

lighthouse | prakāś stambh | प्रकाश स्तंभ

buoy
boyā | बोया

---

vocabulary • śabdāvalī • शब्दावली

coastguard	**dry dock**	**board (v)**
taṭrakṣak	sūkhā bandargāh	charhnā
तटरक्षक	सूखा बंदरगाह	चढ़ना
harbour master	**moor (v)**	**disembark (v)**
bandargāh pramukh	nāv bāndhnā	jahāz se utarnā
बंदरगाह प्रमुख	नाव बांधना	जहाज़ से उतरना
drop anchor (v)	**dock (v)**	**set sail (v)**
laṅgar ḍālnā	bandargāh meṃ lānā	yātrā ārambh karnā
लंगर डालना	बंदरगाह में लाना	यात्रा आरंभ करना

sports
khelkūd
खेलकूद

American football • amerikan football • अमेरिकन फुटबॉल

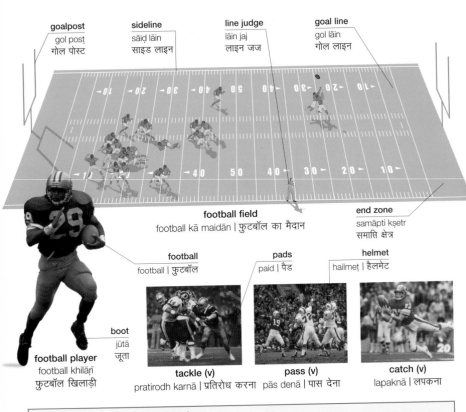

goalpost
gol poṣṭ
गोल पोस्ट

sideline
sāiḍ lāin
साइड लाइन

line judge
lāin jaj
लाइन जज

goal line
gol lāin
गोल लाइन

football field
football kā maidān | फुटबॉल का मैदान

end zone
samāpti kṣetr
समाप्ति क्षेत्र

football
football | फुटबॉल

pads
paid | पैड

helmet
hailmeṭ | हैलमेट

boot
jūtā
जूता

football player
football khilāṛī
फुटबॉल खिलाड़ी

tackle (v)
pratirodh karnā | प्रतिरोध करना

pass (v)
pās denā | पास देना

catch (v)
lapaknā | लपकना

---

vocabulary • śabdāvalī • शब्दावली

time out	**team**	**defence**	**cheerleader**	**What is the score?**
samaya samāpt	ṭīm	bachāv	protsāhak ṭīm netā	kyā skor huā hai?
समय समास	टीम	बचाव	प्रोत्साहक टीम नेता	क्या स्कोर हुआ है?
fumble	**attack**	**score**	**touchdown**	**Who is winning?**
binā soche kik mārnā	hamlā	skor	gend se zamīn chhūnā	kaun jīt rahā hai?
बिना सोचे किक मारना	हमला	स्कोर	गेंद से जमीन छूना	कौन जीत रहा है?

rugby • ragbī • रग्बी

dead ball line
ḍed ball lāin
डेड बॉल लाइन

in-goal area
gol kā kṣetr
गोल का क्षेत्र

touch line
pārśv rekhā
पार्श्व रेखा

flag
jhaṇḍā
झंडा

goal
gol
गोल

rugby pitch | ragbī kā maidān | रग्बी का मैदान

ball
ball
बॉल

rugby strip
ragbī strip
रग्बी स्ट्रिप

throw (v)
ball pheṃknā
बॉल फेंकना

kick (v)
kik mārnā
किक मारना

pass (v)
ball ek-dūsre ko denā
बॉल एक – दूसरे को देना

tackle (v)
pratirodh karnā
प्रतिरोध करना

try
ṭraī | ट्राई

player
khilāṛī
खिलाड़ी

ruck | khilāṛiyoṃ kā dal | खिलाड़ियों का दल

scrum | ball ko ghernā | बॉल को घेरना

soccer • soccer • सॉकर

football
football
फ़ुटबॉल

forward
agrim paṅkti kā khilāṛī
अग्रिम पंक्ति का खिलाड़ी

referee
refrī
रेफ़री

centre circle
kendrīya gherā
केंद्रीय घेरा

goalkeeper
golkīpar
गोलकीपर

football strip
football strip
फ़ुटबॉल स्ट्रिप

footballer
footballer
फ़ुटबॉलर

football pitch
football maidān | फ़ुटबॉल मैदान

goalpost
gol posṭ
गोल पोस्ट

net
jāl
जाल

crossbar
crossbar
क्रॉसबार

dribble (v) | gend dhakelnā
गेंद धकेलना

head (v)
sir se mārnā | सिर से मारना

wall
pratirakṣak
paṅkti
प्रतिरक्षक पंक्ति

goal | gol | गोल

free kick | frī kik | फ़्री किक

penalty area
penalṭī kṣetr
पेनल्टी क्षेत्र

goal line
gol sīmā
गोल – सीमा

goal area
gol kṣetr
गोल–क्षेत्र

goal
gol
गोल

defender
pratirakṣak
प्रतिरक्षक

linesman
lāins main
लाइन्स मैन

corner flag
corner jhaṇḍā
कॉर्नर–झंडा

throw-in
ball pheṃknā | बॉल फेंकना

kick (v) | kik mārnā |
किक मारना

boot
jūtā
जूता

pass (v) | pāss denā |
पास देना

shoot (v) | zor se
mārnā | ज़ोर से मारना

save (v)
gol roknā | गोल रोकना

tackle (v)
pratirodh karnā
प्रतिरोध करना

vocabulary • śabdāvalī • शब्दावली

stadium sṭeḍiyam स्टेडियम	**foul** niyam ullanghan नियम उल्लंघन	**yellow card** pīlā kārḍ पीला कार्ड	**league** līg लीग	**extra time** atirikt samaya अतिरिक्त समय
score a goal (v) gol dāgnā गोल दागना	**corner** corner कॉर्नर	**off-side** off - sāiḍ ऑफ़–साइड	**draw** anirṇit maich अनिर्णित मैच	**substitute** vaikalpik khilāṛī वैकल्पिक खिलाड़ी
penalty penalṭī पेनल्टी	**red card** lāl kārḍ लाल कार्ड	**send off** saiṇḍ off सैंड ऑफ़	**half time** ādhā vakt आधा वक़्त	**substitution** vikalp bulānā विकल्प बुलाना

hockey • hockey • हॉकी

ice hockey • āis hockey • आइस हॉकी

defending zone
rakṣā kṣetr
रक्षा क्षेत्र

goal line
gol lāin
गोल लाइन

attack zone
ākramaṇ kṣetr
आक्रमण क्षेत्र

neutral zone
taṭasth kṣetr
तटस्थ क्षेत्र

goalkeeper
golkīpar
गोलकीपर

goal
gol
गोल

face-off circle
fes off sarkal
फ़ेस ऑफ़ सर्कल

centre circle
kendrīya gherā
केंद्रीय घेरा

pad
paiḍ
पैड

ice hockey rink
āis hockey kā maidān
आइस हॉकी का मैदान

glove
dastānā
दस्ताना

ice-skate
āis skeṭ
आइस स्केट

stick
sṭik | स्टिक

field hockey • fīlḍ hockey • फ़ील्ड हॉकी

puck
ḍisk | डिस्क

ice hockey player | āis hockey khilāṛī
आइस हॉकी खिलाड़ी

hockey stick
hockey sṭik
हॉकी स्टिक

ball
ball
बॉल

skate (v) | skeṭiṅg
karnā | स्केटिंग करना

hit (v)
ball mārnā | बॉल मारना

cricket • krikeṭ • क्रिकेट

wicket
vikeṭ
विकेट

pitch
pich
पिच

batsman
ballebāz
बल्लेबाज़

crease
krīz
क्रीज़

face mask
hailmeṭ
हैलमेट

boundary line
sīmā rekhā
सीमा रेखा

bowler
gendbāz
गेंदबाज़

stump
ṣṭamp
स्टंप

leg pad
paiḍ
पैड

bat
ballā
बल्ला

bowl (v)
gendbāzī karnā
गेंदबाज़ी करना

bat (v)
ballebāzī karnā | बल्लेबाज़ी करना

cricket ball
krikeṭ gend
क्रिकेट गेंद

cricketer
krikeṭ khilāṛī | क्रिकेट खिलाड़ी

field (v) | fīlḍiṅg
karnā | फ़ील्डिंग करना

wicket-keeper | vikeṭ
kīpar | विकेट कीपर

vocabulary • śabdāvalī • शब्दावली		
out	**scoreboard**	**umpire**
āuṭ	skor borḍ	ampāyar
आउट	स्कोर बोर्ड	अंपायर

basketball • bāskeṭ ball • बास्केट बॉल

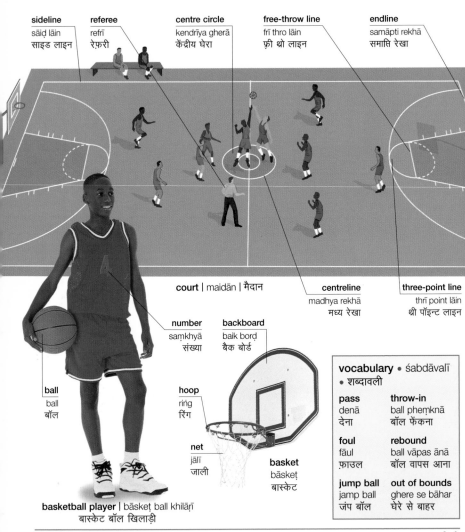

sideline
sāiḍ lāin
साइड लाइन

referee
refrī
रेफरी

centre circle
kendrīya gherā
केंद्रीय घेरा

free-throw line
frī thro lāin
फ़्री थ्रो लाइन

endline
samāpti rekhā
समाप्ति रेखा

court | maidān | मैदान

centreline
madhya rekhā
मध्य रेखा

three-point line
thrī point lāin
थ्री पॉइन्ट लाइन

number
saṃkhyā
संख्या

backboard
baik borḍ
बैक बोर्ड

ball
ball
बॉल

hoop
riṅg
रिंग

net
jālī
जाली

basket
bāskeṭ
बास्केट

basketball player | bāskeṭ ball khilāṛī
बास्केट बॉल खिलाड़ी

vocabulary • śabdāvalī • शब्दावली	
pass denā देना	**throw-in** ball pheṃknā बॉल फेंकना
foul fāul फ़ाउल	**rebound** ball vāpas ānā बॉल वापस आना
jump ball jamp ball जंप बॉल	**out of bounds** ghere se bāhar घेरे से बाहर

actions • gatividhiyāṃ • गतिविधियां

throw (v)
ball pheṃknā
बॉल फेंकना

catch (v)
ball pakaṛnā
बॉल पकड़ना

shoot (v)
gol mārnā
गोल मारना

jump (v)
kūdnā
कूदना

mark (v) | ball niśāne par mārnā | बॉल निशाने पर मारना

block (v) | ball roknā | बॉल रोकना

bounce (v) | ṭappā mārnā | टप्पा मारना

dunk (v) | ball bāskeṭ meṃ ḍālnā | बॉल बास्केट में डालना

volleyball • volleyball • वॉलीबॉल

block (v)
ball roknā
बॉल रोकना

net
jāl
जाल

dig (v)
ball lapakne ko taiyār rahnā
बॉल लपकने को तैयार रहना

referee
refrī
रेफ़री

knee support
nī saporṭ
नी सपोर्ट

court | maidān | मैदान

baseball • baseball • बेसबॉल

field • maidān • मैदान

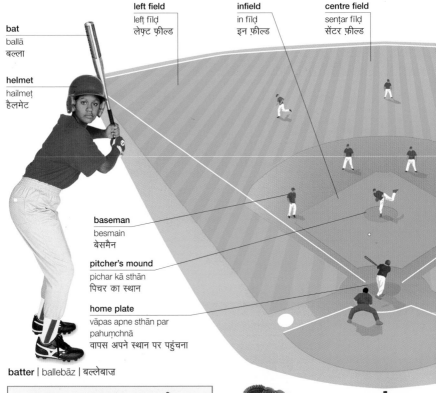

left field
left fīlḍ
लेफ़्ट फ़ील्ड

infield
in fīlḍ
इन फ़ील्ड

centre field
senṭar fīlḍ
सेंटर फ़ील्ड

bat
ballā
बल्ला

helmet
hailmeṭ
हैलमेट

baseman
besmain
बेसमैन

pitcher's mound
pichar kā sthān
पिचर का स्थान

home plate
vāpas apne sthān par
pahuṃchnā
वापस अपने स्थान पर पहुंचना

batter | ballebāz | बल्लेबाज

vocabulary • śabdāvalī • शब्दावली

inning	**safe**	**foul ball**
pārī	surakṣit	fāul gend
पारी	सुरक्षित	फ़ाउल गेंद
run	**out**	**strike**
ran	āuṭ	sṭrāik
रन	आउट	स्ट्राइक

ball
gend
गेंद

mitt | dastānā | दस्ताना

mask | mukhauṭā | मुखौटा

actions • kriyāeṃ • क्रियाएं

outfield
āuṭ fīlḍ
आउट फ़ील्ड

right field
rāiṭ fīlḍ
राइट फ़ील्ड

foul line
fāul lāin
फ़ाउल लाइन

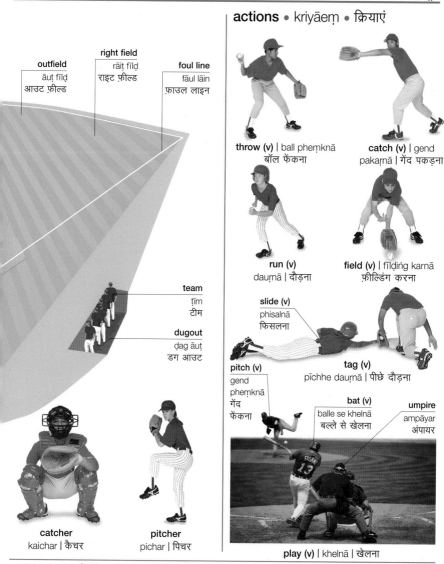

throw (v) | ball pheṃknā
बॉल फेंकना

catch (v) | gend
pakaṛnā | गेंद पकड़ना

run (v)
dauṛnā | दौड़ना

field (v) | fīlḍiṅg karnā
फ़ील्डिंग करना

slide (v)
phisalnā
फिसलना

tag (v)
pīchhe dauṛnā | पीछे दौड़ना

pitch (v)
gend
pheṃknā
गेंद
फेंकना

bat (v)
balle se khelnā
बल्ले से खेलना

umpire
ampāyar
अंपायर

team
ṭīm
टीम

dugout
ḍag āuṭ
डग आउट

catcher
kaichar | कैचर

pitcher
pichar | पिचर

play (v) | khelnā | खेलना

tennis • ṭenis • टेनिस

handle
haiṇḍal
हैंडल

head
haiḍ
हैड

string
striṅg
स्ट्रिंग

umpire
ampāyar
अंपायर

baseline
bes lāin
बेस लाइन

racquet
raikeṭ | रैकेट

service line
sarvis lāin
सर्विस लाइन

sideline
sāiḍ lāin
साइड लाइन

ball
gend
गेंद

wristband
risṭ baiṇḍ
रिस्ट बैंड

tennis court | ṭenis korṭ | टेनिस कोर्ट

---

vocabulary • śabdāvalī • शब्दावली

singles	**set**	**deuce**	**fault**	**slice**	**let!**
ekal	saiṭ	barābarī	galat shot	galat prahār	khilāṛī ko roknā
एकल	सैट	बराबरी	ग़लत शॉट	ग़लत प्रहार	खिलाड़ी को रोकना
doubles	**match**	**love**	**dropshot**	**rally**	**championship**
yugal	maich	śūnya	dropshot	kaṛā pariśram	chaimpiyanśip
युगल	मैच	शून्य	ड्रॉप शॉट	कड़ा परिश्रम	चैम्पियनशिप
game	**spin**	**tiebreak**	**advantage**	**linesman**	**ace**
khel	spin	nirṇāyak aṁk	anukūl sthiti	lāins main	pahlī sarvis se banā aṁk
खेल	स्पिन	निर्णायक अंक	अनुकूल स्थिति	लाइन्स मैन	पहली सर्विस से बना अंक

---

strokes • stroks • स्ट्रोक्स

net
net
नेट

smash
zor se mārnā
जोर से मारना

ballboy
ball boy
बॉल बॉय

serve (v)
sarvis karnā
सर्विस करना

tennis shoes
tenis jūte
टेनिस जूते

player
khilāṛī | खिलाड़ी

serve
sarv | सर्व

volley
volley | वॉली

return
riṭarn | रिटर्न

lob | lob
लोब

forehand
forhaiṇḍ | फ़ोरहैंड

backhand
baikhaiṇḍ | बैकहैंड

racquet games • raikeṭ ke khel • रैकेट के खेल

shuttlecock
chiriyā
चिड़िया

bat
baiṭ
बैट

badminton
baiḍminṭan | बैडमिंटन

table tennis
ṭebal ṭenis | टेबल टेनिस

squash
skvaiś | स्क्वैश

racquetball
raikeṭ ball | रैकेट बॉल

golf • golf • गोल्फ़

hole
hol
होल

swing (v)
shot mārnā
शॉट मारना

teeing ground
ṭīiṅg grāuṇḍ
टीइंग ग्राउंड

green
grīn
ग्रीन

bunker
baṅkar
बंकर

flag
jhaṇḍā
झंडा

fairway
supath
सुपथ

rough
ūbaṛ -
khābaṛ
ऊबड़–
खाबड़

water hazard
jal bādhak
जल बाधक

golf course
golf kors | गोल्फ़ कोर्स

buggy
baggī
बग्गी

stance
shot mārne kā tarīkā
शॉट मारने का तरीक़ा

golfer | golf khilāṛī | गोल्फ़ खिलाड़ी

clubhouse | klab sadan | क्लब सदन

equipment • upkaraṇ • उपकरण

golf ball
golf ball
गोल्फ़ बॉल

umbrella
chhātā
छाता

golf bag
golf baig
गोल्फ़ बैग

spikes
kīlom vāle jūte
कीलों वाले जूते

tee | ṭī | टी

glove
dastānā | दस्ताना

golf trolley
golf trolley | गोल्फ़ ट्रॉली

golf shoe
golf ke jūte | गोल्फ़ के जूते

golf clubs • golf klab • गोल्फ़ क्लब

wood
vuḍ | वुड

putter
paṭar | पटर

iron
āyaran | आयरन

wedge
vej | वेज

actions • gatividhiyāṃ • गतिविधियां

tee-off (v) | khel
ārambh karnā
खेल आरंभ करना

drive (v)
ḍrāiv mārnā
ड्राइव मारना

putt (v) | gend par
prahār karnā
गेंद पर प्रहार करना

chip (v)
chip shot lenā
चिप शॉट लेना

vocabulary • śabdāvalī • शब्दावली

par	over par	handicap	caddy	backswing	stroke
ausat khel	utkṛṣṭ khel	haiṇḍīkaip	golf sahāyak	baiksviṅg	ṣṭrok
औसत खेल	उत्कृष्ट खेल	हैंडीकैप	गोल्फ़ सहायक	बैकस्विंग	स्ट्रोक
under par	**hole in one**	**tournament**	**spectators**	**practice swing**	**line of play**
nimn khel	hol in van	mukābalā	darśak	praikṭis shot	khel rekhā
निम्न खेल	होल इन वन	मुक़ाबला	दर्शक	प्रैक्टिस शॉट	खेल रेखा

athletics • ethleṭiks • एथलेटिक्स

lane
len
लेन

track
paṅkti
पंक्ति

finishing line
samāpti rekhā
समाप्ति रेखा

starting line
prārambhik rekhā
प्रारंभिक रेखा

field
maidān | मैदान

athlete
ethlīṭ
एथलीट

starting blocks
ārambhik avrodh | आरंभिक अवरोध

sprinter
tez dhāvak
तेज़ धावक

discus
chakkā pheṃk
चक्का फेंक

shotput
golā pheṃk
गोला फेंक

javelin
bhālā pheṃk
भाला फेंक

---

vocabulary • śabdāvalī • शब्दावली

race	**record**	**photo finish**	**personal best**
dauṛ	record	barābarī kī dauṛ	apnā viśeṣ pradarśan
दौड़	रिकॉर्ड	बराबरी की दौड़	अपना विशेष प्रदर्शन
time	**pole vault**	**marathon**	**break a record (v)**
samaya	bāṃs kūd	mairāthan	record toṛnā
समय	बांस–कूद	मैराथन	रिकॉर्ड तोड़ना

stopwatch
virām ghaṛī | विराम घड़ी

baton
ḍaṇḍī
डंडी

crossbar
chhaṛ
छड़

relay race
rile dauṛ | रिले दौड़

high jump
ūmchī kūd | ऊंची कूद

long jump
lambī kūd | लंबी कूद

hurdles | bādhā
dauṛ | बाधा दौड़

gymnastics • jimnāsṭik • जिमनास्टिक

springboard
spriṅgborḍ
स्प्रिंगबोर्ड

gymnast
jimnāsṭ
जिमनास्ट

horse
horse
हॉर्स

somersault
kalābāzī | कलाबाजी

beam | bīm | बीम

ribbon
fītā
फ़ीता

mat
chaṭāī | चटाई

vault
chhalāṅg mārnā
छलांग मारना

floor exercises
zamīnī vyāyām
जमीनी व्यायाम

tumble
kalābāzī
कलाबाजी

rhythmic gymnastics
saṅgītmaya jimnāsṭik
संगीतमय जिमनास्टिक

vocabulary • śabdāvalī • शब्दावली

horizontal bar āṛī chhaṛ आड़ी छड़	**pommel horse** pommel horse पॉमेल हॉर्स	**rings** riṅg रिंग	**medals** padak पदक	**silver** rajat रजत
parallel bars samānāntar chhaṛeṃ समानांतर छड़ें	**asymmetric bars** asamān chhaṛeṃ असमान छड़ें	**podium** poḍiyam पोडियम	**gold** svarṇ स्वर्ण	**bronze** kāṃsya कांस्य

combat sports • mall krīṛā • मल्ल क्रीड़ा

opponent
pratidvaṅdī
प्रतिद्वंद्वी

glove
dastānā
दस्ताना

guard
hailmeṭ
हैलमेट

belt
peṭī
पेटी

tae-kwon-do | tāikvāṇḍo | ताइक्वांडो

karate | karāṭe | कराटे

judo | jūḍo | जूडो

mask
mukhauṭā
मुखौटा

sword
talvār
तलवार

aikido
ekāiḍo | एकाइडो

kendo
kenḍo | केनडो

kung fu
kuṅgfū | कुंगफू

kickboxing
kik boxing | किक बॉक्सिंग

wrestling
kuśtī | कुश्ती

boxing
mukkebāzī | मुक्केबाज़ी

actions • darivpench • दांवपेंच

fall
girnā | गिरना

hold
pakaṛnā | पकड़ना

throw
girānā | गिराना

pin | paṭkanī
denā | पटकनी देना

kick
kik | किक

punch
mukkā | मुक्का

strike
mukkā mārnā | मुक्का मारना

jump
kūdnā | कूदना

block
prahār roknā | प्रहार रोकना

chop | nīche vār
karnā | नीचे वार करना

vocabulary • śabdāvalī • शब्दावली

boxing ring boxing riṅg बॉक्सिंग रिंग	**round** charaṇ चरण	**fist** muṭṭhī मुट्ठी	**black belt** blaik belṭ ब्लैक बेल्ट	**capoeira** kepoirā केपोइरा
boxing gloves boxing dastāne बॉक्सिंग–दस्ताने	**bout** śakti parīkṣā शक्ति परीक्षा	**knock out** paṭkanī पटकनी	**self defence** ātmrakṣā आत्मरक्षा	**sumo wrestling** sūmo kuśtī सूमो कुश्ती
mouth guard māuth gārḍ माउथ गार्ड	**sparring** paiṅtrebāzī पैंतरेबाज़ी	**punch bag** pañch baig पंच बैग	**martial arts** mārśal ārṭs मार्शल आर्ट्स	**tai-chi** tāī chī ताई–ची

swimming • tairākī • तैराकी

equipment • upkaraṇ • उपकरण

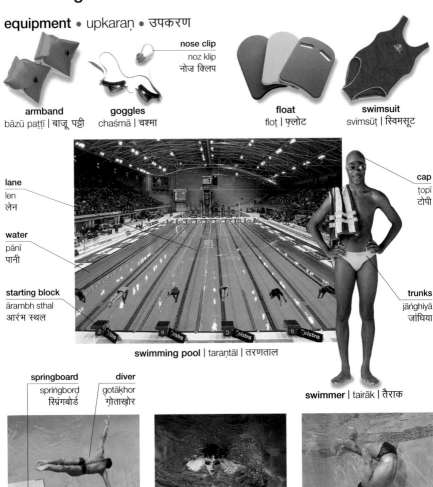

nose clip
noz klip
नोज़ क्लिप

armband
bāzū paṭṭī | बाजू पट्टी

goggles
chaśmā | चश्मा

float
floṭ | फ़्लोट

swimsuit
svimsūṭ | स्विमसूट

lane
len
लेन

water
pānī
पानी

starting block
ārambh sthal
आरंभ स्थल

cap
ṭopī
टोपी

trunks
jāṅghiyā
जांघिया

swimming pool | taraṇtāl | तरणताल

swimmer | tairāk | तैराक

springboard
spriṅgborḍ
स्प्रिंगबोर्ड

diver
gotākhor
ग़ोताख़ोर

dive (v) | ḍāiv mārnā | डाइव मारना

swim (v) | tairnā | तैरना

turn | palaṭnā | पलटना

styles • śailiyāṃ • शैलियां

front crawl | franṭ crawl | फ़्रंट कॉल

breaststroke | bresṭsṭrok | ब्रेस्टस्ट्रोक

stroke
sṭrok | स्ट्रोक

kick
kik | किक

backstroke | baiksṭrok | बैकस्ट्रोक

butterfly | baṭarflāī | बटरफ़्लाई

scuba diving • skūbā ḍāiviṅg • स्कूबा डाइविंग

air cylinder
oxygen slienḍar
ऑक्सीज़न सिलेंडर

flipper
flipar
फ़्लिपर

snorkel
śvās nalī
श्वास नली

mask
naḳāb
नक़ाब

wetsuit
veṭ sūṭ
वेट सूट

weight belt
vazanī peṭī
वज़नी पेटी

regulator
regyūleṭar
रेग्यूलेटर

vocabulary • śabdāvalī • शब्दावली

dive ḍāiv डाइव	**racing dive** resiṅg ḍāiv रेसिंग डाइव	**lockers** lockers लॉकर्स	**water polo** water polo वॉटर पोलो	**shallow end** uthlā chhor उथला छोर	**cramp** nas charhnā नस चढ़ना
high dive ūṃchī ḍāiv ऊंची डाइव	**tread water (v)** pānī meṃ pair mārnā पानी में पैर मारना	**lifeguard** jīvan rakṣak जीवन रक्षक	**deep end** gahrā chhor गहरा छोर	**synchronized swimming** sinkronāizḍ tairākī सिंक्रोनाइज़्ड तैराकी	**drown (v)** ḍūbnā डूबना

sailing • pāl naukāyan • पाल नौकायन

compass
kampās | कंपास

anchor
langar | लंगर

mast
mastūl
मस्तूल

rigging
rasse
रस्से

headsail
aglā pāl
अगला पाल

mainsail
pāl
पाल

cleat
phannī
फन्नी

sidedeck
sāiḍ ḍek
साइड डेक

bow
galhī
गलही

boom
pāldaṇḍ
पालदंड

stern
dumbāl
दुंबाल

tiller
patvār hatthā
पतवार हत्था

hull
peṭā
पेटा

navigate (v) | mārg nirdeśan
karnā | मार्ग निर्देशन करना

yacht | krīṛā naukā | क्रीड़ा–नौका

safety • surakṣā • सुरक्षा

flare
tīvr prakāś saṅketak
तीव्र प्रकाश संकेतक

lifebuoy
jīvan rakṣā ṭyūb
जीवन रक्षा ट्यूब

life jacket
rakṣā jaikeṭ
रक्षा जैकेट

life raft
jīvan rakṣā naukā
जीवन रक्षा नौका

watersports • jalkrīṛā • जलक्रीड़ा

rower
nāvik
नाविक

oar
chappū
चप्पू

kayak
pansuiyā
पनसुइया

paddle
chhoṭā chappū
छोटा चप्पू

row (v) | nāv khenā | नाव खेना

canoeing | naukā vihār | नौका विहार

sail
pāl
पाल

windsurfer
viṇḍ sarfar
विंड सर्फ़र

board
borḍ
बोर्ड

footstrap
fuṭ strep
फ़ुट स्ट्रेप

windsurfing | viṇḍ sarfiṅg | विंड सर्फ़िंग

surfboard
sarf borḍ
सर्फ़ बोर्ड

surfing
sarfiṅg | सर्फ़िंग

ski
skī | स्की

waterskiing | water
skīiṅg | वॉटर स्कीइंग

speed boating | spīḍ
boṭiṅg | स्पीड बोटिंग

rafting
naukāyan | नौकायन

jet skiing
jeṭ skīiṅg | जेट स्कीइंग

---

vocabulary • śabdāvalī • शब्दावली

waterskier	**crew**	**wind**	**surf**	**sheet**	**centreboard**
water skīar	karmīdal	havā	samudrī lahreṅ	naukā pāl	senṭar borḍ
वॉटर स्कीअर	कर्मीदल	हवा	समुद्री लहरें	नौका पाल	सेंटर बोर्ड
surfer	**tack (v)**	**wave**	**rapids**	**rudder**	**capsize (v)**
sarfar	diśā badalnā	lahar	tīvr nadī	patvār	nāv ulaṭnā
सर्फ़र	दिशा बदलना	लहर	तीव्र नदी	पतवार	नाव उलटना

horse riding • ghuṛsavārī • घुड़सवारी

riding hat
haiṭ
हैट

mane
ayāl
अयाल

rider
ghuṛsavār
घुड़सवार

reins
lagām
लगाम

saddle
zīn
जीन

horse
ghoṛā
घोड़ा

jodhpurs
taṅg pajāmī
तंग पजामी

tail
pūṃchh
पूंछ

girth
ghoṛe kī taṅg
घोड़े की तंग

riding boot
ghuṛsavārī ke jūte
घुड़सवारी के जूते

stirrup
rakāb
रकाब

hoof
khur
खुर

pommel
haiṇḍal
हैंडल

browband
sir paṭṭā
सिर–पट्टा

noseband
nakel
नकेल

bit
lagām kī
mukhrī
लगाम की
मुखरी

seat
sīṭ
सीट

horseshoe
ghuṛnāl | घुड़नाल

side-saddle
sāiḍ zīn | साइड जीन

bridle | lagām | लगाम

riding crop | chābuk | चाबुक

242

events • pratispardhā • प्रतिस्पर्धा

racehorse
dauṛ kā ghoṛā | दौड़ का घोड़ा

fence
bāṛ | बाड़

horse race
ghuṛdauṛ | घुड़दौड़

steeplechase
bādhā dauṛ | बाधा दौड़

harness race | ghoṛā gāṛī
dauṛ | घोड़ा गाड़ी दौड़

rodeo
ghuṛsavārī khel | घुड़सवारी खेल

showjumping
śo jamping | शो जंपिंग

carriage race
baggī dauṛ | बग्गी दौड़

trekking
ṭraiking | ट्रैकिंग

dressage
ghoṛā sadhānā | घोड़ा सधाना

polo
polo | पोलो

---

vocabulary • śabdāvalī • शब्दावली

walk	**canter**	**jump**	**halter**	**paddock**	**flat race**
chāl	ghoṛe kī mand chāl	kūd	rassī	ghoṛoṁ kā bāṛā	sīdhī dauṛ
चाल	घोड़े की मंद चाल	कूद	रस्सी	घोड़ों का बाड़ा	सीधी दौड़
trot	**gallop**	**groom**	**stable**	**arena**	**racecourse**
dulkī	sarpaṭ chāl	sāīs	astabal	khel kā maidān	dauṛ kā maidān
दुलकी	सरपट चाल	साईस	अस्तबल	खेल का मैदान	दौड़ का मैदान

fishing • machhlī pakaṛnā • मछली पकड़ना

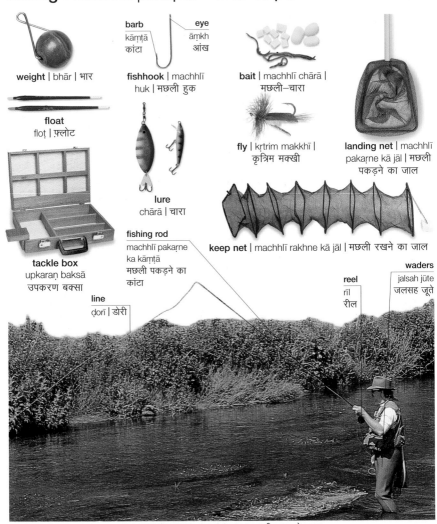

weight | bhār | भार

barb | kāṃṭā | कांटा
eye | āṃkh | आंख
fishhook | machhlī huk | मछली हुक

bait | machhlī chārā | मछली–चारा

float | floṭ | फ़्लोट

lure | chārā | चारा

fly | kṛtrim makkhī | कृत्रिम मक्खी

landing net | machhlī pakaṛne kā jāl | मछली पकड़ने का जाल

tackle box | upkaraṇ baksā | उपकरण बक्सा

fishing rod | machhlī pakaṛne ka kāṃṭā | मछली पकड़ने का कांटा

keep net | machhlī rakhne kā jāl | मछली रखने का जाल

line | ḍorī | डोरी

reel | rīl | रील

waders | jalsah jūte | जलसह जूते

angler | machhlī pakaṛne vālā | मछली पकड़ने वाला

types of fishing • machhlī pakaṛne ke prakār • मछली पकड़ने के प्रकार

freshwater fishing | nadī meṃ machhlī pakaṛnā | नदी में मछली पकड़ना

fly fishing | makkhī se machhlī pakaṛnā | मक्खी से मछली पकड़ना

sport fishing
śaukiyā machhlī pakaṛnā
शौकिया मछली पकड़ना

deep sea fishing
gahre samudr meṃ machhlī pakaṛnā
गहरे समुद्र में मछली पकड़ना

surfcasting | samudr kināre machhlī pakaṛnā
समुद्र किनारे मछली पकड़ना

activities • gatividhiyāṃ • गतिविधियां

cast (v)
jāl ḍālnā
जाल डालना

catch (v)
pakaṛnā
पकड़ना

reel in (v)
ḍorī khīṃchnā
डोरी खींचना

net (v)
jāl se pakaṛnā
जाल से पकड़ना

release (v)
pānī meṃ chhoṛnā
पानी में छोड़ना

---

vocabulary • śabdāvalī • शब्दावली

bait (v)	**tackle**	**waterproofs**	**fishing permit**	**creel**
chārā lagānā	upkaraṇ	jalvārak	fiśiṅg parmiṭ	machhlī kī ṭokrī
चारा लगाना	उपकरण	जलवारक	फ़िशिंग परमिट	मछली की टोकरी
bite (v)	**spool**	**pole**	**marine fishing**	**spearfishing**
chārā khānā	charkhī	bāṃs	samudr meṃ	bhāle se machhlī pakaṛnā
चारा खाना	चरखी	बांस	machhlī pakaṛnā	भाले से मछली पकड़ना
			समुद्र में मछली पकड़ना	

---

skiing • skīing • स्कीइंग

chairlift
cheyarlift
चेयरलिफ़्ट

ski slope
skī slop
स्की स्लोप

cable car
kebal kār
केबल कार

ski suit
skī sūṭ
स्की सूट

ski pole
skī pol
स्की पोल

glove
dastānā
दस्ताना

ski run
skī mārg
स्की मार्ग

ski boot
skī būṭ
स्की बूट

safety barrier
surakṣā bairiyar
सुरक्षा बैरियर

ski
skī
स्की

edge
kinārā
किनारा

tip
nok
नोक

skier
skīyar | स्कीयर

events • pratispardhāeṃ • प्रतिस्पर्धाएं

gate
prārambh sthān
प्रारंभ स्थान

downhill skiing | ḍāun hil
skīiṅg | डाउन हिल स्कीइंग

slalom | barfānī
dauṛ | बर्फानी दौड़

ski jump
skī kūd | स्की कूद

cross-country skiing
cross kanṭrī skīiṅg
क्रॉस कंट्री स्कीइंग

winter sports • śaradiya krīṛāeṃ • शरदीय क्रीड़ाएं

goggles
chaśmā
चश्मा

skate
skeṭ
स्केट

ice climbing
āis klāimbiṅg
आइस क्लाइम्बिंग

ice-skating
āis skeṭiṅg
आइस स्केटिंग

figure skating
figar skeṭiṅg
फ़िगर स्केटिंग

snowboarding
sno borḍiṅg | स्नो बोर्डिंग

bobsleigh
slej gāṛī | स्लेज गाड़ी

luge
him vāhan | हिम वाहन

vocabulary • śabdāvalī • शब्दावली

giant slalom
baṛī barfānī dauṛ
बड़ी बर्फानी दौड़

dog sledding
dog slejiṅg
डॉग स्लेजिंग

curling
karliṅg khel
कर्लिंग खेल

speed skating
spīḍ skeṭiṅg
स्पीड स्केटिंग

off-piste
ṭhos baraf par skīiṅg
ठोस बर्फ पर स्कीइंग

biathlon
skīiṅg pratiyogitā
स्कीइंग प्रतियोगिता

alpine skiing
ucch parvatīya skīiṅg
उच्च पर्वतीय स्कीइंग

avalanche
him skhalan
हिम स्खलन

snowmobile
slej | स्लेज

sledding | slej par
phisalnā | स्लेज पर
फिसलना

other sports • anya khelkūd • अन्य खेलकूद

glider
glāiḍar
ग्लाइडर

hang-glider
haiṅg glāiḍar
हैंग–ग्लाइडर

gliding
glāiḍiṅg
ग्लाइडिंग

parachute
pairāśūṭ
पैराशूट

hang-gliding
haiṅg glāiḍiṅg
हैंग–ग्लाइडिंग

rope
rassī
रस्सी

rock climbing
parvatārohaṇ | पर्वतारोहण

parachuting
pairāśūṭ se utarnā | पैराशूट से उतरना

paragliding
pairāglāiḍiṅg | पैराग्लाइडिंग

skydiving
ākāśīya goṭākhorī | आकाशीय ग़ोताख़ोरी

abseiling
parvat avrohaṇ | पर्वत अवरोहण

bungee jumping
bañjī kūd | बंजी कूद

rally driving
railī ḍrāiving
रैली ड्राइविंग

racing driver
resing ḍrāivar
रेसिंग ड्राइवर

motor racing
moṭar res
मोटर रेस

motorcross
moṭar cross
मोटर क्रॉस

motorbike racing
moṭarbāik res
मोटरबाइक रेस

skateboard
skeṭ borḍ
स्केट बोर्ड

rollerskate
rolar skeṭ
रोलर स्केट

skateboarding
skeṭborḍiṅg
स्केटबोर्डिंग

roller skating
rolar skeṭiṅg
रोलर स्केटिंग

stick
sṭik
स्टिक

lacrosse
cross balle kā khel
क्रॉस बल्ले का खेल

mask
naḳāb
नक़ाब

foil
talvār
तलवार

fencing
talvārbāzī
तलवारबाज़ी

pin
pin | पिन

bowling
boliṅg | बोलिंग

bowling ball
boliṅg ball
बोलिंग बॉल

bow
dhanuṣ | धनुष

arrow
tīr
तीर

quiver
tarkaś
तरकश

archery
dhanurvidyā
धनुर्विद्या

pool
pūl biliyarḍ | पूल बिलियर्ड

target
niśānā | निशाना

target shooting
niśānebāzī
निशानेबाज़ी

snooker
snūkar | स्नूकर

fitness • svasthtā • स्वस्थता

exercise bike
vyāyām
sāikil
व्यायाम
साइकिल

gym machine
jim maśīn
जिम मशीन

bench
bench
बेंच

free weights
vazan
वज़न

bar
chhaṛ
छड़

gym
jim
जिम

rowing machine
roing maśīn
रोइंग मशीन

treadmill
ṭreḍmil
ट्रेडमिल

cross trainer
cross ṭrenar
क्रॉस ट्रेनर

personal trainer
nijī praśikṣak
निजी प्रशिक्षक

step machine
sṭep maśīn
स्टेप मशीन

swimming pool
taraṇtāl
तरणताल

sauna
vāṣp snān
वाष्प स्नान

exercises • vyāyām • व्यायाम

tights
taṅg pajāmī
तंग पजामी

stretch | sṭrech | स्ट्रेच

lunge
āge jhuknā | आगे झुकना

press-up
pres ap | प्रेस अप

dumb bell
ḍambal
डंबल

squat
squat
स्कवॉट

sit-up
siṭ-ap
सिट–अप

bicep curl
ḍole
डोले

leg press
leg pres
लेग प्रेस

trainers
jūte
जूते

weight bar
vazan chhaṛ
वज़न छड़

vest
baniyān
बनियान

chest press
chesṭ pres
चेस्ट प्रेस

weight training
bhārottolan
भारोत्तोलन

jogging
jogging
जॉगिंग

aerobics
airobiks
ऐरोबिक्स

---

vocabulary • śabdāvalī • शब्दावली

train (v) abhyās karnā अभ्यास करना	**circuit training** sarkiṭ ṭreniṅg सर्किट ट्रेनिंग	**extend (v)** baṛhnā बढ़ना	**Pilates** pilāṭīz पिलातीज़	**skipping** rassī kūd रस्सी कूद
warm up (v) māṃspeśiyāṃ garmānā मांसपेशियां गरमाना	**flex (v)** jhukānā झुकाना	**pull up (v)** pul-ap karnā पुल–अप करना	**boxercise** boxing vyāyām बॉक्सिंग व्यायाम	**jog on the spot (v)** ek jagah jog karnā एक जगह जॉग करना

---

leisure
manorañjan
मनोरंजन

theatre • thieṭar • थिएटर

curtain
pardā
पर्दा

wings
pārśv
पार्श्व

set
saiṭ
सैट

audience
darśak
दर्शक

orchestra
orchestra
ऑर्केस्ट्रा

stage | manch | मंच

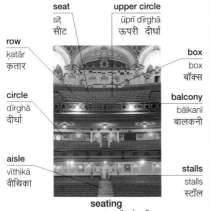

seat
sīṭ
सीट

upper circle
ūprī dīrghā
ऊपरी दीर्घा

row
kaṭār
क़तार

box
box
बॉक्स

circle
dīrghā
दीर्घा

balcony
bālkanī
बालकनी

aisle
vīthikā
वीथिका

stalls
stalls
स्टॉल

seating
baiṭhne kī vyavasthā | बैठने की व्यवस्था

vocabulary • śabdāvalī • शब्दावली		
cast pātr chayan पात्र चयन	**script** paṭkathā पटकथा	**first night** prīmiyar प्रीमियर
actor abhinetā अभिनेता	**backdrop** pṛṣṭhpaṭ पृष्ठपट	**interval** antarāl अंतराल
actress abhinetrī अभिनेत्री	**director** nirdeśak निर्देशक	**programme** kāryakram कार्यक्रम
play nāṭak नाटक	**producer** nirmātā निर्माता	**orchestra pit** orchestra sthal ऑर्केस्ट्रा स्थल

concert
concert | कॉन्सर्ट

musical
myūzikal | म्यूज़िकल

costume
veśbhūṣā
वेशभूषा

ballet
baile | बैले

vocabulary • śabdāvalī • शब्दावली

usher praveśak प्रवेशक	**soundtrack** dhvani paṭṭī ध्वनि पट्टी	**What time does it start?** yah kis samaya śurū hogā? यह किस समय शुरू होगा?
classical music śāstrīya saṅgīt शास्त्रीय संगीत	**applaud (v)** talī bajānā ताली बजाना	**I'd like two tickets for tonight's performance.** mujhe āj rāt ke kāryakram kī do ṭikṭeṃ chāhie
musical score svarlipi स्वरलिपि	**encore** punaḥ prastuti पुनः प्रस्तुति	मुझे आज रात के कार्यक्रम की दो टिकटें चाहिए।

opera
opera | ऑपेरा

cinema • sinemā • सिनेमा

popcorn
popcorn
पॉपकॉर्न

box office
box office
बॉक्स ऑफ़िस

lobby
lobby
लॉबी

poster
posṭar
पोस्टर

cinema hall
sinemā hall | सिनेमा हॉल

screen
pardā | पर्दा

vocabulary • śabdāvalī • शब्दावली

comedy comedy कॉमेडी	**romance** romāns रोमांस
thriller thrilar थिलर	**science fiction film** vijñān kathā film विज्ञान कथा फ़िल्म
horror film ḍarāvanī film डरावनी फ़िल्म	**adventure** romānch kathā रोमांच कथा
western paśchimī पश्चिमी	**animated film** ainimeṭeḍ film ऐनिमेटेड फ़िल्म

orchestra • vādyavṛnd • वाद्यवृंद

strings • tantrī vādya • तंत्री वाद्य

harp
hārp
हार्प

conductor
sanchālak
संचालक

double bass
ḍabal bās
डबल बास

violin
vāyalin
वायलिन

podium
poḍiyam
पोडियम

viola
vāyolā
वायोला

cello
chelo
चेलो

score
svar lipi
स्वर लिपि

treble clef
ṭrebal klaif
ट्रेबल क्लैफ़

note
svar
स्वर

staff
sṭāf
स्टाफ़

bass clef
bās klaif
बास क्लैफ़

Andante

rit.

piano | piyāno | पियानो

notation | svar lipi | स्वर लिपि

vocabulary • śabdāvalī • शब्दावली

overture	**sonata**	**rest**	**sharp**	**natural**	**scale**
pūrvraṅg	sonāṭā	virām	ucch svar	piyāno kā śvet pardā	saptak
पूर्वरंग	सोनाटा	विराम	उच्च स्वर	पियानो का श्वेत पर्दा	सप्तक
symphony	**instruments**	**pitch**	**flat**	**bar**	**baton**
svar saṅgati	vādya yantr	svarmān	komal sur	tālkhaṇḍ	chhaṛī
स्वर संगति	वाद्य यंत्र	स्वरमान	कोमल सुर	तालखंड	छड़ी

woodwind • kāṣṭh vādya yantr • काष्ठ वाद्य यंत्र

piccolo
piccolo | पिकॉलो

flute
bāṃsurī | बांसुरी

oboe
obo | ओबो

cor anglais
aṅgrezī bīn | अंग्रेज़ी बीन

clarinet
klairineṭ
क्लैरिनेट

bass clarinet
mandr klairineṭ
मंद्र क्लैरिनेट

bassoon
basūn
बसून

double bassoon
ḍabal basūn
डबल बसून

saxophone
seksofon
सेक्सोफ़ोन

percussion • tāl vādya • ताल वाद्य

kettledrum
nagāṛā | नगाड़ा

gong
ghaṇṭā | घंटा

bongos
baumgo
बौंगो

snare drum
chhoṭā ḍram
छोटा ड्रम

cymbals
manjīrā | मंजीरा

tambourine
ḍaphlī | डफली

triangle
ṭrāieṅgal
ट्राइएंगल

maracas
marākas
मराकस

vibraphone
vāibrāfon | वाइब्राफ़ोन

brass • pītal ke vādya • पीतल के वाद्य

trumpet
ṭrampeṭ | ट्रम्पेट

trombone
trombone | ट्रॉम्बोन

French horn
french horn | फ़्रेंच हॉर्न

tuba
ṭyūbā | ट्यूबा

concert • concert • कॉन्सर्ट

lead singer
pramukh
gāyak
प्रमुख गायक

microphone
māikrofon
माइक्रोफ़ोन

drummer
ḍramar
ड्रमर

guitarist
giṭār vādak
गिटार वादक

fans
praśansak
प्रशंसक

bass guitarist
bais giṭār vādak
बैस गिटार वादक

speaker
spīkar | स्पीकर

rock concert | rock concert | रॉक कॉन्सर्ट

instruments • vādya yantr • वाद्य यंत्र

pickup
pikap
पिकअप

neck
tanā
तना

fret
freṭ
फ़्रेट

tuning peg
khūmṭī
खूंटी

string
tār
तार

bridge
brij
ब्रिज

drum
ḍram
ड्रम

bass guitar | bais giṭār | बैस गिटार

keyboard
kī borḍ | की बोर्ड

electric guitar
ilekṭrik giṭār | इलेक्ट्रिक गिटार

drum kit
ḍram kiṭ | ड्रम किट

musical styles • saṅgīt śailiyāṃ • संगीत शैलियां

jazz | jaiz | जैज़

blues | blūz | ब्लूज़

punk | paṅk | पंक

folk music
lok saṅgīt | लोक संगीत

pop | pop | पॉप

dance | dāns | डांस

rap
raip | रैप

heavy metal
rock | रॉक

classical music
śāstrīya saṅgīt | शास्त्रीय संगीत

---

vocabulary • śabdāvalī • शब्दावली

song	lyrics	melody	beat	reggae	country	spotlight
gānā	gīt	madhur saṅgīt	thāp	raige	kanṭrī myūzik	spot lāiṭ
गाना	गीत	मधुर संगीत	थाप	रैगे	कंट्री म्यूज़िक	स्पॉट लाइट

---

sightseeing • sair-sapāṭā • सैर–सपाटा

tourist
paryaṭak
पर्यटक

tourist attraction
paryaṭan sthal | पर्यटन स्थल

itinerary
mārg nirdeśikā
मार्ग निर्देशिका

open-top
khulī chhat
खुली छत

This is an official London Sightseeing Bus.

LONDON PRIDE

tour bus | paryaṭan bas | पर्यटन बस

tour guide
paryaṭan gāiḍ
पर्यटन–गाइड

guided tour
mārgdarśit paryaṭan
मार्गदर्शित पर्यटन

statuette
laghu pratimā
लघु प्रतिमा

souvenirs
smṛti chihn
स्मृति चिह्न

---

vocabulary • śabdāvalī • शब्दावली

open khulā खुला	**guide book** nirdeśikā निर्देशिका	**camcorder** haiṇḍīkaim हैंडीकैम	**left** bāyāṃ बायां	**Where is…?** … kahāṃ hai? … कहां है?
straight on sīdh meṃ सीध में	**film closed** band बंद	**camera** kaimrā कैमरा	**right** dāyāṃ दायां	**I'm lost.** maiṃ kho gayā hūṃ मैं खो गया हूं।
film entrance fee praveś śulk प्रवेश शुल्क	**batteries** baiṭriyāṃ बैटरियां	**directions** nirdeśan निर्देशन	**film** film फ़िल्म	**Can you tell me the way to…?** kyā āp mujhe … jāne kā rāstā batā sakte haiṃ? क्या आप मुझे … जाने का रास्ता बता सकते हैं?

---

attractions • ramaṇīya sthal • रमणीय स्थल

painting
peṇṭiṅg
पेंटिंग

exhibit
pradarśit vastu
प्रदर्शित वस्तु

exhibition
pradarśanī | प्रदर्शनी

famous ruin
prasiddh khaṇḍahar
प्रसिद्ध खंडहर

art gallery
kalā dīrghā | कला दीर्घा

monument
smārak | स्मारक

museum
saṅgrahālya | संग्रहालय

historic building
aitihāsik imārat
ऐतिहासिक इमारत

casino
juāghar | जुआघर

gardens
bāg | बाग़

national park
rāṣṭrīya udyān | राष्ट्रीय उद्यान

information • jānkarī • जानकारी

times
samaya
समय

floor plan
bhavan naqśā | भवन नक़्शा

map
naqśā | नक़्शा

timetable
samaya sāriṇī
समय सारिणी

tourist information
paryaṭak sūchnā kendr
पर्यटक सूचना केंद्र

outdoor activities • bāhrī gatividhiyāṃ • बाहरी गतिविधियां

footpath
paidal rāstā
पैदल रास्ता

sundial
dhūp ghaṛī
धूप घड़ी

café
kaife
कैफ़े

park | udyān | उद्यान

grass
ghās
घास

bench
bench
बेंच

formal gardens
bagīchā
बग़ीचा

roller coaster
rolar kosṭar
रोलर कोस्टर

fairground
melā sthal | मेला स्थल

theme park
thīm pārk | थीम पार्क

safari park
safārī pārk | सफ़ारी पार्क

zoo
chiṛiyāghar | चिड़ियाघर

activities • gatividhiyāṃ • गतिविधियां

cycling | sāikil chalānā |
साइकिल चलाना

jogging
jogging | जॉगिंग

skateboarding | skeṭ
bording | स्केट बोर्डिंग

rollerblading | rolar
bleḍiṅg | रोलर ब्लेडिंग

bridle path
aśv mārg
अश्व मार्ग

bird watching | pakṣī
nihārnā | पक्षी निहारना

horse riding
ghuṛsavārī | घुड़सवारी

hiking
padyātrā | पदयात्रा

hamper
ṭokrī
टोकरी

picnic
piknik | पिकनिक

playground • khel kā maidān • खेल का मैदान

sandpit
ret kā akhāṛā
रेत का अखाड़ा

paddling pool
kṛtrim tālāb
कृत्रिम तालाब

swings
jhūlā | झूला

climbing frame
sīṛhīnumā jhūlā | सीढ़ीनुमा झूला

seesaw | seesaw | सीसॉ

slide | phisal paṭṭī | फिसल पट्टी

beach • taṭ • तट

hotel	beach umbrella	beach hut	sand	wave	sea
hoṭal	taṭīya chhātā	taṭīya jhoprī	ret	lahar	samudr
होटल	तटीय छाता	तटीय झोपड़ी	रेत	लहर	समुद्र

beach bag
bīch thailā
बीच थैला

bikini
biknī
बिकनी

sunbathe (v) | sūrya snān karnā | सूर्य स्नान करना

lifeguard
jīvan rakṣak
जीवन रक्षक

lifeguard tower
jīvan rakṣak ṭāvar
जीवन रक्षक टावर

windbreak | havā
rodhak | हवा रोधक

promenade | vihār
sthal | विहार स्थल

deck chair | ḍaik
kursī | डैक कुर्सी

sunglasses | dhūp kā
chaśmā | धूप का चश्मा

sunhat
haiṭ | हैट

suntan lotion | saṇṭain
lośan | सनटैन लोशन

sunblock | san
block | सन ब्लॉक

beach ball
bīch ball | बीच बॉल

rubber ring | rabaṛ kī
ṭyūb | रबड़ की ट्यूब

beach towel
bīch tauliyā | बीच तौलिया

swimsuit
tairākī sūṭ
तैराकी सूट

spade
khurpī
खुरपी

bucket
ṭokrī
टोकरी

sandcastle
ret kā mahal
रेत का महल

shell
sīp
सीप

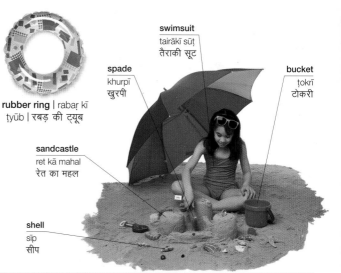

camping • śivir lagānā • शिविर लगाना

toilets śauchālaya शौचालय	**waste disposal** kūṛedān कूड़ेदान	**shower block** snān sthal स्नान स्थल	**electric hook-up** ilekṭrik huk ap इलेक्ट्रिक हुक–अप

flysheet dvār pardā द्वार पर्दा	**tent peg** khūṃṭā खूंटा	**guy rope** rassī रस्सी	**caravan** gāṛī गाड़ी

campsite
śivir sthal | शिविर स्थल

---

vocabulary • śabdāvalī • शब्दावली

camp (v) śivir lagānā शिविर लगाना	**pitch** sthān स्थान	**picnic bench** piknik bench पिकनिक बेंच	**charcoal** kacchā koyalā कच्चा कोयला
site manager's office sāiṭ prabandhak kāryālaya साइट प्रबंधक कार्यालय	**pitch a tent (v)** tambū gāṛnā तंबू गाड़ना	**hammock** jhūlā झूला	**firelighter** āg jalāne kā upkaraṇ आग जलाने का उपकरण
pitches available sthān uplabdh स्थान उपलब्ध	**tent pole** tambū kā khambhā तंबू का खंभा	**camper van** śivir vāhan शिविर वाहन	**light a fire (v)** āg jalānā आग जलाना
full pūrā पूरा	**camp bed** safrī palaṅg सफ़री पलंग	**trailer** ṭrelar ट्रेलर	**campfire** alāv अलाव

frame
frem
फ़्रेम

ground sheet
darī
दरी

backpack
piṭṭhū
पिट्ठू

vacuum flask
vaikyūm flāsk
वैक्यूम फ़्लास्क

water bottle
pānī kī botal
पानी की बोतल

tent
śivir | शिविर

mosquito net
macchhardānī
मच्छरदानी

insect repellent
macchhar avrodhak
मच्छर अवरोधक

torch
torch | टॉर्च

thermals
garm kapṛe
गर्म कपड़े

walking boots
jūte | जूते

waterproofs
waterproofs | वॉटरप्रूफ़

sleeping bag
slīpiṅg baig | स्लीपिंग बैग

sleeping mat
gaddā
गद्दा

camping stove
safrī sṭov | सफ़री स्टोव

barbecue
gril | ग्रिल

air mattress | havā bharā gaddā | हवा भरा गद्दा

home entertainment • gharelū manorañjan • घरेलू मनोरंजन

personal CD player
parsnal CD pleyar
पर्सनल सीडी प्लेयर

mini disk recorder
minī ḍisk recorder
मिनी डिस्क रिकॉर्डर

MP3 player
MP3 pleyar
एम पी श्री प्लेयर

DVD disk
DVD ḍisk
डीवीडी डिस्क

DVD player
DVD pleyar
डीवीडी प्लेयर

record player
record pleyar
रिकॉर्ड प्लेयर

CD player
CD pleyar
सीडी प्लेयर

radio
reḍiyo
रेडियो

amplifier
emplīfāyar
एंप्लीफ़ायर

headphones
haiḍfon
हैडफ़ोन

stand
staiṇḍ
स्टैंड

(loud) speaker
spīkar
स्पीकर

speaker stand
spīkar staiṇḍ
स्पीकर स्टैंड

hi-fi system
hāī fāī sisṭam | हाई–फ़ाई सिस्टम

video tape
vīḍiyo ṭep
वीडियो टेप

video recorder
vīḍiyo recorder | वीडियो रिकॉर्डर

screen
skrīn
स्क्रीन

eyecup
aī kap
आई कप

camcorder
haiṇḍīkaim | हैंडीकैम

satellite dish
upgrah ḍiś | उपग्रह डिश

widescreen television
baṛe skrīn vālā ṭīvī
बड़े स्क्रीन वाला टीवी

console
console
कॉन्सोल

fast forward
fāsṭ forward
फ़ास्ट फ़ॉरवर्ड

pause
pause
पॉज़

record
record
रिकॉर्ड

volume
volume star
वॉल्यूम स्तर

controller
kanṭrolar
कंट्रोलर

rewind
rivāiṇḍ
रिवाइंड

play
ple
प्ले

stop
stop
स्टॉप

video game | vīḍiyo gem | वीडियो गेम

remote control
rimoṭ kanṭrol | रिमोट कंट्रोल

---

vocabulary • śābdāvalī • शब्दावली

compact disc compact ḍisk कॉम्पैक्ट डिस्क	**feature film** fīchar film फ़ीचर फ़िल्म	**programme** kāryakram कार्यक्रम	**change channel (v)** chainal badalnā चैनल बदलना	**turn the television on (v)** ṭelīvizan chalānā टेलीविज़न चलाना
cassette tape kaiseṭ ṭep कैसेट टेप	**advertisement** vijñāpan विज्ञापन	**stereo** sṭīriyo स्टीरियो	**tune the radio (v)** reḍiyo saiṭ karnā रेडियो सैट करना	**turn the television off (v)** ṭelīvizan band karnā टेलीविज़न बंद करना
cassette player kaiseṭ pleyar कैसेट प्लेयर	**digital** ḍijīṭal डिजीटल	**cable television** kebal ṭelīvizan केबल टेलीविज़न	**watch television (v)** ṭīvī dekhnā टीवी देखना	**pay per view channel** prati chainal bhugtān प्रति चैनल भुगतान

---

photography • foṭogrāfī • फ़ोटोग्राफ़ी

frame counter
frem kāunṭar
फ़्रेम काउंटर

flash
flaiś
फ़्लैश

aperture dial
aparchar
niyantrak
अपर्चर नियंत्रक

shutter release
śaṭar rilīz
शटर रिलीज़

shutter-speed dial
śaṭar-spīḍ ḍāyal
शटर–स्पीड डायल

lens
lains
लैंस

SLR camera | SLR kaimrā | एस एल आर कैमरा

filter
filṭar | फ़िल्टर

lens caps
lains kaip | लैंस कैप

flash gun
flaiś gan | फ़्लैश गन

lightmeter
lāiṭmīṭar | लाइटमीटर

zoom lens
zūm lains | ज़ूम लैंस

tripod
tipāyā sṭaiṇḍ | तिपाया स्टैंड

types of camera • kaimre ke prakār • कैमरे के प्रकार

digital camera
ḍijiṭal kaimrā
डिजीटल कैमरा

APS camera
APS kaimrā
ए पी एस कैमरा

instant camera
insṭenṭ kaimrā
इंस्टेंट कैमरा

disposable camera
ḍispozebal kaimrā
डिस्पोज़ेबल कैमरा

photograph (v) • foṭo khīṃchnā • फ़ोटो खींचना

film spool
film rīl
फ़िल्म रील

film
film | फ़िल्म

focus (v) | kendrit
karnā | केंद्रित करना

develop (v)
film dhonā | फ़िल्म धोना

negative
negeṭiv | नेगेटिव

landscape
prakr̥tik dr̥śya
प्राकृतिक दृश्य

portrait
vyakti chitr
व्यक्ति चित्र

photograph | tasvīr | तस्वीर

photo album
foṭo elbam | फ़ोटो एल्बम

photo frame | foṭo
frem | फ़ोटो फ़्रेम

problems • samasyāeṃ • समस्याएं

underexposed
kam udbhāsit
कम उद्भासित

overexposed
atyadhik udbhāsit
अत्यधिक उद्भासित

out of focus | fokas se
bāhar | फ़ोकस से बाहर

red eye
raid āī | रैड आई

vocabulary • śabdāvalī • शब्दावली	
viewfinder dr̥śyadarśī दृश्यदर्शी	**print** foṭo prati फ़ोटो प्रति
camera case kaimrā kes कैमरा केस	**mat** khurdurā खुरदुरा
exposure udbhāsan उद्भासन	**gloss** chiknā चिकना
darkroom ḍārk rūm डार्क रूम	**enlargement** foṭo baṛī karānā फ़ोटो बड़ी कराना

I'd like this film processed
maiṃ ye rīl dhulvānā chāhtī hūṃ
मैं ये रील धुलवाना चाहती हूं।

games • khel • खेल

chessboard
bisāt
बिसात

black
kālā
काला

white
safed
सफ़ेद

queen
vazīr
वज़ीर

king
rājā
राजा

bishop
ūṃṭ
ऊंट

pawn
pyādā
प्यादा

knight
ghoṛā
घोड़ा

rook
hāthī
हाथी

chess
śatranj | शतरंज

square
k̲h̲ānā
ख़ाना

piece
goṭī
गोटी

tile
ṭāil
टाइल

draughts | draughts | ड्रॉट्स

scrabble | skraibal | स्क्रैबल

backgammon
baik gaiman | बैक गैमन

dice
pāsā
पासा

counter
mohrā | मोहरा

monopoly
monopolī
मोनोपोली

board games
borḍ khel | बोर्ड खेल

stamp collecting
ḍāk ṭikaṭ saṅgrah
डाक टिकट संग्रह

jigsaw puzzle | chitrakhaṇḍ
pahelī | चित्रखंड पहेली

dominoes
ḍominos | डोमिनोस

dartboard
ḍārṭ borḍ
डार्टबोर्ड

bullseye
lakṣya
लक्ष्य

darts
ḍārṭs | डार्ट्स

joker
jokar
जोकर

jack
gulām
गुलाम

queen
begam
बेगम

king
bādśāh
बादशाह

ace
ikkā
इक्का

diamond
īṇṭ
ईंट

spade
hukum
हुकुम

heart
pān
पान

club
chiṛī
चिड़ी

cards
tāś | ताश

shuffle (v)
tāś pheṃṭnā | ताश फेंटना

deal (v)
patte bāṃṭnā | पत्ते बांटना

vocabulary • śabdāvalī • शब्दावली

move	**win (v)**	**loser**	**point**	**bridge**	**Roll the dice.**
chāl	jītnā	parājit	nambar	brij	pāsā pheṃko
चाल	जीतना	पराजित	नंबर	ब्रिज	पासा फेंको
play (v)	**winner**	**game**	**score**	**pack of cards**	**Whose turn is it?**
khelnā	vijetā	khel	arjit aṃk	tāś kī gaḍḍī	kiskī bārī hai?
खेलना	विजेता	खेल	अर्जित अंक	ताश की गड्डी	किसकी बारी है?
player	**lose (v)**	**bet**	**poker**	**suit**	**It's your move.**
khilāṛī	hārnā	śart	pokar	tāś raṅg	ab tumhārī chāl hai
खिलाड़ी	हारना	शर्त	पोकर	ताश रंग	अब तुम्हारी चाल है।

arts and crafts 1 • kalā aur śilp 1 • कला और शिल्प 1

paints • raṅg • रंग

artist
chitrakār
चित्रकार

painting
chitr
चित्र

easel
chitrādhār
चित्राधार

canvas
kainvas
कैनवस

brush
braś
ब्रश

palette
tūlikā
तूलिका

painting | chitrakārī | चित्रकारी

oil paints
tail raṅg | तैल रंग

watercolour paint
pānī ke raṅg | पानी के रंग

pastels
raṅgīn khaṛiyā | रंगीन खड़िया

acrylic paint
aikrilīk raṅg | ऐक्रिलीक रं

poster paint
pōsṭar raṅg | पोस्टर रंग

colours • raṅg • रंग

red lāl	लाल	**blue** nīlā	नीला	**yellow** pīlā	पीला	**green** harā	हरा
orange nāraṅgī	नारंगी	**purple** baiṅganī	बैंगनी	**white** safed	सफ़ेद	**black** kālā	काला
grey slēṭī	स्लेटी	**pink** gulābī	गुलाबी	**brown** bhūrā	भूरा	**indigo** nīl	नील

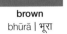

other crafts • anya kalāeṃ • अन्य कलाएं

sketch pad
rekhāṅkan paṭal
रेखांकन पटल

sketch
k̲hākā
ख़ाका

ink
syāhī
स्याही

pencil
pensil
पेंसिल

charcoal
koyalā battī
कोयला बत्ती

drawing | rekhāṅkan | रेखांकन

printing
chhapāī | छपाई

engraving
utkīrṇan | उत्कीर्णन

stone
patthar
पत्थर

mallet
muṅgrā
मुंगरा

chisel
chhainī
छैनी

wood
lakṛī
लकड़ी

sculpting
mūrti śilp | मूर्ति शिल्प

woodworking
kāṣṭh-kalā | काष्ठ–कला

modelling tool
hastkalā upkaraṇ
हस्तकला उपकरण

potter's wheel
chāk
चाक

clay
chiknī miṭṭī
चिकनी
मिट्टी

glue
gond
गोंद

cardboard
gattā
गत्ता

collage | kolāj | कोलाज

pottery
kumhār karm | कुम्हार कर्म

ewellery making | ābhūṣaṇ-nirmāṇ | आभूषण निर्माण

papier-mâché | paipya māśe | पैप्य माशे

origami
aurigāmī | औरिगामी

model making | model banānā | मॉडल बनाना

arts and crafts 2 • kalā aur śilp 2 • कला और शिल्प 2

thread guide
dhāgā
धागा

thread reel
dhāge kī rīl
धागे की रील

needle
sūī
सूई

balance wheel
pahiyā
पहिया

presser foot
kapṛā dabāne vālā
कपड़ा दबाने वाला

needle plate
sūī ke nīche
kī pattī
सूई के नीचे
की पत्ती

stitch selector
silāī chayan baṭan
सिलाई चयन बटन

sewing machine
silāī maśīn | सिलाई मशीन

scissors
kaiṃchī
कैंची

pattern
k͟hākā
ख़ाका

pincushion
pinkuśan
पिनकुशन

pin
pin
पिन

tape measure
inchṭep
इंचटेप

material
kapṛā | कपड़ा

sewing basket
silāī kī ṭokrī | सिलाई की टोकरी

thread
dhāgā
धागा

eye
āī | आई

bobbin
phirkī
फिरकी

hook
huk
हुक

thimble
amguśtānā
अंगुश्ताना

tailor's chalk
darzī kā chalk
दर्ज़ी का चॉक

tailor's dummy
darzī kī ḍamī
दर्ज़ी की डमी

thread (v)
dhāgā ḍālnā
धागा डालना

stitch
bakhiyā
बखिया

sew (v)
silnā
सिलना

darn (v)
rafū karnā
रफू करना

tack (v)
ṭāṃknā
टांकना

cut (v)
kāṭnā
काटना

needlepoint
sūī kī nok
सूई की नोक

embroidery
kaṛhāī
कढ़ाई

crochet hook
krośiyā huk
क्रोशिया हुक

crochet
krośiyā
क्रोशिया

macramé
jhālar
झालर

patchwork
paiband
पैबंद

quilting
parat lagānā
परत लगाना

lace bobbin
les bobbin
लेस बॉबिन

lace-making
les banānā
लेस बनाना

loom
karghā
करघा

weaving
bunnā
बुनना

knitting needle
bunne kī slāī
बुनने की सलाई

knitting
bunāī | बुनाई

skein
lacchhī | लच्छी

wool
ūn
ऊन

---

vocabulary • śabdāvalī • शब्दावली

unpick (v)	**nylon**
udheṛnā	nāyalon
उधेड़ना	नायलोन
fabric	**silk**
kapṛā	reśam
कपड़ा	रेशम
cotton	**designer**
sūtī kapṛā	ḍizāinar
सूती कपड़ा	डिज़ाइनर
linen	**fashion**
linen	faiśan
लिनेन	फ़ैशन
polyester	**zip**
polyester	zip
पॉलीएस्टर	ज़िप

---

environment
paryāvaraṇ
पर्यावरण

space • antarikṣ • अंतरिक्ष

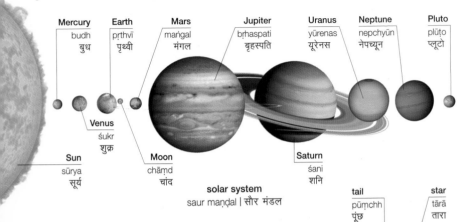

Mercury
budh
बुध

Earth
pṛthvī
पृथ्वी

Mars
maṅgal
मंगल

Jupiter
bṛhaspati
बृहस्पति

Uranus
yūrenas
यूरेनस

Neptune
nepchyūn
नेप्च्यून

Pluto
plūṭo
प्लूटो

Venus
śukr
शुक्र

Sun
sūrya
सूर्य

Moon
chāṃd
चांद

Saturn
śani
शनि

solar system
saur maṇḍal | सौर मंडल

tail
pūṃchh
पूंछ

star
tārā
तारा

galaxy
tārāsamūh | तारासमूह

nebula
nihārikā | निहारिका

asteroid
grahikā | ग्रहिका

comet
dhūmketu | धूमकेतु

---

vocabulary • śabdāvalī • शब्दावली

universe brahamāṇḍ ब्रह्मांड	**black hole** blaik hol ब्लैक होल	**full moon** pūrā chāṃd पूरा चांद
orbit kakṣā कक्षा	**planet** grah ग्रह	**crescent moon** ardhchandr अर्धचंद्र
gravity gurutv गुरुत्व	**meteor** ulkā उल्का	**new moon** pratipadā kā chāṃd प्रतिपदा का चांद

eclipse | grahan | ग्रहण

space exploration • antarikṣ anveṣaṇ • अंतरिक्ष अन्वेषण

radar
rāḍār
राडार

thruster
thrasṭar
थ्रस्टर

crew hatch
updvār
उपद्वार

space shuttle
antarikṣ yān
अंतरिक्ष यान

space suit
antarikṣ sūṭ
अंतरिक्ष सूट

booster
būsṭar
बूस्टर

astronaut | antarikṣ yātrī | अंतरिक्ष यात्री

lunar module | chandryān | चंद्रयान

launch pad
prakṣepaṇ sthal
प्रक्षेपण स्थल

launch
prakṣepaṇ | प्रक्षेपण

satellite
upgrah | उपग्रह

space station | antarikṣ kendr
अंतरिक्ष केंद्र

astronomy • khagol vijñān • खगोल विज्ञान

telescope
dūrbīn
दूरबीन

tripod
tipāyā sṭaiṇḍ
तिपाया स्टैंड

constellation
tārāmaṇḍal | तारामंडल

binoculars
dūrbīn | दूरबीन

Earth • pṛthvī • पृथ्वी

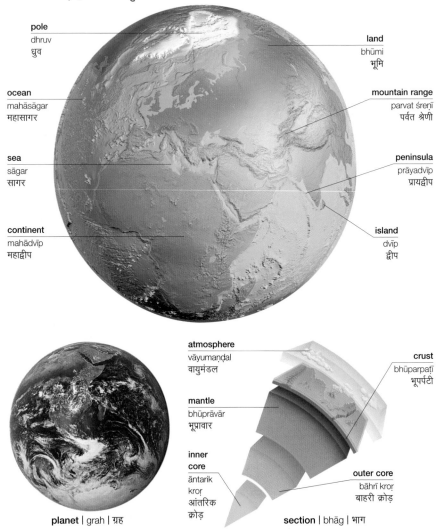

pole
dhruv
ध्रुव

land
bhūmi
भूमि

ocean
mahāsāgar
महासागर

mountain range
parvat śreṇī
पर्वत श्रेणी

sea
sāgar
सागर

peninsula
prāyadvīp
प्रायद्वीप

continent
mahādvīp
महाद्वीप

island
dvīp
द्वीप

atmosphere
vāyumaṇḍal
वायुमंडल

crust
bhūparpaṭī
भूपर्पटी

mantle
bhūprāvār
भूप्रावार

inner core
āntarik kroṛ
आंतरिक क्रोड़

outer core
bāhrī kroṛ
बाहरी क्रोड़

planet | grah | ग्रह

section | bhāg | भाग

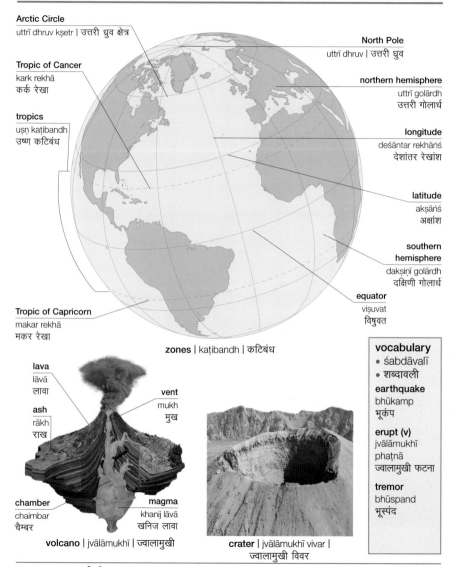

Arctic Circle
uttrī dhruv kṣetr | उत्तरी ध्रुव क्षेत्र

North Pole
uttrī dhruv | उत्तरी ध्रुव

Tropic of Cancer
kark rekhā
कर्क रेखा

northern hemisphere
uttrī golārdh
उत्तरी गोलार्ध

tropics
uṣṇ kaṭibandh
उष्ण कटिबंध

longitude
deśāntar rekhāṅś
देशांतर रेखांश

latitude
akṣāṅś
अक्षांश

southern hemisphere
dakṣiṇī golārdh
दक्षिणी गोलार्ध

equator
viṣuvat
विषुवत

Tropic of Capricorn
makar rekhā
मकर रेखा

zones | kaṭibandh | कटिबंध

lava
lāvā
लावा

vent
mukh
मुख

ash
rākh
राख

chamber
chaimbar
चैम्बर

magma
khanij lāvā
खनिज लावा

volcano | jvālāmukhī | ज्वालामुखी

crater | jvālāmukhī vivar |
ज्वालामुखी विवर

vocabulary
● śabdāvalī
● शब्दावली

earthquake
bhūkamp
भूकंप

erupt (v)
jvālāmukhī
phaṭnā
ज्वालामुखी फटना

tremor
bhūspand
भूस्पंद

landscape • bhūdṛśaya • भूदृश्य

mountain
parvat | पर्वत

slope
ḍhalān
ढलान

bank
kinārā
किनारा

river
nadī
नदी

rapids
tīvr dhārā
तीव्र धारा

rocks
chaṭṭān
चट्टान

glacier
himnad | हिमनद

valley | ghāṭī | घाटी

hill
pahāṛī | पहाड़ी

plateau
paṭhār | पठार

gorge
darrā | दर्रा

cave
guphā | गुफा

plain | maidān | मैदान

desert | registān रेगिस्तान

forest | jaṅgal | जंगल

wood | van | वन

rainforest varṣā van | वर्षा वन

swamp daldal | दलदल

meadow charāgāh | चरागाह

grassland | ghās kā maidān | घास का मैदान

waterfall jalprapāt | जलप्रपात

stream dhārā | धारा

lake jhīl | झील

geyser garm jalsarot | गर्म जलस्रोत

coast samudr taṭ | समुद्र तट

cliff | kharī chaṭṭān खड़ी चट्टान

coral reef pravāl dvīp | प्रवाल द्वीप

estuary | sāgar vilyan सागर विलयन

weather • mausam • मौसम

exosphere
parāmaṇḍal
परामंडल

aurora
dhruvjyoti
ध्रुवज्योति

thermosphere
tāpmaṇḍal
तापमंडल

sunshine | dhūp | धूप

ionosphere
āyan maṇḍal
आयन मंडल

ultraviolet rays
parābaiṅganī kirṇeṃ
पराबैंगनी किरणें

mesosphere
madhya maṇḍal
मध्य मंडल

stratosphere
samtāp maṇḍal
समताप मंडल

ozone layer
ozon parat
ओज़ोन परत

troposphere
nimntāp maṇḍal
निम्नताप मंडल

atmosphere | vayumaṇḍal | वायुमंडल

wind | pavan | पवन

vocabulary • śabdāvalī • शब्दावली

sleet	**shower**	**hot**	**dry**	**windy**	**I'm hot/cold.**
himvarṣā	bauchhār	garm	sūkhā	tūfānī	mujhe garmī / ṭhaṇḍ lag rahī hai
हिमवर्षा	बौछार	गर्म	सूखा	तूफ़ानी	मुझे गर्मी/ठंड लग रही है।
hail	**sunny**	**cold**	**wet**	**gale**	**It's raining.**
ole	dhūpdār	ṭhaṇḍā	gīlā	āndhī	bāriś ho rahī hai
ओले	धूपदार	ठंडा	गीला	आंधी	बारिश हो रही है।
thunder	**cloudy**	**warm**	**humid**	**temperature**	**It's ... degrees.**
garaj	meghācchhann	gungunā	nam	tāpmān	tāpmān ... ḍigrī hai
गरज	मेघाच्छन्न	गुनगुना	नम	तापमान	तापमान... डिग्री है।

cloud | bādal | बादल

rain | bāriś | बारिश

lightning
bijlī | बिजली

storm | tūfān | तूफ़ान

mist | kohrā | कोहरा

fog | dhundh | धुंध

rainbow | indrdhanuṣ | इंद्रधनुष

snow | him | हिम

frost | tuṣār | तुषार

ice | baraf | बर्फ़

icicle
āisikal | आइसिकल

freeze | ṭhaṇḍ | ठंड

hurricane
chakrvāt | चक्रवात

tornado
bavaṇḍar | बवंडर

monsoon
varṣā | वर्षा

flood
bāṛh | बाढ़

rocks • pāṣāṇ • पाषाण

igneous • jvalāmukhīya śail • ज्वालामुखीय शैल

granite
grenāiṭ
ग्रेनाइट

obsidian
obsidiyan
ओबसिडियन

basalt
kālā patthar
काला पत्थर

pumice
jhāmak
झामक

sedimentary • avsādī śail • अवसादी शैल

sandstone
baluā patthar
बलुआ पत्थर

limestone
chūnā patthar
चूना पत्थर

chalk
khaṛiyā
खड़िया

flint
chakmak
चकमक

conglomerate
pāṣāṇit kaṅkaṛ
पाषाणित कंकड़

coal
koyalā
कोयला

metamorphic • rūpāntarit śail • रूपांतरित शैल

slate
sleṭ
स्लेट

schist
starit chaṭṭān
स्तरित चट्टान

gneiss
śail
शैल

marble
saṅgmarmar
संगमरमर

gems • ratan • रत्न

ruby
māṇik | माणिक

amethyst
jambumaṇi
जंबुमणि

jet
lāvā maṇi
लावा मणि

opal
upal
उपल

moonstone
chandrakānt maṇi
चंद्रकांत मणि

diamond
hīrā
हीरा

garnet
raktmaṇi
रक्तमणि

topaz
pukhrāj
पुखराज

aquamarine
haritnīl
हरितनील

jade
jeḍ
जेड

emerald
pannā
पन्ना

sapphire
nīlam
नीलम

tourmaline
turmalī
तुरमली

minerals • khanij • खनिज

quartz
sphaṭik
स्फटिक

mica
abhrak
अभ्रक

sulphur
gandhak
गंधक

hematite
hemeṭāiṭ
हेमेटाइट

calcite
kailsāiṭ
कैल्साइट

malachite
melākāiṭ
मेलाकाइट

turquoise
fīrojā
फ़ीरोजा

onyx
sarpmaṇi
सर्पमणि

agate
akīk
अकीक

graphite
grefāiṭ
ग्रेफ़ाइट

metals • dhātu • धातु

gold
sonā | सोना

silver
chāndī
चांदी

platinum
pleṭinam
प्लेटिनम

nickel
nikal | निकल

iron
lohā | लोहा

copper
tāmbā | तांबा

tin
ṭin | टिन

aluminium
alyūminiyam
अल्यूमिनियम

mercury
pārā | पारा

zinc
jastā | जस्ता

animals 1 • paśu 1 • पशु
mammals • standhārī jīv • स्तनधारी जीव

rabbit
ḳhargoś
ख़रगोश

whiskers
mūṃchheṃ
मूंछें

hamster
haimsṭar | हैम्स्टर

mouse
mūṣak | मूषक

tail
pūṃchh
पूंछ

rat
chūhā | चूहा

hedgehog
sāhī | साही

squirrel
gilahrī
गिलहरी

bat
chamgādaṛ
चमगादड़

raccoon
raikūn
रैकून

fox
lomṛī
लोमड़ी

wolf
bheṛiyā
भेड़िया

puppy
pillā
पिल्ला

kitten
billī kā bacchā
बिल्ली का बच्चा

pup
śiśu sīl
शिशु सील

dog
kuttā | कुत्ता

cat
billī | बिल्ली

otter
ūdbilāv | ऊदबिलाव

seal
sīl | सील

flipper
mīn paṅkh
मीन पंख

blowhole
śvās chhidr
श्वास छिद्र

dolphin
dolphin
डॉल्फिन

sea lion
samudr siṅh
समुद्र सिंह

walrus
hāthī sīl
हाथी सील

whale
vhel | व्हेल

antler
sīṅg
सींग

mane
ayāl
अयाल

hump
kūbar
कूबड़

hoof
khur
खुर

deer
hiran | हिरन

zebra
zebrā | ज़ेबरा

giraffe
jirāf | जिराफ़

camel
ūṃṭ | ऊंट

trunk
sūṃṛ | सूंड़

tusk
hāthī dāṃt
हाथी दांत

horn
sīṅg | सींग

hippopotamus
dariyāī ghoṛā | दरियाई
घोड़ा

elephant
hāthī | हाथी

rhinoceros
gaiṇḍā | गैंडा

tiger
bāgh | बाघ

mane
ayāl | अयाल

lion
babbar śer | बब्बर शेर

monkey
bandar | बंदर

gorilla
gorillā | गोरिल्ला

koala
koālā | कोआला

pouch
thailī
थैली

panda
pāṃḍā
पांडा

kangaroo
kaṅgārū | कंगारू

bear
bhālū | भालू

claw
panjā
पंजा

polar bear
dhruviya bhālū | ध्रुवीय भालू

animals 2 • paśu • पशु
birds • pakṣī • पक्षी

tail
pūṃchh
पूंछ

canary
chhoṭī pīlī chiṛiyā
छोटी पीली चिड़िया

sparrow
goraiyā | गौरैया

hummingbird | marmar
pakṣī | मर्मर पक्षी

swallow
abābīl | अबाबील

crow
kauā | कौआ

pigeon
kabūtar | कबूतर

woodpecker
kaṭhphoṛvā
कठफोड़वा

falcon
bāz | बाज़

owl
ullū | उल्लू

gull
ghomrā | घोमरा

eagle
uḳāb | उक़ाब

pelican
pelikan | पेलिकन

flamingo
rājhaṃs | राजहंस

stork
bagulā | बगुला

crane
sāras | सारस

penguin
penguin | पेंगुइन

ostrich
śuturmurg | शुतुर्मुर्ग़

goose
bataḵẖ | बतख़

swan
haṃs | हंस

peacock
mor | मोर

pheasant
tītar | तीतर

turkey
ṭarkī | टर्की

cockatoo
kākātū totā
काकातू तोता

bill
choṃch
चोंच

feather
far
फ़र

wing
paṅkh
पंख

claw
panjā
पंजा

parrot
totā | तोता

reptiles • sarīsṛp • सरीसृप

scales
sūkhī chamṛī
सूखी चमड़ी

alligator
ghaṛiyāl | घड़ियाल

lizard
chhipkalī | छिपकली

iguana
goh | गोह

shell
kavach
कवच

turtle | samudrī
kachhuā | समुद्री कछुआ

tortoise
kachhuā | कछुआ

snake
sāṃp | सांप

snout
thūthnī
थूथनी

crocodile
magarmacchh | मगरमच्छ

animals 3 • paśu 3 • पशु

amphibians • ubhayachar jīv • उभयचर जीव

frog
meṃḍhak | मेंढक

toad
thal meṃḍhak | थल मेंढक

tadpole
śiśu meṃḍhak | शिशु मेंढक

salamander
sarṭak | सरटक

fish • machhlī • मछली

eel
bām machhlī | बाम मछली

shark
śārk | शार्क

seahorse
aśvmīn | अश्वमीन

skate
skeṭ machhlī | स्केट मछली

ray
re | रे

goldfish
sonmāchhī | सोनमाछी

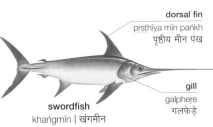

dorsal fin
pṛṣṭhīya mīn paṅkh
पृष्ठीय मीन पंख

pectoral fin
vakṣīya mīn paṅkh
वक्षीय मीन पंख

tail
pūṃchh
पूंछ

gill
galphere
गलफेड़े

scale
śalk
शल्क

swordfish
khaṅgmīn | खंगमीन

koi carp
koi kārp | कोइ कार्प

invertebrates • akaśerukī jīv • अकशेरुकी जीव

ant
chīṃṭī | चींटी

termite
dīmak | दीमक

bee
madhumakkhī | मधुमक्खी

wasp
barr | बर्र

beetle
phūṅgā | फूंगा

cockroach
tilchaṭṭā | तिलचट्टा

moth
pataṅgā | पतंगा

butterfly
titlī | तितली

cocoon
koyā | कोया

caterpillar
illī | इल्ली

cricket
jhīṅgur | झींगुर

grasshopper
ṭiḍḍā | टिड्डा

praying mantis
mantris
मंत्रिस

sting
ḍaṅk
डंक

scorpion
bicchhū | बिच्छू

centipede
kankhajūrā | कनखजूरा

dragonfly
ḍraigan flāī
ड्रैगन फ़्लाई

fly
makkhī | मक्खी

mosquito
macchhar | मच्छर

ladybird
leḍībarḍ | लेडीबर्ड

spider
makṛī | मकड़ी

slug
kambu | कंबु

snail
ghoṃghā | घोंघा

worm
kṛmi | कृमि

starfish
sṭār fiś | स्टार फ़िश

mussel
śambuk | शंबुक

crab
kekṛā | केकड़ा

lobster
lobster | लॉबस्टर

octopus
aṣṭbhuj | अष्टभुज

squid
skviḍ | स्क्विड

jellyfish
jailī fiś | जैली फ़िश

plants • vanaspati • वनस्पति

tree • peṛ • पेड़

leaf
pattī
पत्ती

twig
ṭahnī
टहनी

branch
śākhā
शाखा

bark
chhāl
छाल

trunk
tanā
तना

root
jaṛ
जड़

oak | bāṃj | बांज

willow
śarpat | शरपत

poplar | vilāyatī
pīpal | विलायती पीपल

eucalyptus
nīlgiri | नीलगिरि

larch
śrīdāru | श्रीदारु

beech
bīch | बीच

birch
bhojvṛkṣ | भोजवृक्ष

pine
chīṛ | चीड़

cedar
devdār | देवदार

maple
mepal | मेपल

elm
chirābel | चिराबेल

lime | nībū kā
vṛkṣ | नीबू का वृक्ष

berry
saras phal
सरस फल

holly
śūlparṇī | शूलपर्णी

palm
tāṛ | ताड़

flowering plant • puṣpī paudhe • पुष्पी पौधे

flower
phūl
फूल

stamen
puṅkesar
पुंकेसर

petal
paṅkhuṛī
पंखुड़ी

calyx
karṇikā
कर्णिका

stalk
ḍaṇthal
डंठल

bud
kalī
कली

stem
ḳalam
क़लम

buttercup
baṭarkap | बटरकप

daisy
ḍezī | डेजी

thistle
ikṣugandhā
इक्षुगंधा

dandelion
kukraumdhā
कुकरौंधा

heather
haidar
हैदर

poppy
ahipuṣp
अहिपुष्प

foxglove
apsaroṅguli
अप्सरोंगुलि

honeysuckle
hanīsakal
हनीसकल

sunflower
sūryamukhī
सूर्यमुखी

clover
tinpatiyā
तिनपतिया

bluebells
jaṅglī gomed
जंगली गोमेद

primrose
primroz
प्रिमरोज़

lupins
lyūpin
ल्यूपिन

nettle
bicchhū-būṭī
बिच्छू–बूटी

town · śahar · शहर

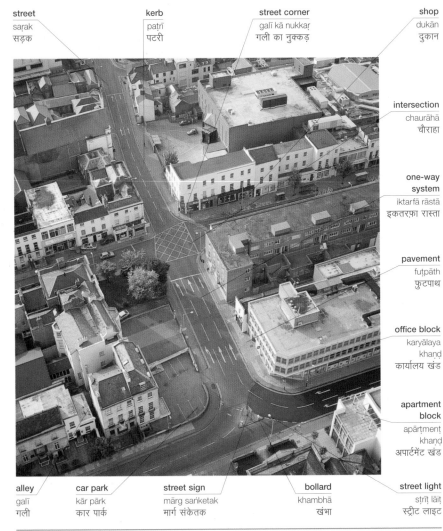

street
saṛak
सड़क

kerb
paṭrī
पटरी

street corner
galī kā nukkaṛ
गली का नुक्कड़

shop
dukān
दुकान

intersection
chaurāhā
चौराहा

one-way system
iktarfā rāstā
इकतरफ़ा रास्ता

pavement
fuṭpāth
फुटपाथ

office block
karyālaya khaṇḍ
कार्यालय खंड

apartment block
apārṭmeṇṭ khaṇḍ
अपार्टमेंट खंड

alley
galī
गली

car park
kār pārk
कार पार्क

street sign
mārg saṅketak
मार्ग संकेतक

bollard
khambhā
खंभा

street light
sṭrīṭ lāiṭ
स्ट्रीट लाइट

buildings • imārat • इमारत

town hall
ṭāun hall | टाउन हॉल

library
pustakālaya | पुस्तकालय

cinema
sinemā | सिनेमा

theatre
thieṭar | थिएटर

university
viśvvidyālaya | विश्वविद्यालय

school
vidyālaya | विद्यालय

skyscraper
gaganchumbī imārat
गगनचुंबी इमारत

areas • kṣetr • क्षेत्र

industrial estate
audyogik kṣetr
औद्योगिक क्षेत्र

city
śahar | शहर

suburb
upnagar | उपनगर

village
gāṃv | गांव

---

vocabulary • śabdāvalī • शब्दावली

pedestrian zone paidal rāstā पैदल रास्ता	**side street** galī गली	**manhole** mainhol मैनहोल	**gutter** nālā नाला	**church** charch चर्च
avenue rāstā रास्ता	**square** chauk चौक	**bus stop** bas stop बस स्टॉप	**factory** kārḳhānā कारख़ाना	**drain** nālī नाली

architecture • vāstuśilp • वास्तुशिल्प

buildings and structures • bhavan evam imāratem • भवन एवं इमारतें

skyscraper | gaganchumbī imārat | गगनचुंबी इमारत

castle
ḳilā | किला

turret
burj
बुर्ज

moat
khāī
खाई

church
girjāghar | गिरजाघर

dome
gumbad
गुम्बद

mosque
masjid | मस्जिद

gable
triyankī chhat
त्रियंकी छत

tower
mīnār
मीनार

temple
mandir | मंदिर

synagogue | yahūdī pūjāsthal
यहूदी पूजास्थल

vault
mehrābdār chhat
मेहराबदार छत

cornice
cornice
कॉर्निस

dam
bāndh | बांध

bridge
pul | पुल

pillar
khambhā
खंभा

finial
stūpikā
स्तूपिका

spire
śikhar
शिखर

cathedral
baṛā girjāghar | बड़ा गिरजाघर

styles · śailī · शैली

architrave
prastarpād
प्रस्तरपाद

gothic
gothic | गॉथिक

renaissance
renesāns | रेनेसान्स

baroque
bārok | बारोक

arch
mehrāb
मेहराब

frieze
chitr vallarī
चित्र वल्लरी

choir
gāyan sthal
गायन स्थल

rococo
rokoko | रोकोको

pediment
trikonikā
त्रिकोनिका

buttress
puśtā
पुश्ता

neoclassical
navśāstrīya | नवशास्त्रीय

art nouveau
ārṭ nūvo | आर्ट नूवो

art deco
ārṭ ḍeko | आर्ट डेको

reference
sandarbh
संदर्भ

time • samaya • समय

minute hand
minaṭ kī sūī
मिनट की सूई

hour hand
ghaṇṭe kī sūī
घंटे की सूई

clock | ghaṛī | घड़ी

vocabulary • śabdāvalī • शब्दावली		
second	**now**	**a quarter of an hour**
saikaṇḍ	abhī	pandrah minaṭ
सैकंड	अभी	पंद्रह मिनट
minute	**later**	**twenty minutes**
minaṭ	bād meṃ	bīs minaṭ
मिनट	बाद में	बीस मिनट
hour	**half an hour**	**forty minutes**
ghaṇṭā	ādhā ghaṇṭā	chālīs minaṭ
घंटा	आधा घंटा	चालीस मिनट

What time is it?
kyā samaya huā haī ?
क्या समय हुआ है?

It's three o'clock.
tīn baj gae haiṃ
तीन बज गए हैं।

 five past one
ek baj kar pāṃch minaṭ
एक बज कर पांच मिनट

 ten past one
ek baj kar das minaṭ
एक बज कर दस मिनट

 quarter past one
savā ek
सवा एक

 twenty past one
ek baj kar bīs minaṭ
एक बज कर बीस मिनट

second hand
saikaṇḍ kī sūī
सैकंड की सूई

 twenty five past one
ek baj kar pacchīs minaṭ
एक बज कर पच्चीस मिनट

 one thirty
ḍerh
डेढ़

 twenty five to two
do bajne meṃ pacchīs minaṭ
दो बजने में पच्चीस मिनट

 twenty to two
do bajne meṃ bīs minaṭ
दो बजने में बीस मिनट

 quarter to two
paune do
पौने दो

 ten to two
do bajne meṃ das minaṭ
दो बजने में दस मिनट

 five to two
do bajne meṃ pāṃch minaṭ
दो बजने में पांच मिनट

 two o'clock
do baje
दो बजे

night and day · rāt aur din · रात और दिन

midnight
ardhrātri | अर्धरात्रि

sunrise
sūryodaya | सूर्योदय

dawn
bhor | भोर

morning
subah | सुबह

sunset
sūryāst | सूर्यास्त

midday
madhyāhn | मध्याह्न

dusk
sāyaṃkāl | सायंकाल

evening
sandhyā | संध्या

afternoon
dopahar | दोपहर

vocabulary · śabdāvalī · शब्दावली

early
jaldī
जल्दी

on time
samaya par
समय पर

late
der
देर

You're early.
āp jaldī ā gae haiṃ
आप जल्दी आ गए हैं।

You're late.
āp der se āe haiṃ
आप देर से आए हैं।

I'll be there soon.
maiṃ jaldī hī pahuṃch
jāūṃgā
मैं जल्दी ही पहुंच जाऊंगा।

Please be on time.
kṛpyā samaya par pahuṃcheṃ
कृपया समय पर पहुंचें।

What time does it start?
yah kis samaya śurū hogā?
यह किस समय शुरू होगा?

I'll see you later.
maiṃ āpse bād meṃ milūṃgā
मैं आपसे बाद में मिलूंगा।

It's getting late.
der ho rahī hai
देर हो रही है।

How long will it last?
yah kab tak chalegā?
यह कब तक चलेगा?

What time does it finish?
yah kab samāpt hogā?
यह कब समाप्त होगा?

calendar · kailendạr · कैलेंडर

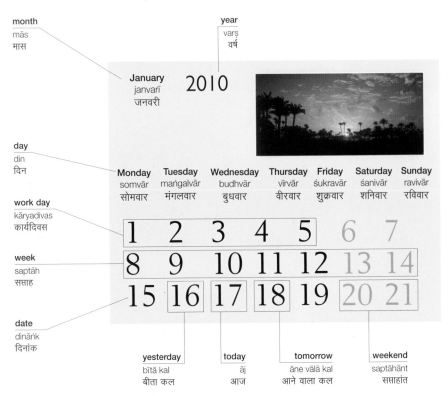

month
mās
मास

year
varṣ
वर्ष

January · janvarī · जनवरी · 2010

day
din
दिन

work day
kāryadivas
कार्यदिवस

week
saptāh
सप्ताह

date
dināṅk
दिनांक

Monday	Tuesday	Wednesday	Thursday	Friday	Saturday	Sunday
somvār	maṅgalvār	budhvār	vīrvār	śukravār	śanivār	ravivār
सोमवार	मंगलवार	बुधवार	वीरवार	शुक्रवार	शनिवार	रविवार
1	2	3	4	5	6	7
8	9	10	11	12	13	14
15	16	17	18	19	20	21

yesterday
bītā kal
बीता कल

today
āj
आज

tomorrow
āne vālā kal
आने वाला कल

weekend
saptāhānt
सप्ताहांत

---

vocabulary · śabdāvalī · शब्दावली

January	March	May	July	September	November
janvarī	mārch	maī	julāī	sitambar	navambar
जनवरी	मार्च	मई	जुलाई	सितंबर	नवंबर

February	April	June	August	October	December
farvarī	aprail	jūn	agast	akṭūbar	disambar
फ़रवरी	अप्रैल	जून	अगस्त	अक्टूबर	दिसंबर

years • varṣ • वर्ष

1900 nineteen hundred • unnīs sau • उन्नीस सौ

1901 nineteen hundred and one • unnīs sau ek • उन्नीस सौ एक

1910 nineteen ten • unnīs sau das • उन्नीस सौ दस

2000 two thousand • do hazār • दो हज़ार

2001 two thousand and one • do hazār ek • दो हज़ार एक

seasons • r̥tuem̐ • ऋतुएं

spring
basant
बसंत

summer
grīṣm
ग्रीष्म

autumn
patjhar
पतझड़

winter
śarad
शरद

vocabulary • śabdāvalī • शब्दावली

century śatābdī शताब्दी	**this week** is hafte इस हफ़्ते	**weekly** sāptāhik साप्ताहिक	**millennium** sahsrābdī सहस्राब्दी	**What's the date today?** āj kyā tārīkh hai? आज क्या तारीख़ है?
decade daśak दशक	**last week** pichhle hafte पिछले हफ़्ते	**monthly** māsik मासिक	**next week** agle hafte अगले हफ़्ते	**It's February seventh,** **two thousand and two.** āj 7 farvarī 2002 hai आज 7 फ़रवरी, 2002 है।
fortnight pakhvāṛā पखवाड़ा	**the day before** **yesterday** bītā parsom̐ बीता परसों	**annual** vārṣik वार्षिक	**the day after** **tomorrow** parsom̐ परसों	

numbers • aṃk • अंक

0 zero • śūnya • शून्य

1 one • ek • एक

2 two • do • दो

3 three • tīn • तीन

4 four • chār • चार

5 five • pāṃch • पांच

6 six • chhah • छह

7 seven • sāt • सात

8 eight • āṭh • आठ

9 nine • nau • नौ

10 ten • das • दस

11 eleven • gyārah • ग्यारह

12 twelve • bārah • बारह

13 thirteen • terah • तेरह

14 fourteen • chaudah • चौदह

15 fifteen • pandrah • पंद्रह

16 sixteen • solah • सोलह

17 seventeen • satrah • सत्रह

18 eighteen • aṭhārah • अठारह

19 nineteen • unnīs • उन्नीस

20 twenty • bīs • बीस

21 twenty-one • ikkīs • इक्कीस

22 twenty-two • bāīs • बाईस

30 thirty • tīs • तीस

40 forty • chālīs • चालीस

50 fifty • pachās • पचास

60 sixty • sāṭh • साठ

70 seventy • sattar • सत्तर

80 eighty • assī • अस्सी

90 ninety • nabbe • नब्बे

100 one hundred • sau • सौ

110 one hundred and ten • ek sau das • एक सौ दस

200 two hundred • do sau • दो सौ

300 three hundred • tīn sau • तीन सौ

400 four hundred • chār sau • चार सौ

500 five hundred • pāṃch sau • पांच सौ

600 six hundred • chhah sau • छह सौ

700 seven hundred • sāt sau • सात सौ

800 eight hundred • āṭh sau • आठ सौ

900 nine hundred • nau sau • नौ सौ

1000 **one thousand** • ek hazār • एक हज़ार

10,000 **ten thousand** • das hazār • दस हज़ार

20,000 **twenty thousand** • bīs hazār • बीस हज़ार

50,000 **fifty thousand** • pachās hazār • पचास हज़ार

55,500 **fifty-five thousand five hundred** • pachpan hazār pāṃch sau • पचपन हज़ार पांच सौ

100,000 **one hundred thousand** • ek lākh • एक लाख

1,000,000 **one million** • das lākh • दस लाख

1,000,000,000 **one billion** • ek arab • एक अरब

first
pahlā
पहला

second
dūsrā
दूसरा

third
tīsrā
तीसरा

fourth • chauthā • चौथा

fifth • pāṃchvāṃ • पांचवां

sixth • chhaṭhā • छठा

seventh • sātvāṃ • सातवां

eighth • āṭhvāṃ • आठवां

ninth • nauvāṃ • नौवां

tenth • dasvāṃ • दसवां

eleventh • gyārahavāṃ • ग्यारहवां

twelfth • bārhavāṃ • बारहवां

thirteenth • terhavāṃ • तेरहवां

fourteenth • chaudhavāṃ • चौदहवां

fifteenth • pandrahavāṃ • पंद्रहवां

sixteenth • solahavāṃ • सोलहवां

seventeenth • satrahavāṃ • सत्रहवां

eighteenth • aṭhārahavāṃ • अठारहवां

nineteenth • unnīsvāṃ • उन्नीसवां

twentieth • bīsvāṃ • बीसवां

twenty-first • ikkīsvāṃ • इक्कीसवां

twenty-second • bāisvāṃ • बाइसवां

twenty-third • teisvāṃ • तेइसवां

thirtieth • tīsvāṃ • तीसवां

fortieth • chālīsvāṃ • चालीसवां

fiftieth • pachāsvāṃ • पचासवां

sixtieth • sāṭhvāṃ • साठवां

seventieth • sattarvāṃ • सत्तरवां

eightieth • assīvāṃ • अस्सीवां

ninetieth • nabbevāṃ • नब्बेवां

one hundredth • sauvāṃ • सौवां

weights and measures • bhār aur māpak • भार और मापक

area • kṣetr • क्षेत्र

square foot	square metre
varg fuṭ	vargmīṭar
वर्ग फुट	वर्गमीटर

distance • dūrī • दूरी

kilometre	mile
kilomīṭar	mīl
किलोमीटर	मील

pan
pain
पैन

pound
pāuṃḍ
पाउंड

kilogram
kilogrām
किलोग्राम

ounce
auṃs
औंस

gram
grām
ग्राम

scales | tarāzū | तराज़ू

vocabulary • śabdāvalī • शब्दावली

yard	tonne	measure (v)
gaz	ṭan	māpnā
गज़	टन	मापना
metre	**milligram**	**weigh (v)**
mīṭar	milīgrām	tolnā
मीटर	मिलीग्राम	तोलना

length • lambāī • लंबाई

foot
fuṭ
फुट

millimetre	centimetre	inch
milīmīṭar	senṭīmīṭar	īnch
मिलीमीटर	सेंटीमीटर	इंच

capacity • kṣamtā • क्षमता

half-litre
ādhā līṭar
आधा लीटर

pint
pāinṭ | पाइंट

volume
āyatan
आयतन

millilitre
milīlīṭar
मिलीलीटर

measuring jug
māpak jag | मापक जग

measure
māp | माप

container • kaṇṭenar • कंटेनर

carton
kārṭan | कार्टन

packet
paikeṭ | पैकेट

bottle
botal | बोतल

bag
thailā
थैला

tub | ṭab | टब

jar | jār | जार

can
kain
कैन

tin | ṭin | टिन

dispenser
ḍispensar | डिस्पेंसर

bar
ṭikiyā
टिकिया

tube | ṭyūb | ट्यूब

roll | rol | रोल

pack | paik | पैक

spray can
spre kain | स्प्रे कैन

english • hindī • हिन्दी

311

world map · viśv mānchitr · विश्व मानचित्र

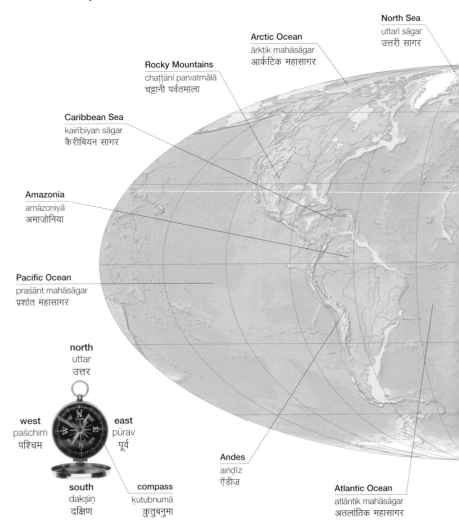

North Sea
uttarī sāgar
उत्तरी सागर

Arctic Ocean
ārkṭik mahāsāgar
आर्कटिक महासागर

Rocky Mountains
chaṭṭānī parvatmālā
चट्टानी पर्वतमाला

Caribbean Sea
kairībiyan sāgar
कैरीबियन सागर

Amazonia
amāzoniyā
अमाजोनिया

Pacific Ocean
praśānt mahāsāgar
प्रशांत महासागर

north
uttar
उत्तर

west
paśchim
पश्चिम

east
pūrav
पूर्व

south
dakṣiṇ
दक्षिण

compass
ḳutubnumā
कुतुबनुमा

Andes
aiṇḍīz
ऐंडीज़

Atlantic Ocean
atlāntik mahāsāgar
अतलांतिक महासागर

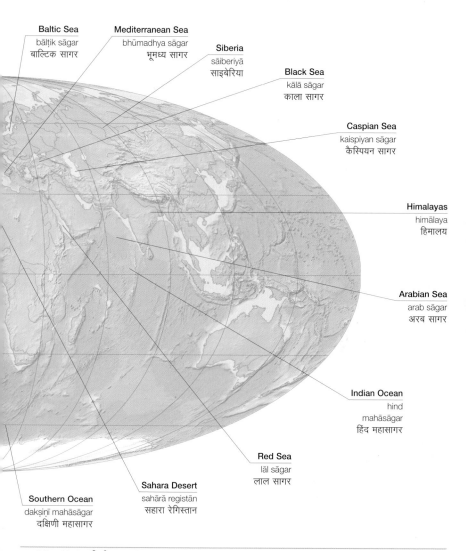

Baltic Sea
bālṭik sāgar
बाल्टिक सागर

Mediterranean Sea
bhūmadhya sāgar
भूमध्य सागर

Siberia
sāiberiyā
साइबेरिया

Black Sea
kālā sāgar
काला सागर

Caspian Sea
kaispiyan sāgar
कैस्पियन सागर

Himalayas
himālaya
हिमालय

Arabian Sea
arab sāgar
अरब सागर

Indian Ocean
hind
mahāsāgar
हिंद महासागर

Red Sea
lāl sāgar
लाल सागर

Sahara Desert
sahārā registān
सहारा रेगिस्तान

Southern Ocean
dakṣiṇī mahāsāgar
दक्षिणी महासागर

North and Central America • uttarī aur madhya amerikā • उत्तरी और मध्य अमेरिका

Hawaii
havāī
हवाई

1 **Alaska** • alāskā • अलास्का
2 **Canada** • kanāḍā • कनाडा
3 **Greenland** • grīnlaiṇḍ • ग्रीनलैंड
4 **United States of America** •
  samyūkt rājya amerikā •
  सयुंक्त राज्य अमेरिका
5 **Mexico** • maiksiko • मैक्सिको
6 **Guatemala** • gvāṭemālā • ग्वाटेमाला
7 **Belize** • belīz • बैलीज़
8 **El Salvador** • el selvāḍor •
  एल सेल्वाडोर
9 **Honduras** • honduras • हॉन्डुरास
10 **Nicaragua** • nikārāguā • निकारागुआ
11 **Costa Rica** • kosṭārīkā • कोस्टारीका
12 **Panama** • panāmā • पनामा
13 **Cuba** • kyūbā • क्यूबा
14 **Bahamas** • bāhāmās • बाहामास
15 **Jamaica** • jamaikā • जमैका
16 **Haiti** • haiṭī • हैटी
17 **Dominican Republic** • ḍomink
  gaṇrājya • डोमिनिक गणराज्य
18 **Puerto Rico** • puerto rīko • पुएरतो रीको
19 **Barbados** • barbados • बारबेडॉस
20 **Trinidad and Tobago** • trinidād evam ṭābāgo •
  त्रिनिदाद एवं टाबागो
21 **St. Kitts and Nevis** • senṭ kiṭs
  enḍ nevis • सेंट किट्स एंड नेविस

22 **Antigua and Barbuda** • enṭīguā aur bārbuḍā •
  एंटीगुआ और बारबुडा
23 **Dominica** • ḍominikā • डोमिनिका
24 **St Lucia** • senṭ luchiā • सेंट लुचिया
25 **St Vincent and The Grenadines** • senṭ vinsenṭ
  enḍ da grenāḍins • सेंट विन्सेंट एंड द ग्रेनाडिन्स
26 **Grenada** • grenāḍā • ग्रेनाडा

South America • dakṣiṇī amerikā • दक्षिणी अमेरिका

1 **Venezuela** • venezuelā • वेनेजुएला
2 **Colombia** • kolambiyā • कोलम्बिया
3 **Ecuador** • ikveḍor • इक्वेडोर
4 **Peru** • perū • पेरु
5 **Galapagos Islands** •
   gālāpāgos dvip samūh •
   गालापागोस द्वीप समूह
6 **Guyana** • guānā • गुआना
7 **Suriname** • sūrīnām • सूरीनाम
8 **French Guiana** •
   french gayānā • फ़्रेंच गयाना
9 **Brazil** • brāzīl • ब्राज़ील
10 **Bolivia** • bolīviyā • बोलीविया
11 **Chile** • chilī • चिली
12 **Argentina** • arjenṭīnā • अर्जेंटीना
13 **Paraguay** • pairāgue • पैरागुए
14 **Uruguay** • urūgue • उरूगुए
15 **Falkland Islands** • falkland
   dvīp samūh • फ़ॉकलैंड द्वीप समूह

vocabulary • śabdāvalī • शब्दावली		
country deś देश	**province** prānt प्रांत	**zone** kṣetr क्षेत्र
continent mahādvīp महाद्वीप	**territory** ilāḳā इलाक़ा	**district** zilā ज़िला
nation rāṣṭr राष्ट्र	**colony** colony कॉलोनी	**region** anchal अंचल
state rājya राज्य	**principality** maṇḍal मंडल	**capital** rājdhānī राजधानी

Europe · yūrop · यूरोप

1 **Ireland** · āyarlaiṇḍ · आयरलैंड
2 **United Kingdom** · yūnāiṭeḍ kiṅgḍam · यूनाइटेड किंग्डम
3 **Portugal** · purtgāl · पुर्तगाल
4 **Spain** · spen · स्पेन
5 **Balearic Islands** · bailirik dvīp samūh · बैलिरिक द्वीप समूह
6 **Andorra** · aṇḍorā · अंडोरा
7 **France** · frāṁs · फ़्रांस
8 **Belgium** · beljiyam · बेल्जियम
9 **Netherlands** · nīdarlaiṇḍ · नीदरलैंड
10 **Luxembourg** · lakzambarg · लक्ज़मबर्ग
11 **Germany** · jarmanī · जर्मनी
12 **Denmark** · ḍenmārk · डेनमार्क
13 **Norway** · nārve · नार्वे
14 **Sweden** · svīḍan · स्वीडन
15 **Finland** · finlaiṇḍ · फ़िनलैंड
16 **Estonia** · esṭoniyā · एस्टोनिया
17 **Latvia** · lāṭviyā · लाटविया
18 **Lithuania** · lithuāniyā · लिथुआनिया
19 **Kaliningrad** · kailinin grāḍ · कैलिनिनग्राड
20 **Poland** · polaiṇḍ · पोलैंड
21 **Czech Republic** · chek gaṇrājya · चेक गणराज्य
22 **Austria** · austria · ऑस्ट्रिया
23 **Liechtenstein** · liśtenastin · लिश्तेनस्तिन
24 **Switzerland** · sviṭzarlaiṇḍ · स्विटज़रलैंड
25 **Italy** · iṭlī · इटली
26 **Monaco** · monāko · मोनाको
27 **Corsica** · corsica · कॉर्सिका
28 **Sardinia** · sārḍīniyā · सार्डीनिया

29 **San Marino** · sān mārino · सान मारिनो
30 **Vatican City** · veṭikan siṭī · वेटिकन सिटी
31 **Sicily** · sislī · सिसली
32 **Malta** · mālṭā · माल्टा
33 **Slovenia** · sloveniyā · स्लोवेनिया
34 **Croatia** · kroeśiyā · क्रोएशिया
35 **Hungary** · haṅgarī · हंगरी
36 **Slovakia** · slovākiyā · स्लोवाकिया
37 **Ukraine** · yūkren · यूक्रेन
38 **Belarus** · belārūs · बेलारूस

39 **Moldova** · moldova · मॉल्डोवा
40 **Romania** · romāniyā · रोमानिया
41 **Yugoslavia** · yugoslāviyā · युगोस्लाविया
42 **Bosnia and Herzogovina** · bosniyā eṇḍ harzogovinā · बोस्निया एंड हर्ज़ोगोविना
43 **Albania** · albāniyā · अल्बानिया
44 **Macedonia** · meseḍoniyā · मेसेडोनिया
45 **Bulgaria** · bulgāriyā · बुल्गारिया
46 **Greece** · grīs · ग्रीस
47 **Turkey** · turkī · तुर्की
48 **Cyprus** · sāipras · साइप्रस

Africa • afrīkā • अफ़्रीका

koengo

1 **Morocco** •
morokko • मोरोक्को

2 **Western Sahara** •
paśchim sahārā • पश्चिम सहारा

3 **Mauritania** •
mauritania • मॉरीटेनिया

4 **Senegal** • sainegāl • सैनेगाल

5 **Gambia** • gaimbiyā • गैंबिया

6 **Guinea-Bissau** •
ginībissāū • गिनीबिस्साऊ

7 **Guinea** • gini • गिनी

8 **Sierra Leone** •
sierā lione • सिएरा लिओने

9 **Liberia** • lāiberiyā • लाइबेरिया

10 **Ivory Coast** •
āivarī kosṭ • आइवरी कोस्ट

11 **Burkina Faso** • burkinā
fāso • बुर्किना फ़ासो

12 **Mali** • mālī • माली

13 **Algeria** • aljīriyā • अल्जीरिया

14 **Tunisia** • ṭyūnīśiyā •
ट्यूनीशिया

15 **Libya** • lībiyā • लीबिया

16 **Niger** • nāijar • नाइजर

17 **Ghana** • ghānā • घाना

18 **Togo** • ṭogo • टोगो

19 **Benin** • benin • बेनिन

20 **Nigeria** • nāijīriyā • नाइजीरिया

21 **São Tomé and Principe**
• são ṭom enḍ princhip
• साओ टोम एंड प्रिंचिप

22 **Equatorial Guinea** •
ikveṭoriyal gini •
इक्वेटोरियल गिनी

23 **Cameroon** •
kaimrūn • कैमरून

24 **Chad** • chād • चाद

25 **Egypt** • misr • मिस्र

26 **Sudan** • sūḍān • सूडान

27 **Eritrea** • eriṭriyā • एरिट्रिया

28 **Djibouti** • jibūtī • जिबूती

29 **Ethiopia** • ithopiyā • इथोपिया

30 **Somalia** • somāliyā •
सोमालिया

31 **Kenya** • kīniyā • कीनिया

32 **Uganda** • yugāṇḍā • युगांडा

33 **Central African Republic** •
madhya afrīkī gaṇrajya •
मध्य अफ़्रीकी गणराज्य

34 **Gabon** • gaibon • गैबोन

35 **Congo** • congo • कॉन्गो

36 **Cabinda** • kebindā • केबिंदा

37 **Democratic Republic of
the Congo** • congo loktāṇtrik
gaṇrājya • कॉन्गो लोकतांत्रिक
गणराज्य

38 **Rwanda** • ruāṇḍā • रुआंडा

39 **Burundi** • burūṇḍī • बुरुंडी

40 **Tanzania** • tanzāniyā • तंज़ानिया

41 **Mozambique** •
mozāmbīk़ • मोज़ाम्बीक़

42 **Malawi** • malāvī • मलावी

43 **Zambia** • zāmbiyā • ज़ाम्बिया

44 **Angola** • aṅgolā • अंगोला

45 **Namibia** • nāmībiyā • नामीबिया

46 **Botswana** • botsvānā • बोत्सवाना

47 **Zimbabwe** • zimbabve • ज़िम्बाब्बे

48 **South Africa** • dakṣiṇ afrīkā •
दक्षिण अफ़्रीका

49 **Lesotho** • lisotho • लिसोथो

50 **Swaziland** •
svāzīlaiṇḍ • स्वाज़ीलैंड

51 **Comoros** • komoro • कोमोरो

52 **Madagascar** •
maiḍāgāskar • मैडागास्कर

53 **Mauritius** • mauritius • मॉरीशस

Asia • eśiyā • एशिया

1 **Russian Federation** • rūs • रूस
2 **Georgia** • georgia • जॉर्जिया
3 **Armenia** • ārmeniyā • आर्मेनिया
4 **Azerbaijan** •
   azarbejān • अज़रबेजान
5 **Iran** • īrān • ईरान
6 **Iraq** • irāk̤ • इराक़
7 **Syria** • sīriyā • सीरिया
8 **Lebanon** • lebnān • लेबनान
9 **Israel** • izrāyal • इज़रायल
10 **Jordan** • jordan • जॉर्डन
11 **Saudi Arabia** •
   saūdī arab • सऊदी अरब
12 **Kuwait** • k̤uvait • कुवैत
13 **Qatar** • k̤atar • क़तर
14 **United Arab Emirates** • sanyukt
   arab amīrāt • संयुक्त अरब अमीरात
15 **Oman** • omān • ओमान
16 **Yemen** • yaman • यमन
17 **Kazakhstan** •
   kazākistān • कज़ाकिस्तान
18 **Uzbekistan** •
   uzbekistān • उज़्बेकिस्तान
19 **Turkmenistan** •
   turkmenistān • तुर्कमेनिस्तान
20 **Afghanistan** •
   afg̤ānistān • अफ़ग़ानिस्तान
21 **Tajikistan** • tajākistān • तजाकिस्तान
22 **Kyrgyzstan** • kirgīstān • किर्गीस्तान
23 **Pakistan** • pākistān • पाकिस्तान
24 **India** • bhārat • भारत
25 **Maldives** • māldīv • मालदीव
26 **Sri Lanka** • śrīlaṅkā • श्रीलंका
27 **China** • chīn • चीन
28 **Mongolia** • maṅgoliyā • मंगोलिया
29 **North Korea** •
   uttarī koriyā • उत्तरी कोरिया
30 **South Korea** •
   dak̤ṣiṇ koriyā • दक्षिण कोरिया
31 **Japan** • jāpān • जापान
32 **Nepal** • nepāl • नेपाल
33 **Bhutan** • bhūtān • भूटान
34 **Bangladesh** • baṅglādeś • बंगलादेश

35 **Burma (Myanmar)** •
   barmā (myānmār) •
   बर्मा (म्यांमार)
36 **Thailand** • thāīlaiṇḍ • थाईलैंड
37 **Laos** • lāos • लाओस
38 **VietNam** •
   viyatnām • वियतनाम
39 **Cambodia** • kamboḍiyā • कंबोडिया
40 **Malaysia** • maleśiyā • मलेशिया

Australasia • australasia • ऑस्ट्रेलेशिया

1 **Australia** • australia • ऑस्ट्रेलिया
2 **Tasmania** • tasmāniyā • तस्मानिया
3 **New Zealand** • nyūzīlaiṇḍ • न्यूज़ीलैंड

41 **Singapore** • siṅgāpur • सिंगापुर
42 **Indonesia** • iṅḍoneśiyā • इंडोनेशिया
43 **Brunei** • bruneī • ब्रुनेई
44 **Philippines** • filīpins • फ़िलीपिंस
45 **East Timor** • pūrvī timor • पूर्वी तिमोर
46 **Papua New Guinea** •
   papuā nyū ginī • पपुआ न्यू गिनी
47 **Solomon Islands** • soloman dvip
   samūh • सोलोमन द्वीप समूह
48 **Vanuatu** • vanuātū • वनुआतू
49 **Fiji** • fijī • फ़िजी

particles and antonyms · upsarg, pratyaya aur vilom śabd · उपसर्ग, प्रत्यय और विलोम शब्द

to ko · को	**from** se · से	**for** ke lie · के लिए	**towards** kī taraf · की तरफ़
over ūpar · ऊपर	**under** nīche · नीचे	**with** sāth · साथ	**without** bagair · बग़ैर
in front of sāmne · के सामने	**behind** pīchhe · पीछे	**before** pahle · पहले	**after** bād mem · बाद में
onto ke ūpar · के ऊपर	**into** ke andar · के अंदर	**by** tab tak · तब तक	**until** jab tak · जब तक
in andar · अंदर	**out** bāhar · बाहर	**early** jaldī · जल्दी	**late** der · देर
above ūpar · ऊपर	**below** nīche · नीचे	**now** abhī · अभी	**later** bād mem · बाद में
inside andar · अंदर	**outside** bāhar · बाहर	**always** hameśā · हमेशा	**never** kabhī nahīm · कभी नहीं
up ūpar · ऊपर	**down** nīche · नीचे	**often** aksar · अक्सर	**rarely** kabhī-kabhī · कभी–कभी
at par · पर	**beyond** pare · परे	**yesterday** bītā kal · बीता कल	**tomorrow** āgāmī kal · आगामी कल
on top of ke ūpar · के ऊपर	**beside** ke pās · के पास	**first** pahlā · पहला	**last** ākhrī · आख़िरी
between ke bīch · के बीच	**opposite** viprīt · विपरीत	**every** harek · हरेक	**some** kuchh · कुछ
near nikaṭ · निकट	**far** dūr · दूर	**about** lagbhag · लगभग	**exactly** saṭīk · सटीक
here yahām · यहां	**there** vahām · वहां	**a little** thoṛā sā · थोड़ा सा	**a lot** bahut sā · बहुत सा
through ārampār · आरम्पार	**around** ghūm kar · घूम कर	**along** sāth-sāth · साथ–साथ	**across** ke pār · के पार

large
baṛā • बड़ा

small
chhoṭā • छोटा

hot
garm • गर्म

cold
ṭhaṇḍā • ठंडा

wide
chauṛā • चौड़ा

narrow
saṅkrā • संकरा

open
khulā • खुला

closed
band • बंद

tall
lambā • लंबा

short
chhoṭā • छोटा

full
bharā • भरा

empty
ḵẖālī • ख़ाली

high
ūṃchā • ऊंचा

low
nīchā • नीचा

new
nayā • नया

old
purānā • पुराना

thick
moṭā • मोटा

thin
patlā • पतला

light
halkā • हल्का

dark
gahrā • गहरा

light
halkā • हल्का

heavy
bhārī • भारी

easy
āsān • आसान

difficult
kaṭhin • कठिन

hard
kaṭhor • कठोर

soft
mulāyam • मुलायम

free
ḵẖālī • ख़ाली

occupied
vyast • व्यस्त

wet
gīlā • गीला

dry
sūkhā • सूखा

fat
moṭā • मोटा

thin
patlā • पतला

good
acchhā • अच्छा

bad
burā • बुरा

young
javān • जवान

old
būṛhā • बूढ़ा

fast
tez • तेज़

slow
dhīre • धीरे

better
behtar • बेहतर

worse
badtar • बदतर

correct
sahī • सही

wrong
ġalat • ग़लत

black
kālā • काला

white
safed • सफ़ेद

clean
sāf • साफ़

dirty
gandā • गंदा

interesting
rochak • रोचक

boring
ubāū • उबाऊ

beautiful
ḵẖūbsūrat • ख़ूबसूरत

ugly
badsūrat • बदसूरत

sick
bīmār • बीमार

well
svasth • स्वस्थ

expensive
mahaṅgā • महंगा

cheap
sastā • सस्ता

beginning
ārambh • आरंभ

end
ant • अंत

quiet
śānt • शांत

noisy • śor karne vālā
शोर करने वाला

strong
mazbūt • मजबूत

weak
kamzor • कमजोर

useful phrases · upyogī vākyāṅś · उपयोगी वाक्यांश

essential phrases
āvaśyak vākyāṅś
आवश्यक वाक्यांश

Yes · hāṃ · हां

No · nahīṃ · नहीं

Maybe · ho saktā hai
हो सकता है।

Please · kṛpyā · कृपया

Thank you
dhanyavād · धन्यवाद

You're welcome
āpkā svāgat hai
आपका स्वागत है।

Excuse me · māf kījiegā
माफ़ कीजिएगा

I'm sorry
maiṃ māfī chāhtā hūṃ
मैं माफ़ी चाहता हूं।

Don't
mat karo · मत करो।

OK · acchhā · अच्छा

That's fine
yah ṭhīk hai · यह ठीक है।

That's correct
yah sahī hai · यह सही है।

That's wrong
yah galat hai · यह ग़लत है।

greetings
abhivādan
अभिवादन

Hello
namaskār · नमस्कार

Goodbye
namaskār · नमस्कार

Good morning
suprabhāt · सुप्रभात

Good afternoon
namaskār · नमस्कार

Good evening
namaskār · नमस्कार

Good night
śubh rātri · शुभ रात्रि

How are you?
āp kaise haiṃ?
आप कैसे हैं?

My name is...
merā nām ... hai
मेरा नाम ... है।

What is your name?
āpkā kyā nām hai?
आपका क्या नाम है?

What is his/her name?
unkā kyā nām hai?
उनका क्या नाम है?

May I introduce...
maiṃ āpko ... se
milvānā chāhtā hūṃ
मैं आपको ... से मिलवाना
चाहता हूं।

This is...
ye ... haiṃ · ये ... हैं।

Pleased to meet you
āpse milkar khuśī huī
आपसे मिलकर ख़ुशी हुई।

See you later
bād meṃ milte haiṃ
बाद में मिलते हैं।

signs · chihn · चिह्न

Tourist information
paryaṭak jānkārī
पर्यटक जानकारी

Entrance
praveś · प्रवेश

Exit · nikās · निकास

Emergency exit
saṅkaṭ dvār
संकट द्वार

Push · dhakeleṃ · धकेलें

Danger · khatrā · ख़तरा

No smoking · dhūmrpān
varjit · धूम्रपान वर्जित

Out of order
kharāb · ख़राब

Opening times
khulne kā samaya
खुलने का समय

Free admission
muft praveś · मुफ़्त प्रवेश

Open all day · pūre
din khulā · पूरे दिन खुला

Reduced price · kam
mūlya par · कम मूल्य पर

Sale · sel · सेल

Knock before entering
praveś karne se pahle
dastak deṃ · प्रवेश करने
से पहले दस्तक दें

Keep off the grass
kṛpyā ghās par na chaleṃ
कृपया घास पर न चलें

help · sahāyatā
सहायता

Can you help me?
kyā āp merī madad kar
sakte haiṃ?
क्या आप मेरी मदद कर
सकते हैं?

I don't understand
maiṃ samjhā nahīṃ
मैं समझा नहीं।

I don't know
mujhe patā nahīṃ hai
मुझे पता नहीं है।

**Do you speak English,
French...?**
kyā āp aṅgrezī, french
... bolte haiṃ?
क्या आप अंग्रेज़ी, फ़्रेंच ...
बोलते हैं?

**I speak English,
Spanish...**
maiṃ aṅgrezī, speniś ...
boltā hūṃ
मैं अंग्रेज़ी, स्पेनिश ...
बोलता हूं।

**Please speak more
slowly**
kṛpyā aur dhīre boleṃ
कृपया और धीरे बोलें।

**Please write it down
for me** · kṛpyā ye mere
lie likh deṃ
कृपया ये मेरे लिए लिख दें।

I have lost...
merā ... kho gayā hai
मेरा ... खो गया है।

directions
nirdeś • निर्देश

I am lost
maiṁ bhaṭak gayā hūṁ.
मैं भटक गया हूं।

Where is the…?
… kahāṁ haiṁ?
… कहां हैं?

Where is the nearest…?
nazdīkī … kahāṁ hai?
नजदीकी … कहां है?

Where are the toilets?
śauchālaya kahāṁ hai?
शौचालय कहां है?

How do I get to…?
maiṁ … kaise pahuṁch saktā hūṁ?
मैं … कैसे पहुंच सकता हूं?

To the right
dāīṁ taraf • दाईं तरफ़

To the left
bāīṁ taraf • बाईं तरफ़

Straight ahead
āge jākar sīdhā
आगे जाकर सीधा

How far is…?
… kitnī dūr hai?
… कितनी दूर है?

road signs • mārg
chihn • मार्ग चिह्न

All directions • sabhī
diśāeṁ • सभी दिशाएं

Caution
sāvdhānī • सावधानी

No entry
praveś varjit • प्रवेश वर्जित

Slow down
raftār dhīmī kareṁ
रफ़्तार धीमी करें

Diversion • parivartit
mārg • परिवर्तित मार्ग

Keep to the right
dāīṁ taraf raheṁ
दाईं तरफ़ रहें

No parking
pārkiṅg niṣedh hai
पार्किंग निषेध है

No through road
ām rāstā nahīṁ hai
आम रास्ता नहीं है

One-way street
iktarfā rāstā
इकतरफ़ा रास्ता

Other directions
anya nirdeś • अन्य निर्देश

Residents only
keval nivāsiyoṁ ke lie
केवल निवासियों के लिए

Dangerous bend
khatarnāk moṛ
ख़तरनाक मोड़

accommodation
āvās • आवास

I have a reservation
mere pās ārakṣaṇ hai
मेरे पास आरक्षण है।

My room number is…
merā kamrā nambar …
hai. • मेरा कमरा नंबर … है।

What time is breakfast?
nāśte kā kyā samaya
hai? • नाश्ते का क्या समय है?

**I'll be back at…
o'clock** • maiṁ … baje
lauṭūṅgā • मैं … बजे लौटूंगा

I'm leaving tomorrow
maiṁ kal jā rahā hūṁ
मैं कल जा रहा हूं

eating and drinking
khānā-pīnā
खाना–पीना

It's delicious • yah
svādiṣṭ hai • यह स्वादिष्ट है।

I don't drink/smoke
maiṁ śarāb/sigreṭ
nahīṁ pītā
मैं शराब/सिगरेट नहीं पीता।

I don't eat meat
maiṁ māṁs nahīṁ khātā
मैं मांस नहीं खाता।

**No more for me, thank
you** • mujhe aur nahīṁ
chāhie, dhanyavād
मुझे और नहीं चाहिए, धन्यवाद

**May I have some
more?** • kyā mujhe
thoṛā aur mil saktā hai?
क्या मुझे थोड़ा और मिल
सकता है?

May we have the bill?
kyā hameṁ bil mil saktā
hai? • क्या हमें बिल मिल
सकता है?

Can I have a receipt?
kyā mujhe rasīd mil saktī
hai? • क्या मुझे रसीद मिल
सकती है?

No-smoking area
dhūmrpān varjit kṣetr
धूम्रपान वर्जित क्षेत्र

health • svāsthya
स्वास्थ्य

I don't feel well • merī
tabīyat ṭhīk nahīṁ hai
मेरी तबीयत ठीक नहीं है।

I feel sick
maiṁ bīmār mahsūs kar
rahā hūṁ
मैं बीमार महसूस कर रहा हूं।

**What is the telephone
number of the nearest
doctor?**
sabse nazdīkī doctor kā
fon nambar kyā hai?
सबसे नजदीकी डॉक्टर का
फ़ोन नंबर क्या है?

It hurts here
yahāṁ dukhtā hai
यहां दुखता है।

I have a temperature
mujhe bukhār hai
मुझे बुख़ार है।

**I'm … months
pregnant**
mujhe … mahīne kā
garbh hai
मुझे … महीने का गर्भ है।

**I need a prescription
for …** • mujhe … ke lie
docterī nuskhā chāhie
मुझे … के लिए डॉक्टरी
नुस्खा चाहिए।

I normally take…
sāmānyataḥ maiṁ …
letā hūṁ
सामान्यतः मैं … लेता हूं।

I'm allergic to…
mujhe … se elarjī hai
मुझे … से एलर्जी है।

hindi pronunciation

the hindi alphabet

The Hindi script, which is called Devnagari, is made up of 12 vowels and 36 consonants. In this book we have adapted the usual romanization of Hindi by dropping the "a" normally used to represent the Hindi vowel "अ" that is attached to all Hindi consonants. Roman consonants, such as "w", only have a sound of their own once they are joined to vowels such as "a" or "e", as in "water" or "wet". In Hindi, however, every consonant incorporates the vowel "अ", so is a complete sound in itself. The sound of the consonant changes when another vowel is added to it. For example, the Hindi consonant "क" is romanized as "ka". When more vowels are added it becomes "की" (kee) or "के" (ke).

In this book we have used Roman consonants to represent each Devnagari consonant, and its accompanying vowel. For example, traditionally "लोग" ("people") would be transcribed as "loga", but we have used "log" to help you pronounce it more accurately. The exception to this is the Hindi consonant "य", represented by the Roman "ya", where we have retained the "a" to keep the pronunciation accurate.

We have kept the Roman spellings for words such as ball, monitor, coffee, and sauce, which are commonly used in everyday Hindi.

hindi vowels

vowel	english equivalent	phonetic symbol	guide to pronunciation
अ	a	a	as "u" in cut
आ	aa	ā	as "a" in class
इ	i	i	as "i" in bit
ई	ee	ī	as "ea" in beat
उ	u	u	as "u" in put
ऊ	oo	ū	as "oo" in hoot
ए	e	e	as "a" in late
ऐ	ai	ai	as "a" in rack
ओ	o	o	as "oa" in goat
औ	au	au	as "o" in floppy
अं	un	ṃ	as "un" in clung
अः	ah	ḥ	as "ah" in blah

hindi consonants

Instances marked with a bullet (•) have no equivalent in English pronunciation.

consonant	english equivalent	phonetic symbol	guide to pronunciation
क	ka	k	as "cu" in cut
ख	kh	kh	as "kh" in Khaki
ग	ga	g	as "g" in girl
घ	gha	gh	as "gh" in Ghana
ङ	angah	ṅ	as "ung" in clung
च	cha	ch	as "chu" in church
छ	chha	chh	•
ज	ja	j	as "ju" in jug
झ	jha	jh	•
ञ	yan	ñ	•
ट	ta	ṭ	as "tu" in turtle
ठ	tha	ṭh	as "th" in lothar
ड	da	ḍ	as "du" in dump
ड़	ra	ṛ	•
ढ	dha	ḍh	as "dh" in Dhaka
ढ़	rha	ṛh	•
ण	na	ṇ	•
त	ta	t	as "t" in Tashkent
थ	tha	th	as "th" in Pythagoras
द	da	d	as "the" in the (pronounced softly)
ध	dha	dh	•
न	na	n	as "nu" in nursing
प	pa	p	as "pu" in puckered
फ	pha	ph	as "fu" in fur
ब	ba	b	as "bu" in bubble
भ	bha	bh	as "bha" in bharat
म	ma	m	as "mu" in mutter
य	ya	ya	as "yu" in yuppie
र	ra	r	as "ru" in rub

... continued on next page

continued from previous page

consonant	english equivalent	phonetic symbol	guide to pronunciation
ल	la	l	as "lo" in love
व	wa	v	as "wo" in word
श	sha	ś	as "shu" in shut
ष	sa	ṣ	•
स	sa	s	as "si" in sin
ह	ha	h	as "hu" in hurt
क्ष	ksha	kṣ	as "ksha" in rickshaw
त्र	tra	tr	as "tr" in trinidad
ज्ञ	jna	jñ	•

combining consonants and vowels

To show how vowel sounds change, we have taken the consonant "क" (ka) and shown how the vowel sound changes when each of the 12 vowels is joined with it.

k क	+	**a** अ	=	**ka** क	**ka** as "cu" in cut
k क	+	**ā** आ	=	**kā** का	**kā** as "ka" in kamikaze
k क	+	**i** इ	=	**ki** कि	**ki** as "ki" in kiss
k क	+	**ī** ई	=	**kī** की	**kī** as "kee" in keen
k क	+	**u** उ	=	**ku** कु	**ku** as "cu" in cushion
k क	+	**ū** ऊ	=	**kū** कू	**kū** as "coo" in cool
k क	+	**e** ए	=	**ke** के	**ke** as "ka" in kate
k क	+	**ai** ऐ	=	**kai** कै	**kai** as "ca" in California
k क	+	**o** ओ	=	**ko** को	**ko** as "coa" in coarse
k क	+	**au** औ	=	**kau** कौ	**kau** as "co" in copy
k क	+	**ṃ** अं	=	**kang** कं	**kang** as "kan" in kangaroo
n न	+	**ḥ** अः	=	**nah** नः	•

You can repeat this exercise with other consonants as the vowel sounds will change in the same way.

key to romanization

अ	आ	इ	ई	उ	ऊ	ऋ	
a	ā	i	ī	u	ū	ṛ	

			ए	ऐ	ओ	औ
			e	ai	o	au

क	क़	ख	ख़	ग	ग़	घ	ङ
k	ḳ	kh	ḳh	g	g̣	gh	ṅ

च	छ	ज	ज़	झ	ञ	
ch	chh	j	z	jh	ñ	

ट	ठ	ड	ड़	ढ	ढ़	ण
ṭ	ṭh	ḍ	ṛ	ḍh	ṛh	ṇ

त	थ	द	ध	न
t	th	d	dh	n

प	फ	फ़	ब	भ	म
p	ph	f	b	bh	m

य	र	ल	व	श
ya	r	l	v	ś

ष	स	ह	:
ṣ	s	h	ḥ

क्ष	त्र	ज्ञ
kṣ	tr	jña

A "~" over a vowel shows it is pronounced nasally.

A consonant with a dot below it, for example "ṃ", is an anuswar, or a half consonant, which means it is a consonant without an accompanying vowel sound.

Certain letters in Hindi, though pronounced differently, have been romanized with the same consonants, as there aren't enough characters in the Roman alphabet to represent similar sounds. For example:

hindi consonant	roman transliteration
द	d
ढ	ḍh
ढ़	ṛh
ध	dh
ड़ & ऋ	ṛ
ड	ḍ

We have used the *nukta* (a dot) below certain consonants to denote Urdu pronunciation. Consonants with *nuktas*, for example, have been romanized as follows:

क़	ख़	ग़	ज़	फ़
ḳ	ḳh	g̣	z	f

Some of these consonants without a *nukta* have been romanized as follows:

क	ख	ग	ज	फ
k	kh	g	j	ph

index • tālikā • तालिका

arm 13
armband 238
armchair 63
Armenia 318
armpit 13
armrest 200, 210
aromatherapy 55
around 320
arrangements 111
arrest 94
arrivals 213
arrow 249
art 162
art college 169
art deco 301
art gallery 261
art nouveau 301
art shop 115
artery 19
artichoke 124
artist 274
arts and crafts 274, 276
ash 283
ashtray 150
Asia 318
assault 94
assistant 24
assisted delivery 53
asteroid 280
asthma 44
astigmatism 51
astronaut 281
astronomy 281
asymmetric bars 235
at 320
athlete 234

athletics 234
Atlantic Ocean 312
atmosphere 282, 286
atrium 104
attachment 177
attack 220
attack zone 224
attend v 174
attic 58
attractions 261
aubergine 125
auburn 39
audience 254
August 306
aunt 22
aurora 286
Australasia 319
Australia 319
Austria 316
autocue 179
automatic 200
automatic door 196
autumn 31, 307
avalanche 247
avenue 299
avocado 128
awning 148
axe 95
axle 205
ayurveda 55
Azerbaijan 318

B

baby 23, 30
baby bath 74
baby care 74
baby changing

facilities 104
baby monitor 75
baby products 107
baby sling 75
babygro 30
back 13
back brush 73
back seat 200
backboard 226
backdrop 254
backgammon 272
backhand 231
backpack 31, 37, 267
backstroke 239
backswing 233
bacon 118, 157
bad 321
badge 94
badminton 231
bag 311
bagel 139
baggage reclaim 213
baggage trailer 212
bags 37
baguette 138
Bahamas 314
bail 181
bait 244
bait v 245
bake v 67, 138
baked 159
baker 139
baker's 114
bakery 107, 138
baking 69

baking tray 69
balance wheel 276
balcony 59, 254
bald 39
bale 184
Balearic Islands 316
ball 75, 221, 224, 226, 228, 230
ballboy 231
ballet 255
balsamic vinegar 135
Baltic Sea 313
bamboo 86,122
banana 128
bandage 47
Bangladesh 318
banister 59
bank 96, 284
bank charge 96
bank manager 96
bank transfer 96
bap 139
bar 150, 152, 250, 256, 311
bar code 106
bar counter 150
bar mitzvah 26
bar snacks 151
bar stool 150
barb 244
Barbados 314
barbecue 267
barber 39, 188
bark 296
barley 130, 184
barman 191
barn 182

baroque 301
bars 74
bartender 150
basalt 288
base 164, 229
base station 99
baseball 228
baseline 230
baseman 228
basement 58
basil 133
basin 50
basket 106, 207, 226
basket of fruit 126
basketball 226
basketball player 226
basque 35
bass clarinet 257
bass clef 256
bass guitar 258
bass guitarist 258
bassoon 257
bat 225, 228, 231, 290
bat v 225, 229
bath mat 72
bath towel 73
bathrobe 73
bathroom 72
bathtub 72
baton 235, 256
batsman 225
batter 228
batteries 260
battery 167, 202
battery pack 78
battleship 215

english • hindī • हिन्दी

acknowledgments • ābhār • आभार

DORLING KINDERSLEY would like to thank Tracey Miles and Christine Lacey for design assistance, Georgina Garner for editorial and administrative help, Sonia Gavira, Polly Boyd, and Cathy Meeus for editorial help, and Claire Bowers for compiling the DK picture credits.

The publisher would like to thank the following for their kind permission to reproduce their photographs:
Abbreviations key:
t = top, b = bottom, r = right, l = left, c = centre

Abode: 62; **Action Plus:** 224bc; **alamy. com:** 154t; A.T. Willett 287bcl; Michael Foyle 184bl; Stock Connection 287bcr; **Allsport/Getty Images:** 238cl; **Alvey and Towers:** 209 acr, 215bcl, 215bcr, 241cr; **Peter Anderson:** 188cbr, 271br. **Anthony Blake Photo Library:** Charlie Stebbings 114cl; John Sims 114tcl; **Andyalte:** 98tl; **apple mac computers:** 268tcr; **Arcaid:** John Edward Linden 301bl; Martine Hamilton Knight, Architects: Chapman Taylor Partners, 213cl; Richard Bryant 301br; **Argos:** 41tcl, 66cbl, 66cl, 66br, 66bcl, 69cl, 70bcl, 71t, 77tl, 269tc, 270tl; **Axiom:** Eitan Simanor 105bcr; Ian Cumming 104; Vicki Couchman 148cr; **Beken Of Cowes Ltd:** 215cbc; **Bosch:** 76tcr, 76tc, 76tcl; **Camera Press:** 27c, 38tr, 256t, 257cr; Barry J. Holmes 148tr; Jane Hanger 159cr; Mary Germanou 259bc; **Corbis:** 78b; Anna Clopet 247tr; Bettmann 181tl, 181tr; Bo Zauders 156t; Bob Rowan 152bl; Bob Winsett 247cbl; Brian Bailey 247br; Carl and Ann Purcell 162l; Chris Rainer 247ctl; ChromoSohm Inc. 179tr; Craig Aurness 215bl; David H.Wells 249cbr; Dennis Marsico 274bl; Dimitri Lundt 236bc; Duomo 211tl; Gail Mooney 277ctcr; George Lepp 248c; Gunter Marx 248cr; Jack Fields 210b; Jack Hollingsworth 231bl; Jacqui Hurst 277cbr; James L. Amos 247bl, 191ctr, 220bcr; Jan Butchofsky 277cbc; Johnathan Blair 243cr; Jon Feingersh 153tr; Jose F. Poblete 191br; Jose Luis Pelaez.Inc 153tc, 175tl; Karl Weatherly 220bl, 247tcr; Kelly Mooney Photography 259tl; Kevin Fleming 249bc; Kevin R. Morris 105tcr, 243tl, 243tc; Kim Sayer 249tcr; Lynn Goldsmith 258t; Macduff Everton 231bcl; Mark Gibson 249bl; Mark L. Stephenson 249tcl; Michael Pole 115tr; Michael S. Yamashita 247ctcl; Mike King 247cbl; Neil Rabinowitz 214br; Owen Franken 112t; Pablo Corral 115bc; Paul A. Sounders

169br, 249ctcl; Paul J. Sutton 224c, 224br; Peter Turnley 105tcr; Phil Schermeister 227b, 248tr; R. W Jones 309; R.W. Jones 175tr; Richard Hutchings 168b; Rick Doyle 241ctr; Robert Holmes 97br, 277ctc; Roger Ressmeyer 169tr; Russ Schleipman 229; Steve Raymer 168cr; The Purcell Team 211ctr; Tim Wright 178; Vince Streano 194t; Wally McNamee 220br, 220bcl, 224bl; Yann Arhus-Bertrand 249tl; **Demetrio Carrasco / Dorling Kindersley (c) Herge / Les Editions Casterman:** 112ccl; **Dixons:** 270cl, 270cr, 270bl, 270bcl, 270bcr, 270ccr; **Education Photos:** John Walmsley 26tl; **Empics Ltd:** Adam Day 236br; Andy Heading 243c; Steve White 249cbc; **Getty Images:** 48bcl, 100t, 114bcr, 154bl, 287tr; 94tr; **Dennis Gilbert:** 106tc; **Hulsta:** 70t; **Ideal Standard Ltd:** 72r; **The Image Bank/Getty Images:** 58; **Impact Photos:** Eliza Armstrong 115cr; John Arthur 190tl; Philip Achache 246t; **The Interior Archive:** Henry Wilson, Alfie's Market 114bl; Luke White, Architect: David Mikhail, 59tl; Simon Upton, Architect: Phillippe Starck, St Martins Lane Hotel 100bcr, 100br; **Jason Hawkes Aerial Photography:** 216t; **Dan Johnson:** 26cbl, 35r; **Kos Pictures Source:** 215cbl, 240tc, 240tr; David Williams 216b; **Lebrecht Collection:** Kate Mount 169bc; **MP Visual. com:** Mark Swallow 202t; **NASA:** 280cr, 280ccl, 281tl; **P&O Princess Cruises:** 214bl; **P A Photos:** 181br; **The Photographers' Library:** 186bl, 186bc, 186t; **Plain and Simple Kitchens:** 66t; **Powerstock Photolibrary:** 169tl, 256t, 287tc; **Rail Images:** 208c, 208 cbl, 209br; **Red Consultancy:** Odeon cinemas 257br; **Redferns:** 259br; Nigel Crane 259tc; **Rex Features:** 106br, 259tc, 259tr, 259bl, 280b; Charles Ommaney 114tcr; J.F.F Whitehead 243cl; Patrick Barth 101tl; Patrick Frilet 189cbl; Scott Wiseman 287bl; **Royalty Free Images:** Getty Images/Eyewire 154bl; **Science & Society Picture Library:** Science Museum 202b; **Skyscan:** 168t, 182c, 298; Quick UK Ltd 212; **Sony:** 268bc; **Robert Streeter:** 154br; **Neil Sutherland:** 82tr, 83tl, 90t, 118, 188ctr, 196tl, 196tr, 299cl, 299bl; **The Travel Library:** Stuart Black 264t; **Travelex:** 97cl; **Vauxhall:** Technik 198t, 199tl, 199tr, 199cl, 199cr, 199ctcl, 199tccr, 199tcl, 199tcr, 200; **View Pictures:** Dennis Gilbert, Architects: ACDP Consulting, 106t; Dennis Gilbert,

Chris Wilkinson Architects, 209tr; Peter Cook, Architects: Nicholas Crimshaw and partners, 208t; **Betty Walton:** 185br; **Colin Walton:** 2, 4, 7, 9, 10, 28, 42, 56, 92, 95c, 99tl, 99tcl, 102, 116, 120t, 138t, 146, 150t, 160, 170, 191ctcl, 192, 218, 252, 260br, 260l, 261tr, 261c, 261cl, 271cbl, 271cbr, 271ctl, 278, 287br, 302, 401.

DK PICTURE LIBRARY:
Akhil Bahkshi; Patrick Baldwin; Geoff Brightling; British Museum; John Bulmer; Andrew Butler; Joe Cornish; Brian Cosgrove; Andy Crawford and Kit Hougton; Philip Dowell; Alistair Duncan; Gables; Bob Gathany; Norman Hollands; Kew Gardens; Peter James Kindersley; Vladimir Kozlik; Sam Lloyd; London Northern Bus Company Ltd; Tracy Morgan; David Murray and Jules Selmes; Musée Vivant du Cheval, France; Museum of Broadcast Communications; Museum of Natural History; NASA; National History Museum; Norfolk Rural Life Museum; Stephen Oliver; RNLI; Royal Ballet School; Guy Ryecart; Science Museum; Neil Setchfield; Ross Simms and the Winchcombe Folk Police Museum; Singapore Symphony Orchestra; Smart Museum of Art; Tony Souter; Erik Svensson and Jeppe Wikstrom; Sam Tree of Keygrove Marketing Ltd; Barrie Watts; Alan Williams; Jerry Young.

Additional Photography by Colin Walton.

Colin Walton would like to thank:
A&A News, Uckfield; Abbey Music, Tunbridge Wells; Arena Mens Clothing, Tunbridge Wells; Burrells of Tunbridge Wells; Gary at Di Marco's; Jeremy's Home Store, Tunbridge Wells; Noakes of Tunbridge Wells; Ottakar's, Tunbridge Wells; Selby's of Uckfield; Sevenoaks Sound and Vision; Westfield, Royal Victoria Place, Tunbridge Wells.

All other images are Dorling Kindersley copyright. For further information see www.dkimages.com